"This is a prophetic book. Scilla Elworthy turns her sharp intellect and long experience of holding the hands of those in power, to both illuminate the great problems facing mankind and to show how, by an inner transformation, we can all become 'pioneers of the possible.' With a wealth of examples she shows how we can, regardless of gifts or background, give the future our own best shot."

—**GENERAL SIR HUGH BEACH,**
former Master General of the Ordnance, the British Army

"We had the great privilege to work with Scilla Elworthy to turn The Elders into a reality in partnership with Richard Branson, Peter Gabriel, and a host of other wonderful partners. We all found Scilla to be an incredibly insightful leader. Her ability to see the big picture, yet bring this back to practical action for individuals is a wonderful gift. Her new book shares her rich wisdom about a new type of leader that has a deep level of awareness of their inner power. This book is certainly a powerful catalyst toward the new world of consciousness founded in listening and empathy that the world needs to embrace."

—**JEAN OELWANG,** CEO of Virgin Unite,
the entrepreneurial foundation of the worldwide Virgin Group

"A work of lasting impact. *Visionary* is much too small to describe Scilla Elworthy. . . . With a rare grasp of today's realities, she not only sees what's coming but also shares her pragmatic vision of what life *could* be like. From physics to farming, mystical traditions to social entrepreneurship, 'Simpol' to Time Dollars, her wide-ranging descriptions illuminate hope amid crises. Alongside an empathetic analysis of 'some of the giants who have shown the way,' this wise woman—herself a towering figure—offers readers a huge and motivating gift: an explanation of how ordinary individuals can change the world, and why they must wake up and do it."

—**AMBASSADOR SWANEE HUNT,** chair, Hunt Alternatives; chair and founder,
The Institute for Inclusive Security; Eleanor Roosevelt Lecturer of Public Policy,
Harvard Kennedy School of Government

"This is a book about radical leadership; it will give you the essential skills and inner power to help build a world that works for all, and to have a great time doing it."

—**CHADE-MENG TAN,** Jolly Good Fellow of Google and bestselling author of
Search Inside Yourself

"This book by Scilla Elworthy is worthy of a strong push from all of us. If we are to create a sustainable civilization at his point in history (and we must, in order to survive) it is precisely this thinking and writing that must prevail. She has my strong support and concurrence with her efforts."

—**EDGAR MITCHELL, SCD,** NASA astronaut,
pilot of Apollo 14 and the sixth person to walk on the moon

"The world is in crisis, but what can each of us do about it? This book will help you to envision the kind of future that is possible—a lift-off into *life as it could be*. It provides a series of steps to get us from here to there, by bringing in pragmatic view points that can help us on our path. It will inspire you. . . ."

—JOCHEN ZEITZ, director of Kering and
chairman of the Kering board's sustainable development committee

"I have long been a fan of Scilla Elworthy—she's always pushing boundaries and thinking ahead. It has been a joy working with her over the years, especially introducing her to The Elders where she helped us at Virgin Unite design its form and function. We need women like Scilla to challenge us to reorder our perspectives by drawing on the feminine in us all, including men, and finding the 'balance between the inner and the outer, between the psychological and the political, between reflection and action' so vital to a new world in which peace, equity, and justice might prevail."

—JANE TEWSON, founder of Charity Projects, Pilotlight UK,
and Igniting Change Australia; cofounder of Comic Relief

"They say it is better to light a candle than curse the dark. In this great book Scilla Elworthy sets the context of where we are as a society and shines a veritable searchlight on many practical and positive suggestions to some of today's most intractable problems. A must-read for all those who want to be part of the solution!"

—LAWRENCE BLOOM, former chairman of the World Economic Forum,
Global Agenda Council on Urban Management

"In this brilliant and thrilling work, Dr. Elworthy brings her enormous experience and intelligence to the deepest understanding of current challenges, mated with the most profound spectrum of workable solutions. She calls us to become stewards of both Earth and soul, to use this precious incarnation for the enhancement of our interior life so that our exterior life can move toward the creation of a world that works for all. This remarkable book also serves as an intense course in human development in the light of social and ecological change. . . . Some books are miracles. This is one of them . . . the finest offering I know for those who really want to make a difference."

—JEAN HOUSTON, PHD, consultant to the United Nations in human development,
author of *The Wizard of Us*

"This book shows not only that we are living in a time of great challenges for humanity but that we are birthing a 'new we' of participation, caring and innovation that brings forth a powerful answer that can only come through us. Through the internet and global challenges we are forced to become global citizens, and we cannot any more say 'I don't know'; we are being called to contribute our gift to an amazing movement that is happening all over the world. Scilla Elworthy is full of life wisdom. Through her caring, courage, and love for the world, she shines a light on how to be a global citizen in our time."

—**THOMAS HÜBL,** founder of the Academy of Inner Science, Germany

"This extraordinary book is a model of incandescent leadership, inspiring us to imagine a different kind of world and the means of bringing it into being. . . . [I]t carries the power to move us from ignorance and paralysis to informed, dynamic action. The causes and effects of climate change and the unbalanced culture and values contributing to them are now indisputable, but here they are explored in a clear and accessible way, offering an agenda for practical action that could halt the Sixth Great Extinction now in progress. Scilla Elworthy's own life has been lived with immense courage and a visionary commitment to the service of others, as well as to her own inner transformation. Assimilate her wise and urgent message and discover your innate potential to become an awakened human being, participating in the change of consciousness directed towards rescuing the planet and future generations from the calamitous effects of our ignorance."

—**ANNE BARING,** author of *The Dream of the Cosmos: A Quest for the Soul*

PIONEERING

the

POSSIBLE

Awakened Leadership for a World That Works

SCILLA ELWORTHY, PHD

Forewords by Desmond Tutu *and* Andrew Harvey

North Atlantic Books
Berkeley, California

North Atlantic Books
P.O. Box 12327
Berkeley, California 94712

Cover photo © Dan Collier/Shutterstock.com
Cover design by Jasmine Hromjak and Mary Ann Casler
Book design by Mary Ann Casler
Illustrations in chapter 7 by shtiggy.wordpress.com

Photograph credits: Thich Nhat Hanh © Copyright Unified Buddhist Church; Ellen MacArthur by Liot Vapillon/ DPPI / Offshore Challenge; Henri Bura Ladyi by Fiona Lloyd-Davies, courtesy of Peace Direct; Aung San Suu Kyi by Christopher Lunch; Thomas Hübl by Markus Heinbach; Pema Chodron by K. Mortensen; photos of Desmond Tutu and Scilla Elworthy by Rosie Houldsworth; Anupam Jalote by Shrey Jalote; Sarah Ingamells and Yvonne Blankley by Miranda Allen; Felia Salim by Desi Harahap.

NOTE: Every effort has been made to locate the photographer to acquire permission to reprint the photograph of Dekha Ibrahim Abdi. Please contact North Atlantic Books if you are the photographer or have information about how to locate him or her.

Printed in the United States of America

Pioneering the Possible: Awakened Leadership for a World That Works is sponsored and published by the Society for the Study of Native Arts and Sciences (dba North Atlantic Books), an educational non-profit based in Berkeley, California, that collaborates with partners to develop cross-cultural perspectives, nurture holistic views of art, science, the humanities, and healing, and seed personal and global transformation by publishing work on the relationship of body, spirit, and nature.

North Atlantic Books' publications are available through most bookstores. For further information, visit our website at www.northatlanticbooks.com or call 800-733-3000.

ISBN 978–1-58394-862-0—e-book ISBN 978-1-58394-863-7

Library of Congress Cataloging-in-Publication data is available from the publisher upon request.

1 2 3 4 5 6 7 8 9 United 19 18 17 16 15 14

To my beloved daughter, Polly

CONTENTS

ACKNOWLEDGMENTS

Andrew Harvey initiated the Sacred Activism series and introduced me to North Atlantic Books. His compassionate ability to take the time to understand what I wanted to convey in this book has moved me to my core. Not only does he have a unique command of vocabulary and tone, but he also has a meticulous eye for the shape of a book and an ability to hold the whole structure in his mind—these skills make one stand back in awe. His passionate courage inspired me constantly. And as a bonus, Andrew is more fun to work with than anyone I know.

The team at North Atlantic Books have been consistently helpful, practical, and expert in their advice. I would particularly like to thank Doug Reil for initially recognizing the usefulness of the book, Hisae Matsuda for her calm guidance, her deep knowledge of the field, and her resourceful ways of meeting my needs for illustration and photographs, and Jennifer Eastman for her sensitive, meticulous, and wise editing, based on a real understanding of the text.

There are so many people who have given their time and knowledge to the book that it would not be possible to thank every one. May I mention especially: Anne Baring for her deep friendship, for commenting with care and great wisdom on several drafts, for allowing me to excerpt from the *Dream of the Cosmos* and *Awakening to the Feminine,* and for sending a steady stream of ideas; Rama Mani for her warmth and compassion, her seemingly bottomless faith in me, her skill as a colleague and as a poet, and her visionary ideas; Gabrielle Rifkind for the honesty and insights she brings to our friendship, for weekend walking conversations that have enriched the writing process, and for excerpts from *The Fog of Peace;* Rohan Narse for his meticulous reading of the text and practical ideas based on his background in the City of London; Karen Downes for detailed, caring, insightful suggestions on the text; Francis Wilson for crucial advice on reordering the chapter sequence; Florian Hoffmann for the experience of the Do School and for guidance on chapter 4; Kalypso Nicolaïdis for organizing a reading of draft text at the Department of International Relations, University of Oxford; Lisa Braun Dubbels for her tireless work on publicity, and her great skill and original ideas for promotion; Felia Salim for providing details of her work in transforming banking practice in Indonesia; Sujata Khandekar and the Leaders' Quest team and fellows for their work in Mumbai and Rajasthan; Sarah Ingamells and Yvonne Blankley at Sherborne Village Shop for allowing me to interview them in their kitchen; Anupam Jalote for taking me to see his anaerobic digester near Jaipur, India; John Bunzl for contributing his piece on Simpol; Maude Barlow, for excerpts from her forthcoming book *Blue Future, Protecting Water for People and the Planet Forever;* Hazel Henderson for excerpts from *Enacting and Telling the New Story;* Monica Sharma for excerpts from her writing on the future; Jean Houston for her immediate and generous enthusiasm for the book and for excerpts from *The Possible Human and the Possible World;* Thais Corral and Vicki Robin for excerpts from *Women Strengthening Local Food Systems;* Elisabet Sahtouris for her work on imaginal cells and for excerpts from *Ecosophy—Nature's Guide to a Better World;* Annie MacIntyre for excerpts from her writing on Ayurveda; Alexander Schieffer for all his moral support and for allowing me to quote from his article about Sekem; Wei Liu and Ruiqi Zeng for early edits of the text; Sally Dearman-Cummings for her insights on the functioning of the left and right brain; Vandana Shiva for her personal report on the devastation of Uttarakhand; Walter Link for his description of Sarvodaya; Bev Reeler for her elephant poem and her description of the *Tree of Life* in Zimbabwe; Lawrence Bloom for his constant encouragement and ideas on cities of the future; Gulalai Ismael for her extraordinary work in Pakistan; Asha Hagi Elmi for her courage in Somalia; Thomas Hübl for his work on the Unified Field and for excerpts from his teaching; Alison Yiangou for her good ideas and encouragement; Deirdre Burton for her wisdom and her sane advice in exploring energy; Liz Kingsnorth for attempting to stop me taking myself too seriously and for introducing me to her students in Chennai; Lorna Collins, Soraya Abouleish, and Paul King for reading drafts and making suggestions; Nicholas Janni for his astute nudges to make me grow, and for his good ideas; Andrew Powell for suggestions on health and for allowing me to excerpt from *Technology and Soul in the Twenty-First Century;* Allegra Wint for her knowledge of Chinese medicine, her wisdom, and her skill; Shelley Reciniello for allowing me to quote from her work; Mimi Quaife, acting personal assistant to Ellen MacArthur, Ellen MacArthur Foundation; my colleagues at Peace Direct and the Oxford Research Group for all that they inspire, and, finally, my daughter, Polly McLean, for her constant encouragement toward truthful relationship, and for her love and unfailing support.

FOREWORD BY DESMOND TUTU

The world is in crisis. It needs people who have the skill to combine inner power with outer action. Inner power comes from self mastery, observing and controlling the ego, and deepening integrity through a regular practice of reflection or meditation. This generates not only the ability to transform conflicts, listen to others, communicate clearly and develop trust, but also the creative innovation and energy to resolve local and global problems.

This is the current evolutionary process that most people don't yet see: namely that the desired outer changes cannot come about without the inner change, as Einstein said. The quality of your awareness will directly affect the quality of the results you produce. This book demonstrates—steadily and sensibly—how anyone can develop this inner power to build their own personal contribution to the future, and to a world that works for all. It will wake you up to the challenges now facing the planet, and inspire you with sparkling accounts of what people are already doing to meet those challenges. It will show you how to build your own vision of the kind of future you want for your children, and the energy to make that vision real. I suggest you use this book as a guide, so that you too can become a twenty-first-century pioneer of the possible.

DESMOND TUTU

FOREWORD BY ANDREW HARVEY

Scilla Elworthy is one of the great elders and sacred activists of our time, a quiet-voiced woman to whom it would be stupid not to listen. Nominated for the Nobel Peace Prize three times, she has been "pioneering the possible" in her groundbreaking work on nuclear disarmament, in her involvement with The Elders, and as the founder of Peace Direct, an organization that supports locally led peace building in areas of hot conflict. Scilla has worked intimately both with world leaders such as Desmond Tutu and with extraordinary "ordinary" people doing dogged, heroic service against grueling odds all over the world. For four decades now, she has surrendered her whole being and life to the task of helping humanity come to its senses and start building a world of peace, joy, justice, and compassion.

All the qualities that characterize Scilla herself, as I have come to know and love her, inform and irradiate *Pioneering the Possible,* her magisterial distillation of a lifetime's experience of finding and implementing pragmatic, visionary solutions to seemingly intractable problems. Scilla is elegant; understated but laser-like; compassionate but unsentimental; exalted in her vision, but astringently grounded; always curious about and open to others' perspectives, but adamant about what she has learned from her own fierce conscience and experience. This is the book on the

New Leadership that we have been waiting for, not only because of its wise and simply presented content, but also because of its authenticity of address, the kind that can only be forged in the fires of committed action, and at great secret cost.

Four main themes circle around each other in various configurations throughout the book: (1) a vision of Pioneering Leadership as grounded in presence—the mystery of embodied faith, generosity, courage, and radical humility that we saw in Nelson Mandela; (2) the necessity of ceaselessly sustaining such presence through inner work, spiritually and psychological; (3) the living reality of a worldwide, multifaceted movement of heroic, ordinary sacred activists who are in every realm pioneering visionary and pragmatic alternatives to our hubristic insanity; and (4) a challenge to the far deeper honoring of the Sacred Feminine to empower women on all levels and help both women and men integrate glowingly within themselves the deep masculine and full feminine. To each of these themes, Scilla brings her beadily hopeful eye, her knowledge won from four decades of persistence in the trenches of sacred activism, and a lightness of touch that is both moving in its refusal of theatrics and strangely elating.

I had the honor of working with Scilla throughout the process of shaping *Pioneering the Possible*. I learned a tremendous amount about clarity, groundedness, calm, and resolve, and about what it is possible for us all to do in a time like ours. You will too. Buy this book and share its downhome but profound wisdom with all those you know who are daring to wake up to the terrible danger we are all in and with those who want to know what we need to do urgently and in what adult and surrendered joy we need to do it.

ANDREW HARVEY

CHAPTER I

RIDING THE DRAGON

The whole world mourned when Nelson Mandela died. Consciously or not, everyone knew that the world had lost a leader of extraordinary radiance. This man, during twenty-seven years in jail, made the profound shift from believing that violence would end South Africa's apartheid system to committing himself to the much more demanding path of mediation and negotiation with the regime that had imprisoned him and his colleagues. Mandela inspired our imagination not only because of his great achievements but also because of what permeated everything he did—a mighty core of presence and integrity. His very bearing emanated solidity, serenity, and a humble, unshakable majesty.

I shall never forget how palpable and physical was the effect of his presence, witnessed at first hand during the development of The Elders initiative, described later in this chapter. Already in his late eighties, he entered the room in one of his brightly-colored shirts and without any fanfare, yet everyone instantaneously felt the grandeur of his being. He sat down with a slightly mysterious smile and began to speak simply, with no oratorical flourishes and in a slightly rasping voice. My whole body trembled, and this trembling continued for the entire forty minutes that he spoke—an experience I had never had before and haven't since. This sensation was not merely physical but also mental, emotional, and spiritual—the whole of my being vibrated with the electricity of this level of integrity.

That moment crystallized my understanding that authentic leadership —the kind so deeply needed now—begins in the radical mastery of one's inner being. Brilliance, charisma, eloquence, vision—these are wonderful gifts that a leader can possess—but these gifts gain ultimate effect and coherence only when fueled and sustained by inner power. Inner power is the diamond formed by years of honing self-awareness, practicing self-lessness, and observing and controlling the ego. It results from developing the essential skill of empathy—even for those who oppose you—and the humble commitment to keep learning the skills of deep listening and mediation.

What I'm expressing here has been known in all the great spiritual traditions, but it needs to be reclaimed for a secular world in crisis—and in language that all can understand. Without leaders of this kind in every sphere and institution of our world, our chances of survival are grim. With such leaders, you and I can build a world that our grandchildren will be proud of. This is what my book is dedicated to.

Why This Book, Why Now?

We live in a world that is miserable and frightening for most of its inhabitants. Many of the rich are not happy, while the gap between rich and poor gets wider. The richest three hundred people in the world now have more wealth than the poorest three billion—that's nearly half of humanity. And we are ruining our planet at such a rate that—sooner than most people can imagine—large parts of it will become uninhabitable. Soils and forests are disappearing, oceans are literally being vacuumed of fish, disastrous crises lurch through unstable financial markets, the disenfranchised vent their anger at oppressive governments, an economic system rewards only the most greedy and amoral among us, and more than a billion people—no longer able to support themselves in rural areas—are swarming toward cities where there is no work for them. The world is in crisis.

Yet this crisis is a vast opportunity.

At the core of this book is the certainty that a different future for all of humanity is possible, *if humans wake up*. Waking up starts with you and me. It means increasing our knowledge of ourselves by using reflection, mindfulness, and inner work. These tools, in turn, enable us to become more alert to others and their needs, to move from our own concerns to compassion for the world—and to give us the strength and the skill to know what we need to do and how we need to do it.

In half a century of work in the world, the most important lesson I've learned is that inner work is a prerequisite for outer effectiveness—*the quality of our awareness directly affects the quality of results produced*. The new brand of leaders that we need—those who are actually able to meet the challenges of today and thrive in the world of tomorrow—are the ones who know and live the connection between inner self-development and outer action. If we want to communicate clearly, transform conflicts, generate energy, and develop trust within our families and in our places of work, our first challenge is to do the inner work. This is the current evolutionary challenge that most people don't yet grasp: how the desired outer changes cannot come about without the inner change.

If a critical mass of humanity can make this shift, an entirely different way of living could emerge. We could live in a world that is safe, where the earth has regenerated itself, where streams run clear again and you can drink the water anywhere. Where you can breathe clear air. Where children can be secure, not scared. Where creatures are protected from cruelty and extinction. Where people communicate with each other rather than fight. Where women are educated, safe, and respected. Where money holds its value, and companies compete to be trustworthy, because consumers insist on this. Where we find a way to elect to government the kind of people who want to serve rather than to abuse power.

This is not a utopia. It's happening. There are examples all over the world, and a global movement of creativity is beginning, of which you are potentially a part.

This book envisages the kind of future that human beings are now capable of and investigates the steps needed to get to that kind of future, so that very large numbers of people can see the point of change and be drawn toward a future that is not just desirable and exciting, but also possible.

Building this different future will nevertheless require a process of waking up, amounting to nothing less than a leap in consciousness. Only a leap in consciousness can provide the perspective—the bird's eye view, if you like—to take the necessary actions to resolve the problems we have created. As Einstein famously said, "You cannot solve a problem from the consciousness that created it."

There are giants who have shown the way, and we shall examine what they did and how they did it. Doing this will take us to the next step and enable us to contrast the value systems that underpin our current decision making with the kind of values that would inspire us to make better decisions—decisions that can free us from the chaos we're in.

These values or norms build a foundation from which we can envisage the kind of future that is possible—a dynamic lift-off into life *as it could be*. What is required is to build a series of steps to get us from here to there. This is the practical part: this is where we bring in the visionary pragmatists who know what to do in their special area, because they've done it—they've tried it, tested it, and made it work. The notion of this book is to pull all these parts of the picture together. This is, of course, a collaborative exercise. The future will be envisioned and built collaboratively—or not at all.

In the final chapters, we return to the necessary leap in consciousness and how large numbers of people are now able to make that leap. We examine the ways people have found to develop their inner power, to become self-aware, active, and responsible for what happens to the planet—and to find infectious joy in doing so. These methodologies have helped them develop the ability to serve, to be part of this change to a secure and satisfying future.

Have you ever dared to imagine what life *could* be like . . . if we used our skills to transform conflict, to clean up the environment, and to invent a financial system that is fair? How it would be if we set up systems for wise governance, if we kicked out the cynics and gave medals to people who outlaw corruption? What would life be like if we were to bring the feminine and masculine into balance, to free women from millennia of oppression and release their creativity? What if we were able to have a pace of life that suited the soul?

This book is your invitation.

How This Book Works

The foundation of this book is the leap in human consciousness. This first chapter introduces the ideas that propelled me to write it and describes my own journey. Chapter 2 will try to get as close as possible to a vision of what this leap is. Chapter 3 then takes us to meet some living examples of people who have done this—great people who have developed their self-awareness, shifted their consciousness, and become able to work for change in the world in a powerfully effective way. These are individuals who have dealt with the doubts and challenges of being a pioneer, such as speaking truth to power and picking yourself up when things fall apart. They have also, crucially, learned when skepticism is useful and when cynicism is pointless and destructive. Some are household names, but others are local heroes the larger world has never heard of. We shall search out some of their secrets, examine their experiences, and mine their wisdom.

Doing this will enable us, in chapter 4, to define the value systems that underpin our current decision making and to examine some of the results of these kind of decisions. Examining the beliefs or norms that have governed our actions for centuries will help us to see what has contributed to the state of the planet today. These beliefs are important, because they form the assumptions—the foundation—on which many large institutions, businesses, and governments currently make decisions.

In chapter 5, the other side of the coin is revealed; we examine the kind of values that could enable us to make better decisions—decisions that could get us out of the mess we're in. Then, in chapter 6, we begin to think in practical terms about strategies to get from here to there—how to create a more benign future.

Chapter 7 brings us back to *us*—it shows how people wake up to their own energetic potential, meaning that they can then have access to the self-awareness that is an essential part of building a positive future. That chapter spells out eleven signposts—with clues, messages, maps, and poetry—that can set you on this path.

In chapter 8, you will discover a process that will enable you to leave behind the assumptions and prejudices of the past, free up your deepest natural creativity, and open up your own vision of how you want the future to be. Finally, in chapter 9, we shall observe the company you're in: how this "waking up" is taking place worldwide, and how this radically different global future is already emerging.

My Journey

My passion to do something about the state of the world and the suffering of people—and the sense that my life's fulfillment was inseparable from it—began quite young. I had four big brothers, and when I was eleven, they taught me to fire a shotgun. I took the gun out to the woods near our house and saw a bird sitting on a nest high in the trees. I went underneath the nest, pointed the gun straight up, and fired. I felt daring and adventurous. Sticks rained down on me—then pieces of shell, pieces of embryo chicks, and the sky-blue feathers of the mother bird. It had been—was no longer—a beautiful blue jay. I was so shocked at what I had done that I took the gun home and never touched it again.

About two years later I was sitting in our living room watching a grainy black-and-white television. It was 1956 and Soviet tanks were rolling into Budapest to crush the uprising. Kids my age were throwing themselves against the tanks. I rushed upstairs and started packing my suitcase. My mother came in and asked what I was up to.

I said, "I'm going to Budapest" (having no idea where Budapest was).

"What on earth for?"

"Kids are getting killed there, and I have to go."

"Don't be silly."

I burst into tears.

Bless her, she got it—she got how much I minded.

"You're too young, and you'll have to get trained if you're going to be any use. I'll help you, if you just unpack your suitcase."

And she did. When I was sixteen, I went to work in a holiday home for people who had been in camps for "displaced persons" since the end of World War II. Some had been in concentration camps. I sat peeling potatoes, listening to an old man talking about a guard's boot crushing his neck, his face in the snow. This showed me the extent of potential brutality in human beings, which I had never before imagined.

In 1962 I went to university in Dublin to study social science. In my vacation after my first year I worked in a camp for Vietnamese refugees in France, looking after the bewildered children of families who had escaped the escalating war. From there I went to Algiers—then emerging from years of torture, terror, and guerrilla warfare—to work with children who had lost both parents in the fighting. My university training hadn't taught me about the human fallout of war, about the desperation of refugees, or about what happens to abandoned children. What I found made me feel sick and angry every day, furious that nothing effective had been done to stop this wrecking of the children's lives and futures.

After university, I decided to explore my fascination with Africa, then emerging from colonial rule. When I was nine years old, my mother had taken me to East Africa, and its history and grandeur had captured my soul—I couldn't forget the aroma of giant piles of pineapples on Mombasa harbor or the sight of huge lilies growing wild in hills roamed by gorillas. So after university, I boarded a cargo boat from Bordeaux that went around the west coast of Africa, calling in at the ports and, amazingly, unloading champagne and steak for the French expats. We called at Conakry in Guinea, where I watched the new president, Ahmed Sékou Touré, speaking from atop a pillar in the main square to a crowd of thousands. I looked around and found myself a witness to history unfolding.

The boat ended up in Pointe-Noire in the former French Congo, which was at the time at war with the former Belgian Congo. To get from one to the other was almost impossible, but I found out that the French ambassador, like me, needed to cross the Congo River, which was several miles wide. And he had a boat. But we had to go in secrecy, at midnight, because of the war. When we arrived at the other side, the dawn light glinted on the row of machine guns pointing in our direction. Gingerly, I got off the boat and made my way to the airport—through streets teeming with trucks full of crazed soldiers firing rifles into the air—to catch a plane to South Africa, where I had a boyfriend. (There's always a reason. . . .)

SOUTH AFRICA

This was now 1966, when Prime Minister Verwoerd—the "architect of Apartheid"—was stabbed to death in Parliament. It was only three years after Nelson Mandela had been condemned to life in prison on Robben Island. In South Africa I soon realized that if I did manage to get a job in social work (the only training I had), I would be in jail in weeks.

So I temporarily abandoned my determination to be useful and went in the opposite direction, getting a job in retail fashion. I did what so many South African whites do: I closed my eyes to what was happening around me, lived a blinkered luxurious life in a flat on Clifton beach, and drove a sports car. I introduced the Mary Quant range to South Africa, got photographed a good deal, and simply ignored the political situation.

After three years I met Murray McLean, who was selling street-cleaning equipment. He was the most entrepreneurial man I had ever met—and the most charming—and he made me laugh, and we got married. I stopped working and went to university to learn Zulu and then began to understand something of what was going on around me.

Doing voluntary work for a nutrition-education organization called Kupugani ("self-help") involved work in the so-called homelands. My eyes opened to the starkness of starvation, which was denied by the apartheid government. Children with distended bellies from kwashiorkor stared at white men pouring surplus milk down the mines. Kupugani bought the surplus milk, dried it into powder, and shifted it to places where it saved lives. We found a derelict building near the main station in Johannesburg, where commuters left for Soweto, and we set up a shop selling soup powder, peanut butter, surplus oranges, and other cheap, nutritious foods.

Becoming chair of Kupugani, I realized the pressing need for a regular source of income for the organization that didn't involve constant fundraising. By that time, my husband employed about five thousand migrant workers in various enterprises, who were given money at Christmas, before they went home for their annual holiday. Often this money did not reach their families, so we developed a scheme to offer employers in the Johannesburg area the possibility of giving their staff a box of nutritious food instead. We bought food in bulk, used white volunteers to pack the boxes, and were able to sell them for a profit—a classic win-win-win, because the food reached the families, employers felt good, and Kupugani got a regular source of funds. The first year we raised about $90,000 (adjusted to today's US dollars), and that amount doubled every year, enabling us to expand our work accordingly.

The political tension in South Africa took its toll on our marriage—my husband was a substantial employer (albeit a fairly enlightened one), and I was beginning to organize black trade unions. Not a good mix. To save our marriage, we left South Africa and went to live in France for five years.

My husband saw an ad in the paper saying a volunteer was needed to help establish the Minority Rights Group in France. Soon I found myself immersed in the problems of minorities and working with five Arab and African women to write the first substantive report on female genital mutilation, published in 1980, leading to the World Health Organization's first (and unsuccessful) campaign to eradicate the practice.

THE UNITED NATIONS

In 1979 I started working for UNESCO, and as a consultant on women's issues, I was commissioned to research and write UNESCO's submission to the 1980 World Conference of the United Nations Decade for Women in Copenhagen. It had an immensely long title—*The Role of Women in Peace Research, Peace Negotiations and the Improvement of International Relations*—and since I knew almost nothing about any of that, I set out to meet women who did. The women I met were intellectually precise, feisty visionaries, grounded in an earthy pragmatism. Who they were and how they operated was to influence and shape the rest of my life.

In the early 1980s the public was waking up to the huge buildup of nuclear weapons under Thatcher, Brezhnev, and Reagan. The study for UNESCO had woken me up to the real dangers of accidental nuclear war. The British government issued a pamphlet recommending that in the event of a nuclear attack, you should put a paper bag over your head and crawl under a table. It was entitled "Protect and Survive." Cue a perfect opportunity for disarmament activists to mount a campaign entitled "Protest and Survive."

And that's exactly what I did. In 1982 I was in New York for the United Nations Second Special Session on Disarmament, lobbying delegates. After a week of no progress, there was a massive demonstration through the city, which filled Central Park with a million people, all in favor of nuclear disarmament. The *New York Times* gave it five pages. But back in the United Nations the next morning, it was clear that not one delegation had changed its position one inch.

I was shocked. There had never in history been such a big demonstration. What more could people do to get their leaders to listen? What would it take? Straphanging on a bus on Broadway that night, I had one of those sudden illuminations that shift your entire life. It went something like this: "Nuclear decisions clearly are made by people, and probably not those in the United Nations. If the people in the streets—who care so much—could get really well informed and go and talk calmly, one to one, with the people who actually make the decisions on nuclear weapons, perhaps the dynamics might change."

But who *were* the people who made the decisions on nuclear weapons?

OXFORD RESEARCH GROUP

So I went back to the United Kingdom and started a research group round my kitchen table to find out.[1] I called it, simply, the Oxford Research Group, because that's where I lived. My researchers and I started the task of mapping the entire decision-making process on nuclear weapons in the United States, Britain, Russia, France, and China—a task we were told was impossible. This meant understanding who designed the warheads, who built the submarines and aircraft, who provided the data for targeting and deployment, and who had authority to give the orders and sign the checks.

If you want to find out who the decision makers are, you have first to identify the important organizations (ministries, design labs, military strategists, defense companies, and intelligence committees) and the key groups within them. We never used any classified material, but we were fortunate to be guided by scholars and librarians in official institutes. My own savings were used to fund the first two researchers working at my kitchen table. When those savings ran out, we raised funds from Quaker trusts and hired six researchers with good insight into the five countries we focused on. We worked round the clock and managed to have quite a lot of fun as well. Four years later we published our first book, entitled simply *How Nuclear Weapons Decisions Are Made*.[2]

In the meantime, we began to test out whether groups of concerned citizens might develop fruitful dialogue with nuclear decision makers. We contacted a range of groups—women's groups, Quaker groups, peace groups, and church groups—and supplied those interested with an information pack about one British decision maker and his counterpart in China, as we believed it was important to tackle this as a world problem, not just a British or Western one.

We learned that the groups needed to become extremely well informed before they opened the dialogue, so that the first letter they wrote to their decision maker would carry weight and have sound, powerful points for discussion. We also learned that it was vital for the groups to deal with their own anger or frustration before they started, because you could not expect someone in a position of power to listen to you if you approached them with an accusing tone or from the moral high ground.

We made many mistakes, but we learned from them. Some of the groups, after fierce internal debates, refined their ideas, found out new information, and became skilled in dialogue. As they became expert in their chosen area, they soon discovered that they knew as much as, if not more than, their decision maker. This had a powerful effect. It undermined the notion that nuclear issues were too complicated for ordinary members of the public and ought to be left to those in authority.

The project continued for ten years, involving citizens in Britain, France, Sweden, and the United States. I have no hard evidence on the results, because, of course, all the conversations—to take place at all—had to be confidential, but there is some evidence that the project hastened an acceptance among those closely involved in defense policy of the desirability of substantial reductions in the numbers of nuclear weapons. Most particularly, the project made us more convinced than ever that the views of the public could—and should—be made known to those with the heavy responsibility of decisions on defense. And it became obvious that on an issue affecting the future of humanity, the decision-making process should be made accountable.

As a result, I soon found myself in NATO headquarters in Brussels with Margarita Papandreou, the wife of the Greek prime minister, and a battalion of women members of Parliament from East and West Europe, asking questions of NATO leaders, and then in the Kremlin in Moscow, asking Mikhail Gorbachev equally searching questions. For example, we wanted to know why there was (at the time: 1986–1987) no hotline between NATO and the Warsaw Pact, even after mistakes that could have triggered accidental nuclear war. For example, on September 26, 1983, the nuclear early warning system of the Soviet Union twice reported the launch of American Minuteman ICBMs from bases in the United States. Luckily for all of humanity, Stanislav Yevgrafovich Petrov, an officer of the Soviet Air Defense Forces, correctly identified them as a false alarm. His alertness prevented a retaliatory nuclear attack on the United States and its NATO allies, which would have resulted in the deaths of millions of people. Investigation of the satellite warning system later confirmed that the system had malfunctioned.

By this time, we knew enough about the possibility of accidental nuclear war—and the numbers of nuclear warheads that had gone missing—to realize the urgency of talking with those in authority. My doctoral thesis, undertaken at that time, involved in-depth interviews with a number of senior policy makers—ministers, civil servants, military leaders, warhead designers, and weapons contractors. I listened to them talk for several hours and then drew cognitive maps of their thought patterns, which we then discussed. This allowed us to understand each other's thought processes, and speaking to them straightforwardly helped to develop trust.

With some trust established, it was possible to invite them or their colleagues to spend two days in a medieval manor house near Oxford to talk with their most knowledgeable critics on key issues of nuclear weapons policy. For example, we would bring together a leading warhead designer from the Los Alamos National Laboratory in the United States with a physicist who had quit his senior post at Aldermaston (the UK warhead lab) to become director of an internationally respected peace research institute in Stockholm. The subject under discussion might, for example, be a *No First Use* policy—a pledge that country would not use nuclear weapons unless it had been attacked with nuclear weapons—or control of fissile materials. After the initial suspicion and mistrust had subsided (which will be discussed in greater depth in chapter 3), participants were rolling up their sleeves and thrashing out possible terms for treaties.

It took about fifteen years to get to this point. One key ingredient was complete confidentiality—there were no press releases, no communiqués, and nothing of these meetings was ever reported in the media. Building trust between participants was essential. The same is true of the nuclear dialogues conducted by the Oxford Research Group today.

CHINA

I have always felt at home in China. I first went there in 1978, soon after the end of the Cultural Revolution, by smuggling myself into a delegation of doctors studying acupuncture anesthesia. Then in Geneva in 1986, I met Mr. Shu, secretary general of the newly formed Chinese People's Association for Peace and Disarmament—a Chinese version of an NGO, but really part of the foreign office. Mr. Shu was delightful, and we invited him to our home in Oxford and took him cycling around the parks and colleges with the our kids.

Mr. Shu invited us back to Beijing to discuss the possibility of a series of dialogues between Chinese defense decision makers and their US and British counterparts on the most sensitive of issues: the proliferation of nuclear weapons and fissile materials. These dialogues gradually gained traction, hosted in Beijing by the Chinese and in the United Kingdom by the Oxford Research Group, and they continued for nearly two decades. The British, European, and American policy makers that we took to China were dumbfounded by the access to the key actors in Chinese nuclear policy that we were able to arrange. This access built human bridges across ideological divides that were effective and lasting.

Building these bridges involved a long process of learning how to mobilize sufficient *inner* power to sustain the demanding work on *outer* political issues. For example, we gradually learned how to bring the power of silence into contentious meetings. During the visit of one Chinese delegation, there was a heated exchange during a public meeting in an Oxford college. As chair, I suggested that we take three minutes of complete silence to digest what had been said; everyone complied, and when discussion resumed, the tone was markedly calmer. Participants began to see the value of actually listening to one another.

Although we were deeply angry about the dangers to which nuclear weapons exposed humanity, we had to develop the self-awareness not to take a confrontational approach, while maintaining an understanding of the facts. We learned painfully that the moral high ground is not a useful place to stand. Being righteous doesn't change the world, because righteousness so easily becomes a theater for the ego. As we studied the lives of Gandhi, Aung San Suu Kyi, and Mandela, we saw there was another way—a way of patient power that, over time, could bring about more profound change than destroying or demonizing. Later in this book I shall try to analyze what this patient power consists of—this level of consciousness and awareness—and how it can be developed by anyone.

PEACE DIRECT

By the turn of the century, we had become aware of a number of grassroots peace initiatives that were having a real effect on some of the fiercest conflicts in the world. These were led by local people who knew exactly what was needed to prevent or heal violence in their locality, who were brave enough to get up and do something about it. We wanted to know more about them and let others know. I asked a brilliant young researcher, Dylan Mathews, to find out the extent of this locally led peace building. Over the course of a year, Dylan identified 350 viable and effective initiatives, of which he wrote up fifty in a book, *War Prevention Works: 50 Stories of People Resolving Conflict*. The accounts he wrote—of what ordinary people were achieving in war situations—were so stunning that momentum grew to find a way to support them and to enable them to be better known. A small group of us set up Peace Direct to do just that.

Peace Direct was launched in September 2002, when we took over the Royal Opera House in Covent Garden for three nights to celebrate *Transforming September 11th*. We created this program because we calculated, rightly, that the first anniversary of 9/11 would be taken over by obsession with the War on Terror. We wanted to demonstrate, live and before a large audience, how people were transforming conflicts without violence, in real time. Interspersed with fabulous live music by Chloe Goodchild and a full choir, we presented a series of dialogues with people with direct experience of hot conflict in the Congo, Northern Ireland, and Pakistan. The most moving moment for me was when I introduced IRA bomber Pat McGee and the woman whose father he had killed with a bomb planted at the Conservative Party conference in Brighton, for which he had served a long jail sentence. It was only the third time they had met, so we were witnessing—live on stage—the start of a reconciliation process, which led to their long collaboration in building peace in Northern Ireland.

Peace Direct went on to be nominated the Best New Charity at the British Charity Awards in 2005, by which time I had handed over the directorship of the organization to Carolyn Hayman, who not only instantly understood what we wanted to do but also used her extensive experience to make it work effectively. The website now reads:

> We believe that local people have the power to find their own solutions to conflict. Our mission is to help them to make this happen. Local people are the key to preventing, resolving and healing conflicts. They are the best way to break recurrent cycles of violence and make peace last. And increasingly they want to move away from depending on outside help, towards building their own futures.[3]

As an example of the achievements of local peace builders supported by Peace Direct, the following was accomplished in 2013.

- 28,642 people participated in peace-building projects in Sri Lanka.
- 50,000 villagers were given access to justice in DR Congo.
- 965 combatants were demobilized in DR Congo.
- 1,258 volunteers were trained against religious and political extremism in Pakistan.
- 1,257 young people were provided with training and events in east London.

IRAQ

Late in 2002 it became clear that George W. Bush was hell bent on war with Iraq. So I called the wisest political head that I knew—Margarita Papandreou—who, as the widow of the former prime minister of Greece, had good contacts in the region. We agreed that the only thing to do was to go to Iraq and talk to as many leaders as possible to discover if there might still be a way out.

After a long struggle to get visas and an equal struggle to actually get to Baghdad, we finally arrived on January 3, 2003. To enter the hotel you had to walk over a mosaic in the entrance floor that was the face of George Bush—a piece of Iraqi irony not lost on the many journalists staying there. Margarita had sensibly brought with her women leaders from Turkey and Syria, and we teamed up with senior UN officials whom we knew and trusted. We were able to meet with Iraqi cabinet ministers and officials including Deputy Prime Minister Tariq Aziz, Foreign Minister Nagi Sabri, and Oil Minister Amer Mohammed Rashid, as well as with doctors, teachers, and scientists. We had plenty of opportunity to meet ordinary Iraqis and visit sites recently inspected for weapons of mass destruction.

After seven days, during which I wrote my first daily blog,[4] we had collected enough information to come home and write a two-page proposal to Tony Blair, outlining how war could be avoided. A friend put it in Blair's hands a few days later. Apparently he read it quickly and said, "It's too late." For Blair, it was. We later discovered that irreversible machinery for the US/UK invasion had been set in motion the previous October and that Blair had given Bush his unconditional support a year previously.

We were outraged at the duplicity, the failure to inform Parliament of a decision to go to war, and the way that the vast antiwar demonstration in February 2003 was manipulated and ultimately ignored. The invasion of Iraq took place on March 19, 2003.

THE ELDERS

One day in 2004 the phone rang, and someone said, "Richard Branson wants to talk to you." It turned out that Branson, the founder of the Virgin Group, and the musician and philanthropist Peter Gabriel had an idea to assemble The Elders, a group of wise people from all over the world who could guide better decisions for the future of humankind. Since the world was now a global village, it needed global elders. They had first taken the idea to Nelson Mandela, who liked the idea and said, "go away and work out exactly what it is you want to do." Then came what they called the "washing machine period," when ideas went back and forth, and it was difficult to decide exactly what The Elders should do. Hence the phone call—they wanted to see if I could help.

With the brilliant team at Virgin Unite, we eventually defined the qualities an Elder should possess, worked out the options for what kind of organization it would be, how it would be funded, and what issues it might take on. It was challenging for everyone to combine their different visions and expectations, and I made many mistakes. But good ideas emerged, and partners came forward. We developed a list of three hundred potential elders that was whittled down and Nelson Mandela, becoming the founder of The Elders, made the final selection of twelve. We launched The Elders on Mandela's eighty-ninth birthday, July 18, 2007, with Archbishop Desmond Tutu as chair and with members including President Jimmy Carter, human rights supremo Mary Robinson, and former secretary-general of the United Nations Kofi Annan.

The Future Belongs to Those Who Can See It

Working on the transformation of conflict means spending time with people whose lives have been ravaged and shattered by war, as well as with those who are risking their lives daily so that others don't get killed. I also now work with the executive leadership teams of several large companies who realize that the value systems underpinning their actions have to change, not least because the planet can no longer support current levels of resource consumption.

Working with people at both ends of the comfort spectrum—the well fed in elegant boardrooms and the desperate—I see that what they have in common is high levels of stress, a loss of meaning in their lives, and no positive idea of what the future will bring. When I ask people what they think their future will be like, some look blank, others express their worries about getting or holding a job, and others simply shrug.

One of my mentors was a nuclear physicist, Professor Sir Joseph Rotblat, who won the Nobel Peace Prize because he refused to continue working on the Manhattan Project and instead worked with his counterparts in the Soviet Union to minimize the dangers of nuclear war. Once Jo said to me, "the future belongs to those who can see it."

This simple statement made me realize that—amazingly—we have no images for a positive future, no convincing pictures of a world that we'd like our children to inhabit, no pragmatic vision of what life *could* be like. Instead we have an endless stream of doom movies, in which mega-tech battles leave a devastated, uninhabitable earth. We are systematically numbed by reality shows on television and celebrity culture. We have political leaders who make decisions geared to the next opinion poll or the next election, decisions with such a short-term perspective that they do not serve the interests of the next generation, never mind the planet or the biosphere. You could say we have abandoned hope.

Hope, we know well enough, is not a strategy. What's needed is not just hope, but vision grounded in pragmatism and in a humble receptivity to new ideas. Lately I've been lucky enough to come across people who pioneer ways of living that both work in the present day and also build a better future: farmers who transform the desert into oases for growing organic food; businessmen who provide renewable sources of energy on a vast scale; economists who develop new currencies and ways of making financial systems accountable; doctors who combine Eastern and Western medicine to keep their patients healthy; mediators who help rebuild shattered war-torn societies; young women who risk their lives so that other girls can go to school; teachers who enable children to be creative as well as successful; artists who dedicate their passion to waking people up; brilliant authors who give up the academic stratosphere for the challenge of championing new visions; and journalists who risk their careers to blow the whistle on corruption.

Thanks to these heroic innovators, we can paint a picture of a future that could work and inspire people to help build it. That is what this book is about. This picture draws on tested examples of how current problems—overcrowding, hunger, illiteracy, corruption, or violence—are being resolved. It indicates how these efforts could now be scaled up. It identifies the value systems that underpin our current decision making, and it asks how those value systems can change. And, most particularly, it begins to describe the leap in consciousness that will be needed to unlock the mysteries of the future pathway.

How Inner Work Became My Fuel

From the time I was thirteen, I have known deep inside me what I needed to do and to be. I had no choice. I had to stand up for people harmed by extreme violence. I had to understand what was going on and to try for better solutions to what was happening. I wanted the truth.

Like many people trying to change the world, I have run into huge obstacles. Some are the external challenges you have to face—the need to raise money, the constant disappointments, the cynicism. I often found myself on the "losing" side—from my car tires being slit to projects that I started stalling because they were before their time and not understood. I poured energy into a book or a play or a plan and then nothing happened—just no response; no one was interested (there's a list at the end of chapter 7). People greeted my ideas with "that's impossible!"—and quite often that very disbelief made the project impossible. But sometimes it wasn't. Sometimes it worked.

Working in the voluntary sector, in nongovernmental organizations, I notice a distressing drain of energy. People become emotionally exhausted and burned out. This is often due to the sheer pressure of the work, dealing with the toughest of human problems with entirely inadequate resources. However, I also observe that the energy drain is often the result of internal misunderstandings, feuding, bad communication, and lack of self-knowledge. This is one of the reasons that I'm writing this book. It's clear to me that work in the world, however passionate and genuine, is far more effective if it is based on inner intelligence, on self-awareness, and thus on the ability to understand others. This means being able to listen deeply and to do the work on the basis of empathy.

It took years and years for this to dawn on me. I had always been encouraged by the Quakers, whose courage in addressing the toughest issues—slavery, violence in prisons, cruelty to women—had inspired me. Their ability to speak truth to power is extraordinary. It demands a steady cultivation of the ability to be silent and the ability to listen to a greater intelligence. It requires honesty and integrity of high order and the employment of inner power.

About twenty years ago, I was clearing out a cupboard and came upon a large rolled-up scroll. I had never set eyes on it before and to this day I don't know where it came from. The scroll revealed the image of a ferocious red dragon thrashing its way through a storm at sea. Poised on his back is a serene woman in white with a tall headdress, her bare feet resting lightly on the spikes of the dragon's supercharged spine. Immediately I was struck by this powerful and mysterious image of balance.

I knew just enough to recognize the woman in white as Kwan Yin—the Divine Feminine aspect revered for centuries by Buddhists right across East Asia and by Taoists in China and Taiwan. Kwan Yin is the face of the loving Mother. The Mother appears in other belief systems as Mary, Isis, Kali, and Shakti. In her left hand she holds a willow branch, symbol of healing, and in her right, a bottle, from which she pours a stream of compassion into the raging waves.

Without at first knowing why, I was mesmerized by the power this image conveyed. I learned that her full name means "she who listens to the cries of the world" and that she has vowed to remain in the earthly realms until all other living souls have completed their own enlightenment. I framed the scroll and kept staring at it, without quite understanding why I was so fascinated. Gradually I came to perceive that the image of a serene woman standing on the back of a dragon represented an archetypal balance between the calm, centered, grace-filled power of Kwan Yin—her deep feminine power—with the masculine energy, majesty, and the courage of the dragon Yang.

What I was so mysteriously drawn to—and this makes me smile now—was the revelation that the balance between the deep feminine and the deep masculine is the key to any effective social change or truly creative "world work." Why? Because it combines reflection with action, psychological insight with political realism, emotional empathy with clear analysis, and inner spiritual maturity with outer achievement. As our exploding crisis makes absolutely clear, all the latter qualities without all the former can be disastrous. After half a century working on the front line of conflict and societal change, I know that this is the balance that can fuel humanity in helping the earth regenerate, and that could—if deepened and developed—inspire the building of a brilliant future.

I've been struggling to ride the dragon all my life, sometimes balancing but quite often falling off. I'm always finding myself acting as a bridge between those who say, "we need to dream more . . . we need to heal ourselves" and those who sternly say, "face reality and act now!" Being a bridge can be a painful and exhausting occupation—and quite lonely—because it means constantly trying to translate the language of reflection into tools that activists can honor and use. It also means enabling the spiritually inclined to wake up to the urgency of applying their awareness to the crises that so desperately need insight.

I want to make this book as personal and authentic as I can and be honest about the challenges and the darkness, as well as the inspiration and light. Giving birth to my daughter Polly and watching her grow has taught me more about the importance of honesty and openness than anything else in my life. Polly is a living example of truth in action, and the arrival of her new twins has made it all the more urgent in my mind to help build a world that is safe for all. Polly and I believe passionately that the parallel development of inner awareness and outer action—the marriage of the two—is the only effective way to bring about positive change. I know also from experience that being involved in creating a safer and more satisfying future is the source of the greatest and most lasting joy imaginable—a joy that can sustain you through all the ordeals of working for a new world.

CHAPTER 2

THE LEAP IN CONSCIOUSNESS

Edgar Mitchell was a pragmatic young US Navy captain who flew as lunar module pilot on Apollo 14; he was the sixth person to walk on the moon. On the return trip, as he watched the earth float freely in the vastness of space, he realized that the story of the world and humanity as told by science was incomplete and likely flawed. "I recognized that the Newtonian idea of separate, independent, discreet things in the universe wasn't a fully accurate description. What was needed was a new story of who we are and what we are capable of becoming."[1] What new story is Mitchell talking about? What are human beings capable of becoming?

I'm neither a philosopher nor an expert on consciousness, so I will try to keep things as clear and simple as possible, offering from my experience, my studies, and from working with leaders around the world some indications of what this leap in consciousness might be. I will ask what it looks like, how fast it's happening, and whether it actually is essential to human survival.

As far as I can see, this is not a shift in consciousness; this is not something incremental. This is a great leap into a fundamentally different way of perceiving ourselves and the world we inhabit. It will alter everything, and I believe its time has come.

At this point I should also make clear that what I'm talking about has nothing to do with religion. This leap in consciousness is spiritual as well as practical, emanating from a deep desire in human beings for meaning in life and for a profound connection with a greater intelligence, the divine source of All That Is.

What Is This New Consciousness?

My experience tells me that there are many aspects to this leap in consciousness and that there are four essential elements: perspective, interconnectedness, blazing intelligence, and balance between the masculine and the feminine.

PERSPECTIVE

What Edgar Mitchell saw from space was our exquisite planet in its entirety. That sight of our home floating in space allows us humans to perceive the wholeness of our home—the weather systems swirling around it, the vast oceans held to its surface by gravity, and its agonizing beauty. Here we are, sitting on this planet, and we are also able to see it. We are conscious that we are an active part of something vast—living, interconnected cells in one huge body. We can no longer claim to be millions of tiny entities whirling about randomly, victims of circumstances beyond our control. No longer does a person need to be a scientist to begin to grasp the enormity of the planetary systems that our home is part of and the interconnectedness of all things.

For the first time, we have a bird's eye view of the human race. We can see where we live and whom we live among, and we can begin to see what effect our actions have on our home.[2] We are the first species on this earth to be aware that we can destroy not only ourselves but also our habitat by the decisions we make. This alone is a huge wake-up call to consciousness, to the miraculous universe we're part of, and to the responsibility that brings. It is vastly accelerated by the internet, which now means that the majority of the earth's human population can find out, in seconds, what's happening anywhere—and what's happening to our planet as a whole.

Many people experience this kind of perspective when they climb high mountains. For me this was in the Himalaya, when, after a strange series of events, I found myself alone with a depressed guide and two Ladakhi pony men on a twenty-four-days trek, climbing up and over seven passes between 15,000 and 17,000 feet high. It was the beginning of a spiritual journey, and like all worthwhile spiritual journeys, it got tough at times. At the halfway mark—a dilapidated village called Padum—I was asked if I wanted to carry on walking or catch a bus. I sat on a hillock to contemplate this matter. When I opened my eyes, a bird was hovering, fluttering its wings, right in front of my face. And I wasn't sitting on its nest. I closed my eyes again for some time, and when I opened them again, the same thing happened. I took this to mean "get up and fly," and I got up and went on. Little did I know what was about to happen.

The next pass was the toughest we'd faced yet—and the highest; after a steep, fifteen-mile trek, I crawled the last distance to the summit on hands and knees. When I got to the top, all I could see was more of the same—arid, barren, spiky mountains—for miles. No relief of green. No single resemblance to the photos I had seen of wide, fertile Zanskari valleys.

"Where do we go now?" I asked.

"Down," came the reply. "And then up."

What I saw at my feet was an almost vertical drop to a gorge far below and a vertical mountainside opposite, up which was a zigzag path going considerably higher than we already were.

I said, "I don't want to go there."

What I actually wanted was to go home. I cried all the way down the vertical mountainside, put up my tent, and sobbed myself to sleep.

The next day we began the dreaded ascent. About halfway up, we came upon willow trees, which meant water. And, indeed, there was water, a gurgling stream. I sat down, put my feet in the icy water, and began to laugh. I washed my clothes and stretched them on stones to dry. I washed my hair for the first time in two weeks, climbed on a rock, and lay in the sun. Later that night I cooked dinner for the four of us with dried mushrooms that I had brought and felt a sense of well-being. I wrote in my journal:

I realize I'm here to understand the power of the deep feminine. First, it's the ability to bend and not be stiff. There are, of all trees, willows in these jagged hills. Second, the need is for stamina rather than physical strength. Third is the absolute necessity of surrender: because whenever you think things are really bad, you can be socked with something exquisite—right in the middle of the awfulness. In this moment I am totally and completely happy. Hopping in and out of the icy water in the hot sun is delicious, feeling the breeze over my body after all those days of sweaty clothes. And this blessed spot is right in the middle of that mountain that I regarded with such fear and loathing yesterday.

The next morning brought the real wonder. We climbed a high gorge; after three hours, the gorge opened into a stony ascent with perfectly symmetrical sides. As I walked, I began to feel that I did not seem to have a head. It was a strange, inexplicable feeling, full of lightness.[3] Energy seemed to be resonating everywhere and entering my body through the top of my shoulders. Soon I could see the pass itself—always a sacred place—with a stupa decked with prayer flags carrying messages of love on the mountain winds. When I got to the stupa, I fell on my knees, eyes closed. When I opened my eyes, what I saw took my breath away. Below me, stretched out for hundreds of miles, was the entire exquisite panorama of the snow-clad Himalaya.

What this experience gave me was perspective. It gave me a new perspective on life; I saw everything through an entirely different lens, one belonging not to my brain, but to my awakened heart. I wished for everyone on earth to have that experience of spaciousness and peace. I drank in a whole new understanding of the boundless beauty of this planet, seen from the highest place on it that I had ever visited. Everything I saw, I fell in love with.

INTERCONNECTEDNESS

Unless we have gone numb and want only to turn a blind eye to what's happening to the earth, we cannot avoid the reality that we are affecting our own evolution with everything we do. We have learned, for example, that the gases produced by refrigerators destroy the ozone layer; the thinning of the ozone layer, in turn, permits harmful ultraviolet rays to reach our bodies.

This kind of awareness may be jarring and demanding, but it's real. And it's exciting. It is the most unusual opportunity to move toward what some people call "unity consciousness"—a direct, intuitive awareness of the oneness of reality. With this realization comes—inescapably— the knowledge that whatever we think, however we react, and whatever we do has an immediate and positive or negative effect on others. This affects not only those close to us but also those far away whom we have never met.

This is not a new idea; it has been the core realization of all the great mystical traditions. In the Chandogya Upanishad, one of Hinduism's most inspired scriptures, the sage Uddalaka reveals the essential secret of the relationship between the human and the Divine to his son, Shvetaketu.

In the beginning was only Being,
One without a second.
Out of itself Being brought forth the cosmos
And entered into everything in it.
There is nothing that does not come from Being.
Of everything Being is the inmost Self.
Being is the truth; Being is the Self supreme.

You are that, Shvetaketu; you are that.[4]

Thousands of years later, Western teachers echo this: "We are afraid to lose who we think we are. To really receive 'I love you' is to be the love that is loving, and in that there is no room for who you think you are. When there is a surrender to the hugeness of love, to the annihilation of who you think you are, then you are intimate with yourself as what is here, as the whole universe."[5]

Fritjof Capra is a theoretical physicist who demonstrated in 1975 the striking parallels between Eastern and Greek mystical traditions and the discoveries of twentieth century physics.[6] Since then, some of the world's greatest mystics and scientists have combined to marry the global mind to the global heart. Now they're joined by international civil servants at the highest level. Dr. Robert Muller, former assistant secretary-general of the United Nations, said:

See the world with global eyes.
Love the world with a global heart.
Understand the world with a global mind.
Merge with the world through a global spirit.[7]

In the discovery of the quantum vacuum, says Jungian analyst Anne Baring, we have a scientific foundation for the reality of this global spirit, and a challenge to all of us to embody it.

> It seems that we may be immersed in a sea or field or web of energy that is co-inherent with the immensity of the visible universe and the minutest particles of matter. This invisible web connects every one of us to each other and to every aspect of life in the cosmos. Just as we are now discovering that consciousness is distributed through every cell of our body, so we are discovering that it may be present in every photon or particle of light throughout the universe. This discovery tells us that we are literally bathed in a sea of light, invisible to us, yet permeating every cell of our being.[8]

People across the planet are discovering processes that increase awareness—meditation, reflection, creativity, attention to intuition, and bodywork such as yoga or martial arts. Moreover, they are discovering that these practices are enabling them to connect with others in intriguing ways. Thousands of people around the globe now meditate together, at coordinated times, and observe the results.[9]

This sense of interconnectedness is driving change, even in the poorest places on earth—the "informal settlements" in major cities all over Africa and Asia, where thousands arrive every day, desperate to find work. In Mumbai, for example, Shaheen Mistri is the founder and CEO of Teach for India, a movement of young people that has, over the past four years, placed more than seven hundred teachers in under-resourced classrooms. These teachers are willing to forego more lucrative posts because they feel a sense of connectedness to children in need of education.

Explaining this, Shaheen stopped fifty Western visitors in their tracks when she said that when we face a challenge, we can use either a mirror or a magnifying glass. The magnifying glass reveals the detail of the problem, which can be useful if we want to externalize it, but the mirror shows us who *we* are. Seeing who we are and how we interact with the problem is the fastest and most efficient route to transforming it. She says, "When I walk out in the street, do I see the kids as my kids? Do I clean out my house and dump the garbage in the street?"

Imagine a world in which activists on the front line are supported by activist meditators dedicated to the marriage of radical action with inner meditation. This could ultimately stop war. In fact, it has already. An experiment, described by quantum physicist Dr. John Hagelin, was conducted in the Middle East during the war in Lebanon in the 1980s.[10] The hypothesis was that if enough people were collectively stimulating peace within, that would be reflected in the wider society. The results, as illustrated in graphs, showed that the numbers of people meditating correlated exactly with lessening violence and progress toward peace.

Eventually, after endless review processes, this was published in the Yale University *Journal of Conflict Resolution,* with an accompanying letter requesting that other studies be carried out, since the results were so unexpected. In about six different studies at different times and in several different countries, the fluctuations in the size of the meditating groups were compared to officially collected data on daily rates of crime, violence, war deaths, and other problems. The correlation between the size of the meditating group and reductions in violence and crime was dramatic and statistically significant. The statistical likelihood that the results were due to chance was one in ten million—which is a far higher level of significance than most pharmaceuticals or other social interventions have been required to show to prove that their products work as claimed.

Evolutionary biologist Elisabet Sahtouris writes, "When physicists discovered that all the universe was composed of energy waves, and that every instance of our human reality was a wave function collapsed from sheer probability by a conscious observer, everything changed. It meant that our world is produced in our consciousness—that realities are not fixed scenarios in which we grope our way about, but the ever-changing creations we ourselves "bring forth" both individually and collectively."[11]

Something astonishing is becoming clear in this evolving marriage of science and mysticism, and it is this. The whole universe is being recognized as a "Unified Field" of brilliantly intelligent, interconnected energy.

Like many others, I've had my own personal experiences of this field. What happened in 2012 however showed me the enormity of the resources this field makes available for exactly the kind of social and political transformation we now need.

In the summer of 2012, at the Celebrate Life Festival in northern Germany, a teacher named Thomas Hübl explained the Unified Field to an audience of about eight hundred people. Hübl said the Unified Field was a social process for higher understanding. At the festival, my colleagues and I were facilitating a five-day working group of about sixty people, and we were curious to investigate whether this Unified Field had any effect on the transformation of conflict.

During the next few days, our experience was as follows: as conflicts erupted in the group, we found that a key decision on the part of individuals was whether to move "toward" the conflict or to shy away from it. Those willing to move toward the conflict—to unearth it, face it, and listen to others involved in it—found that they could move through the conflict to a place where it was transformed. A key factor seemed to be that they were supported in doing this by a number of people consistently meditating.

As a result of this experience, which was documented, Thomas Hübl asked me if I knew of a community in a zone of hot conflict who might like to work on a further experiment. He wanted to be connected with a community who were thoughtful and reflective, so I put him in touch with the Tree of Life in Zimbabwe.[12] The Tree of Life is a network of five different community groups comprising several hundred people, who have been meeting across the country for years of dedicated work to heal the victims of electoral brutality, torture, rape, and murder that have proliferated under the vicious political regime of Zimbabwean president Robert Mugabe. At the time, they were also gearing up to support activists and community organizers to prevent violence in the run-up to the elections announced for July 2013.

Thomas suggested that those in Zimbabwe meet in meditation at specific times on the first and third Tuesday of every month, connecting with his group sitting in meditation in Germany. As he said, "Many people sitting at the same time generates a very strong energy field. I think this will be very supportive for you. . . . I would suggest that everyone invite consciously that a new level of awakening or light or consciousness will take place. This invitation will draw the energy in." The coordinated meditation groups started in March 2013. In mid July came this email from Zimbabwe:

> The Tree of Life circle this Friday was a feedback from the facilitators who had been either visiting or running workshops in 9 of our different communities both rural and urban. Apart from a few skirmishes between supporters of the two political parties, there is an extraordinary message of peace and calm. In one area they ran a workshop with a large group of youth, many of whom had, 5 years ago, been used to perpetrate the violence—often on their own families—and they spoke of the effects it had had on them. They spoke with firm conviction that this time, they would be part of the peace—this was what they wanted.
>
> The councilors from different parties met with the head of police in a particularly troubled urban community and between them declared non-partisan determination to hold peace. These are agreements and conversations that could not have taken place even 6 months ago.
>
> In most of our communities the Tree of Life facilitators, councilors, police and headmen are now in conversation. The communities all felt very strongly that there was a different possibility this time—and that the election violence could be held at bay. The huge difference is that now they are speaking to one another, as opposed the fearful separation that divided them last election.
>
> It is also clear that there are still irregularities in the voters' role (particularly the exclusion of the youth), and concerns about the placement of polling stations, etc. These are already reported to the election observers—this is also a first as previously this research was more difficult both to execute, and publicize.[13]

Zimbabweans lined up to vote on July 31, and the absence of violence was noted by all observers; this election was quite different to previous ones. Then came the official result of an overwhelming victory to Mugabe. Most non-African observers expressed concern over electoral fraud, including alleged bribery, bussing of voters to opposition strongholds and manipulation of the electoral roll. Nevertheless, the peaceful atmosphere continued. The Tree of Life wrote:

> This time was different
> we have recorded every step of this unlawful process
> we have voiced our findings and spoken our frustrations
> we have used public media
> we have written of the inconsistencies and travesties
> spoken our truth, been heard across the world.
>
> This time, we are different
> . . . we have been to workshops learning of our civic rights/human
>   rights/women's rights/food rights
> learned the language of conflict resolution and sustainable dialogue
> we have begun to take care of our own AIDS victims
> begun circles of support to take care of our orphaned children
> begun community gardens growing organic vegetables.
>
> And we have seen that we have been able to cross the cracks and gaps
> and deep divides
> that have disabled us
>
> and seen ourselves grow into wider people
>
> able to look at things from a longer perspective . . .
>
> looking for a way to live the responsibility of empowered people.[14]

What's emerging has several names: it's known by biochemist Rupert Sheldrake as the Morphogenetic Field, and it's also called the Amplified Field and the Unified Field. This field develops when people choose to come together to communicate with the intention to tell their deepest heart truth.

Sally Dearman Cummings was the first woman to pilot fast jets in the

British Royal Air Force. She writes, "Whenever an authentic truth is told it sets up a resonance that can be felt by others, as a feeling of warmth or comfort within, a flowing or lift in energy, a solidity, an inner sense of 'yes' or congruence or completeness." Cultivating and sustaining this resonance demands a special kind of discipline that is essential to experiencing the Amplified Field and to drawing on its extraordinary power. "The more people train themselves to their highest degree of discernment, by practicing this skill in groups that have highest integrity as their aim, the more truth emerges, and the deeper, richer, fuller and more effective the amplified field becomes."[15]

Frontier scientists from across the planet have produced remarkable evidence that an energy field connects everything in the universe and that humanity is part of this vast exchange of energy. Lynne McTaggart, in her remarkable explanation of how this field was discovered and how it works, says that some scientists suggest that all of our higher cognitive processes result from an interaction with this field, and that this "might account for intuition or creativity—and how ideas come to us in bursts of insight, sometimes as fragments but often as a miraculous whole."[16]

McTaggart records how the Transcendental Meditation organization had systematically tested—through dozens and dozens of studies conducted over a twenty-year span—whether group meditation could reduce violence and discord in the world. The organization had elected to call this "Super Radiance"—after the super-radiance in the brain or in a laser that creates coherence and unity—because they believed meditation would have the same effect on society.

Many of the studies were published in peer-reviewed journals. One study of twenty-four US cities "showed that whenever a city reached a point where 1 percent of the population was carrying out regular [Transcendental Meditation], the crime rate dropped [by] 24 percent. In a follow up study of 48 cities, half of which had a 1 percent population which meditated, the 1 percent cities achieved a 22 percent decrease in crime, compared with an increase of 2 percent in the control cities."[17]

Our understanding of this field is in its infancy, but it is clear to me and to many others that an extraordinary power of transformation awaits us if we can establish a humble and transparent relationship with it.

BLAZING INTELLIGENCE

One day not so long ago I suddenly saw the amazing feat that is a tree. In this case, it was a towering oak tree near where I live; it was in April. It dawned on me that this massive edifice, which has been standing there for at least two hundred winters, was conveying liquids and nourishment vertically upward through solid wood. In a few weeks, this rich moisture was going to produce tiny leaves from the buds I could already see swelling. In autumn there would be acorns falling to the ground, each one carrying a four-hundred year blueprint plan of its own.

I stood there stunned.

As I look around me now, there are literally thousands of such organisms and plants and animals and insects, all going through the most intricate cycles, without any instruction from anyone. I saw the exquisite perfection of a butterfly's wing and realized that however hard we humans try, we can't produce that level of live beauty. When my daughter became the mother of twins, I stared in awe at these beautiful beings who—at the moment of taking their first breath—possessed functioning internal organs that would last them for perhaps a hundred years, who had genes reaching back over millions of years, who had nervous systems and endocrine glands and hormones perfectly designed to function smoothly with no instruction from a human or a computer.

Daniel Siegel, clinical professor of psychiatry at the UCLA School of Medicine, makes the following observations: "Given the number of synaptic connections, the brain's possible on-off firing patterns—its potential for various states of activation—has been calculated to be ten to the millionth power—or ten times ten one million times. This number is thought to be larger than the number of atoms in the known universe. It also far exceeds our ability to experience in one lifetime even a small percentage of these firing possibilities."[18]

Observing these things, I woke up to the sheer extent of the blazing intelligence that must have produced everything that we see around us. We and everything else are made from the stardust of the Big Bang. I remain astounded by the beauty of this system, in the midst of which we humans live.

Any day, any one of us can go into a public park—or even a patch of waste ground—and see the extravagant elegance of what nature has produced over billions of years. A two-year-old child looking at a snail or a wildflower is rightly mesmerized and astonished. If an adult—gazing out of the window of a jet passing over the remaining great tropical forests of the earth—is not astonished and mesmerized, something is . . . well . . . not in working order.

> It comes down to this.
> Thinking we are the most intelligent, the most evolved life form
>   thrown up
> by a foaming, mechanical universe, we commune only with
>   ourselves and
> keep the world at bay.

> But if we were to open to a world in which we recognized the blazing
> intelligence of the cosmic womb that birthed us and everything
>   we see
> around us, if we began to glimpse the scale and scope of her project
> and the depth of love that underwrites it, we would turn
>   and face this
> mysterious world. . . .

> We would build up commerce with it until contact deepened into
> communion, and communion is a sacramental exchange that
>   transforms
> both parties.

> With this pivot, history would turn.
> We would begin to value and cultivate the skills of alignment.
> We would begin to recognize the symptoms of misalignment in
>   individuals,
> institutions and ideologies.[19]

BALANCE BETWEEN THE MASCULINE AND THE FEMININE

For three thousand years—at least—power and decision making worldwide has been in the hands of men. While this has brought us obvious advances in science and great discoveries in many fields, it has also led to an imbalance, a distorted way of doing things that excludes or marginalizes essential aspects of human intelligence.

When I was researching a book on power and sex in 1995, I found that nearly all recorded thinking on power and the use of power has been androcentric—that is, done by men and based on male values. The male norm and the human norm, even today, tend to be thought of as identical. Nations operate according to distorted male notions of power, and that is the way they assume others will respond. There is a whole set of preconceptions underlying this way of thinking, including the conviction that humans are inherently aggressive, inveterately competitive, and socially separate and independent, and that they have no need to be responsible in a collective manner.[20]

This has led to a dangerous imbalance between the masculine and feminine in most of us today—regardless of gender—and it is prevalent almost everywhere in the world. For example, we see women in the City of London and on Wall Street dressing exactly like men (except for the high heels) and competing to outperform men in focus, logic, ruthlessness, and achievement.

What has become devalued in this way of living are essential elements of being human:

- the skill of listening
- the ability to nurture and to include
- the choice to exercise "power with" rather than "power over"
- the attention to intuition and the creative imagination that makes for great art and invention
- the ability to stand in the shoes of another person
- the practice of dialogue with our inner world
- the compassion and stamina to look after those who are weak or in need
- reverence for the sacredness of creation and of our bodies

This loss of the feminine principle of the soul has also resulted in the devaluation of the deep masculine, also known as the sacred masculine and exemplified in the great saints and sages of our global traditions. In our contemporary world's lethal addiction to the grasping and dominating aspects of the male, we have lost sight of the more profound and life-nurturing gifts of the masculine. These include the passion to protect life and the vulnerable, the sense of honor in duty to the community; the profound depth of brotherhood in goals that transcend personal agendas; the courtesy and modesty of the code of chivalry; the rigorous patience devoted to discovery and verification in scholarship and science; the love of order, clarity, and law (not as goals in themselves, but as a way of structuring life); the capacity for one-pointed focus and the stamina to complete the task; and the courage to be in the service of the rights of the weak, to stand up and be counted, and to blow the whistle on corruption.

This devaluation of the qualities of the deep feminine and the deep masculine—in women as in men—has led to untold suffering all over the world. It is a fundamental cause of the dissociation from ourselves, our bodies, and the natural world—and the avalanche of disasters caused by that dissociation.

What is essential for human survival now is the rebalancing of the masculine and feminine qualities possessed by both men and women. We recognize and admire the extraordinary power of individuals who have managed it, who can call equally on their courage and their compassion, on their logic and their love, on their intention and their intuition. Think of how Nelson Mandela had the empathy to understand the needs of the white supremacists in South Africa, combined with a steely courage such as the world has rarely seen. Think of how the compassionate heart of Mother Teresa worked in tandem with a mind as sharp as a razor. In the next chapter, we shall visit other great world changers who have reached this new level of consciousness through their ability to develop and use their masculine and feminine sides equally.

This principle of balance between the feminine and masculine parts of ourselves has long been recognized. For thousands of years, Eastern spiritual traditions have worked with the balance of *yin* and *yang* and Eastern health practices and medical expertise—such as acupuncture—are based on achieving this balance in the body's energy. The balance is superbly evoked in the Kabbalah, the eloquent archive of Jewish mysticism, and it is found in the Hindu tradition of Shiva and Shakti, as well as in ancient

Egypt, and in the stories and folklore of indigenous peoples the world over.

This rebalancing of the masculine and feminine over time creates a being that, like a great dancer, combines peace and passion, rigor and spontaneity, discipline and surrender, being and doing, heart and head, and clear interaction between the right and left hemispheres of the brain. It can be illustrated by the Vesica Piscis—the ancient symbol covering the Chalice Well in Glastonbury, Somerset.

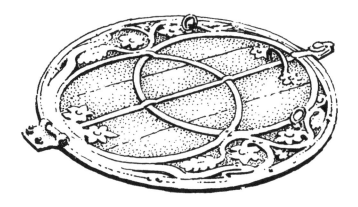

Cover of the Chalice Well, Glastonbury.*

The "wise mind" is in the space created where the two circles overlap. It is this mind that can be the vehicle of the leap in consciousness that Einstein called for, because by its nature, it is connected to all modes of being and becoming in the Unified Field, and it able to draw on whatever is needed for the situation in hand. Imagine for a moment what resources we would discover for the regeneration of the planet if our educational systems were devoted to drawing out this wise mind.

With all its challenges, the age we face now demands that human beings access their wholeness—their ability to use body, soul, and spirit, as well as mind. Women and men of wisdom have a key part to play in showing how this rebalanced power works, awakening in humanity the

---

* Scilla Elworthy, *Power and Sex* (London: Element Books, 1990).

love of and devotion to life on earth that will enable not just survival, but transformation and a future full of possibility. This can be an evolutionary awakening of global proportions.

What Does This Leap in Consciousness Look Like, and Has It Happened Before?

Major shifts in values, possibly even in consciousness, may have taken place in recorded human history; examples cited by historians include the Renaissance and the period of the sixth and fifth centuries BCE, a period that saw early Greek philosophy, the life of the Buddha, the writings of Lao Tzu, and the beginnings of Taoism.

The kind of leap in consciousness we're interested in could be compared to the transformation of a caterpillar into a butterfly. A caterpillar eats hundreds of times its weight in a day—day after day—until it is too bloated to continue and hangs itself up, its skin then hardening into a chrysalis. Inside this chrysalis, deep in the caterpillar's body, tiny things that biologists call "imaginal discs" begin to form. These discs contain the blueprint of a whole new being. At first they are attacked and resisted by the caterpillar, but they keep coming faster and faster, becoming the "imaginal cells" that build the butterfly by feeding on the soupy meltdown of the caterpillar's body.

It took a long time for biologists to understand the reason for the immune system attack on the incipient butterfly cells, but eventually they discovered that the butterfly has its own unique genome, carried by the caterpillar, inherited from long ago in evolution, yet not part of it as such.[21]

Elisabet Sahtouris writes, "If we see ourselves as imaginal discs working to build the butterfly of a better world, we will understand that we are launching a new 'genome' of values and practices to replace that of the current unsustainable system. We will also see how important it is to link with each other in the effort, to recognize how many different kinds of imaginal cells it will take to build a butterfly with all its capabilities and colors."

Before we examine the speed of the leap in consciousness that is occurring, we need to understand the paradoxical nature of our current crisis. It is at once a great birth and a great death. On the one hand, we are living in a time of stupendous scientific discoveries and spiritual renaissance that are transforming our concept of the universe and shattering old ideas about the nature of reality. On the other, our mindless plundering of the earth's resources and our destruction of nature's balance are threatening the delicate organism of life on our planet and the survival of our species as never before.

Since 1900, the percentage of the world's overexploited or fully exploited or oceans has risen from less than 10 percent to 87 percent. "Fully exploited" means there are no fish left in the sea. Ivan MacFadyen has twice raced a yacht from Melbourne to Japan. The first time, ten years ago, his isolation was relieved by regular sightings of turtles, dolphins, and flurries of feeding birds. "But this time, for 3,000 nautical miles there was nothing alive to be seen," he says. What modern mariners do notice plenty of, however, is floating plastic debris. That—along with overfishing, of course—explains the scarcity of maritime creatures. Albatrosses, for example, mistake plastic debris for food and give it to their young. "Chicks starve with full bellies, and when their bodies rot away, they leave tragic piles of bottle tops, pens, cigarette lighters and plastic fragments to bleach in the sun."[22]

The International Union for the Conservation of Nature—the world's leading authority on biodiversity—estimates that, as of 2013, species at imminent risk of extinction include 196 mammals, 197 birds, 151 reptiles, 519 amphibians, 413 fishes, 120 insects, 548 mollusks, and 1920 plants.[23] It doesn't take much imagination to realize the effect such disappearances have on food chains—and thus on human survival.

There is an accelerating change in our entire earth system, of which climate is but one component. Without realizing it, molecule by molecule, we have upset the earth's climatic balance. Arctic coastlines, for example, are retreating by fourteen meters per year. Greenland's surface ice melt season reached peak levels in late July 2013.[24] This will contribute to rising sea levels.[25]

The World Meteorological Organization reports that the first decade of the twenty-first century was the warmest ever recorded for both northern and southern hemispheres. According to the WMO, the rate of temperature rise in the past two decades has been unprecedented.

The combination of the melting of the Antarctic and Greenland ice sheets and the thermal expansion of the oceans as they warm means not only are sea levels rising but also that the rate of this rise is speeding up. In the decade just gone, the rise averaged 3 millimeters per year, nearly double the yearly average of 1.6 millimeters in the twentieth century. The global sea level average in 2010 was 20 centimeters (nearly 8 inches) above the level in 1880. Rising sea levels mean that vast populations will have to move. On an already grotesquely overcrowded planet, where will they go?

Melting sea ice is now, in turn, causing the release of vast quantities of methane from the Arctic Ocean. For the first time, hundreds of plumes of methane—many of them over a mile wide—have been observed rising from previously frozen methane stores in the Lapdev Sea, off the East Siberian Arctic shelf. This may just be the beginning of what increased global warming can release, and because methane is many times more potent a greenhouse gas than carbon dioxide, this could pose the ultimate death knell to our environment.

To summarize, here are the figures quoted by the 2009 award-winning film *Home,* made by Yann Arthus-Bertrand:[26]

1. In fifty years—a single lifetime—the earth has been more radically changed than by all previous generations of humanity combined.
2. Before the end of this century, excessive mining will have exhausted nearly all the planet's reserves of minerals.
3. The Arctic icecap has lost 40 percent of its thickness in forty years.
4. Across the planet, one major river in ten no longer flows into the sea for several months of the year.
5. In India 30 percent of wells have had to be abandoned because the underground aquifers have dried out.
6. It takes nearly 3,500 gallons of water to produce a little over two pounds of beef.
7. One billion people worldwide have no access to clean water.
8. Fish is the staple diet of one in five humans, yet three-quarters of fishing grounds worldwide are depleted or in dangerous decline.

9. Half the world's poor live in resource-rich countries.
10. Half the world's wealth is in the hands of the richest 2 percent of the world's population.
11. Every week over a million people swell the population of the world's cities.
12. In one hour the sun gives the earth the same amount of energy as that consumed by all of humanity in one year. Yet in some countries bathed by the sun, you see almost no solar panels.

Every one of these examples shocks and frightens me. These are examples of human violence—unconsciousness violence, but on a massive scale. Added to that lack of awareness is the desperate race to make money and the hubris of thinking that advanced technology has no consequences.

Andrew Harvey says, "I know that the world is in terrible trouble. I am not going to pretend. I know that if we continue to operate from our current level of collective consciousness we are going to destroy ourselves."[27] How can humans wake up to the mortal danger of our interference with the fragile web of relationships upon which life on this planet depends? Is there a way that we can see that we are an integral part of this great web of life, formed over countless millions of years? That we certainly cannot control it? That we will not survive unless we respect it?

It is now clear to many observers that this mortal danger is challenging us to take a great leap in our evolution—one that we might not have confronted, were we not pushed right up against chaos and collapse. We have never had to think as a planet before. Why? Because our capacity for destruction—whether military, societal, or environmental—is now so much greater than it was fifty years ago. Because the advances we have made in the technology of destruction—combined with our belief in our right to ravage the planet for our own purposes—means that this destruction will be greater tomorrow. We have, at most, only a few decades in which to heal ourselves and help regenerate the planet.

Historian Karen Armstrong has written more than twenty books on faith and the major religions, studying how they have shaped world history and how they drive current events. In *The Great Transformation*, she writes, "We risk environmental catastrophe because we no longer see the earth as holy, but regard it simply as a resource." She goes on: "Unless there is some kind of spiritual revolution that can keep abreast of our technological genius, it is unlikely we will save our planet."[28] More and more outstanding writers and broadcasters are now saying the same thing.[29]

How Fast Is This Leap Happening?

I don't know the answer to this question, and I want to know. I'm astonished that there are no serious studies of the growth in global awareness, since it is the key to human survival.

In 2010 I asked the head of Google's School of Personal Growth if Google could set up a simple poll, asking five questions to determine awakening, such as: "Do you have a daily practice of reflection?" "Do you feel you'd like to contribute to the planet in some way?" "Do you take actions to conserve energy?"

Then, if people ticked all five boxes, they would appear on a Google map of the world as a dot of light, with the result that

- they could then be contacted by other points of light in their neighborhood, and they could take initiatives together;
- people worldwide could see that the planet is lighting up because of individuals waking up to their personal role in the future of all; and
- over a short time, it would become apparent how fast this waking up is taking place.

Needless to say, this could have all sorts of potentially beneficial effects. It might show politicians where future votes lie, encouraging them to change their policies. It might influence the type of consumer goods produced and how they are sourced. And it might challenge the media to cover aspects of change far more responsibly.

The idea didn't seem to get traction—at least it hasn't yet. I'm now at work on having this technology made available on a global scale to inspire and connect those who have taken on making the leap in consciousness.

The next obvious question is, aren't governments and world organizations dealing with global warming and climate change? The organizations that we would hope could do this—like the United Nations, the

International Monetary Fund, and the World Bank—are taking stabs at it, but these have been disastrously ineffective.

The UN Framework Convention on Climate Change, whose job for the past twenty years has been to ensure the stabilization of greenhouse gases, has failed in its goals. Likewise, the Convention on Biological Diversity, whose job has been to reduce the rate of biodiversity loss, has failed. And the UN Convention to Combat Desertification has also failed. Governments either cannot make the necessary agreements to halt the devastation of the planet, or they cannot stick to them.

A recent article in the *Economist* concludes, in effect, that no one wants to be responsible unilaterally, since all want to profit from the world's resources. We are in the grip of a classic—and this time global—case of the "tragedy of the commons," which is the depletion of a shared resource by individuals acting independently and "rationally," each according to his or her own self-interest. Given the extent and complexity of the crisis and the lack of leadership in response, it is hardly surprising that most people feel helpless and allow their instinctive common sense to be dulled by the media.

Andrew Harvey says that 95 percent of us are in denial and 4 percent are beginning to wake up, but then getting lost in magical thinking (by "magical thinking," he means New Age dreaming). In his view, only 1 percent of us are actually waking up to the extent of what must be done and girding ourselves with the powerful energy of the new consciousness.[30]

What is clear is that time is running out. Now, more than ever before, we have to wake up and act from a new consciousness. Only such a consciousness can give us the guidance, wisdom, and strength we need to transform our future. As Eckhart Tolle says, "The history of Communism, originally inspired by noble ideals, clearly illustrates what happens when people attempt to change external reality—create a new earth—without any prior change in their inner reality, their state of consciousness."[31]

So, what would happen if we were able to access the consciousness of the Unified Field—and how can we gain this access? How people do this—how they discover and use a higher level of human consciousness—is what the following chapters are about.

CHAPTER 3

LEARNING HOW WORLD CHANGERS USE INNER POWER

This chapter profiles some surprising examples of individuals who have begun to chart a new future. They awoke to the energy of their own spiritual potential—their inner power—and they gained the self-knowledge that is the essential part of building a positive future. They started out to make a difference in the world and then experienced a leap in their consciousness that empowered them to take the right actions that could transform the problems they faced. By elevating their awareness, they became powerful and wise enough to work for change in the world in a brilliantly effective way.

Some of these people have become household names, and others are local heroes the world may never have heard of. Their stories demonstrate that you don't have to be a media celebrity, a world-class academic, or a gifted talent to have a huge impact on the world. In this chapter, I shall search out some of their secrets, examine their experiences, and mine their wisdom. They are like tuning forks for the consciousness of humankind. In each case, I shall try to identify what the particular leap in consciousness was and how the development of inner power increased the effectiveness of this person's work in the world.

These are individuals who have wrestled deeply with the doubts, ordeals, and challenges of being a pioneer. They have dared to speak truth to power. They have learned to resurrect themselves from the kind of suffering that would have annihilated others. We shall see how valiantly they faced the doubts and dark times. They have also, crucially, learned when skepticism is valuable and when cynicism is destructive.

Meditation and Speaking Truth to Power— ## THICH NHAT HANH

Thich Nhat Hanh became a monk in Vietnam at the age of sixteen. He learned in depth the meditation disciplines of Buddhism and became introduced to the nature of his own mind.

When the Vietnam War broke out, the monasteries were confronted with an agonizing choice—stay in the contemplative life, meditating, or go out and help the villagers. Thich Nhat Hanh chose to do both. His leap in consciousness enabled him to fuse the strength of a warrior with an inner and outer calm. He founded the engaged Buddhism movement—a way of life that embraces peaceful activism for the purpose of social reform. With his disciples, fellow monks and nuns, he rebuilt bombed villages and schools, established medical centers, and resettled families left homeless during the war. And they meditated as they did it.

In the midst of the war, he made a visit to the United States on a mission of reconciliation. He persuaded Martin Luther King to oppose the Vietnam War and made the case for peace to Pentagon officials. This was a risky task; imagine a monk in robes—from the country that was at war with the United States of America—calmly and directly speaking the truth about peace to uniformed generals. Nevertheless, it had a positive effect. He was asked to be the delegate for the Buddhist Peace Delegation at the Paris Peace Talks in 1969—eventually helping to establish peace in Vietnam. But there was a price—his opposition to both his own government's and the American government's involvement in the war forced him into exile from his own country and when the war was over the new government still refused his return.

Eventually he settled in France and established a Buddhist community known as Plum Village, where residents describe their way of life as living mindfully—being conscious in everything they do—eating, walking, working, talking. He continues his work—teaching, writing, and supervising the monasteries and nunneries that have sprung up to practice his insights—and his books sell hundreds of thousands of copies.

This man stayed in the still center of peace while working in the midst of horror, in the toughest areas of the Vietnam war, seeing comrades, families, children, and fellow monks suffering horribly before his eyes, and dying. His response was always pragmatic; he set up welfare schemes, feeding stations, medical services, and peace missions. His activity never stopped; it was always urgent, but never rushed.

He brought extraordinary organizing capacity to a landscape of devastation and terror; he was calm and mysteriously happy. In a remarkable act of compassion after the war, he regularly travelled to the United States to work with war veterans, helping to heal the internal mental torment of the men who bombed and shot the villagers he had spent his early life trying to protect. When I found out that he had done this, my heart cracked open.

The core essence of his life radiates from the opening lines of his book *Being Peace:*

Life is filled with suffering, but it is also filled with many wonders, like the blue sky, the sunshine, the eyes of a baby. To suffer is not enough. We must also be in touch with the wonders of life. . . . If we are not happy, if we are not peaceful, we cannot share peace and happiness with others.[1]

Using the Energy of a Network— DEKHA IBRAHIM ABDI

I can picture my friend Dekha Ibrahim Abdi in her kitchen in Mombasa, surrounded by children, animals, and many pots and pans. Dekha loved to cook—preferably to cook up a feast. One of her maxims for effective peace building was "feast with your enemies," and her feasts were famous for increasing the well-being and energy of anyone lucky enough to be there.

When Dekha was growing up, in a simple rural town in northeastern Kenya, pupils at her secondary school were separated into groups along religious and ethnic lines, but Dekha and her friends created a unity between these opposing camps by sticking together. This childhood experience informed her philosophy that interreligious cooperation was essential to achieving durable peace.

She graduated and became a head teacher of a school in Wajir, where she started a grassroots initiative to end the cattle-rustling disputes, which had taken many lives, by developing a peace plan with women from other clans and encouraging the male clan elders to carry the plan out. Dekha developed this model for mediation, and it has been copied in many countries where she has taught. The Kenyan government asked her to work as an adviser on mediation all over the country, and for this she received many awards.

What was striking about her approach was, firstly, her presence. When she walked into a room, a sense of calm and dignity entered with her. That meant that before a word was spoken, everyone felt a little safer. Tensions began to subside. This kind of presence cannot be invented or conjured up; it's the result of years of self-examination, reflection, listening, and learning.

Dekha's spiritual identity as a Muslim formed a strong foundation for her peace work and I believe her consciousness was expanded through her exploration of the Qu'ran's teaching on understanding the soul. Indeed, she encouraged individuals and communities in conflict to examine themselves using verses from the Qu'ran.

Young people immediately warmed to her. From 2002 Dekha was patron of our London-based NGO *Peace Direct*. In this capacity, after the London bombings she co-facilitated a project to provide a platform for young Muslims to explore the challenges around being a Muslim and being British.

People resonated with her absolute conviction that peace was possible. I remember her addressing a group of hard-headed journalists in London after the post-election violence in Kenya in early 2008. She held them spell-bound with her account of how the strategy for violence reduction was put into action, minute by minute.

"She was called to the Serena Hotel in Nairobi, where two retired generals, an ambassador, and two other civil society leaders were already gathered. She walked in, gravely, in her golden yellow floor-length dress, and everyone breathed more deeply. The ambassador pointed to an empty chair and said, "Dekha, please take the chair. We have immediately to design a way to stop the killing."

One of the methods they used was to ask the sixty thousand members of a women's organization, who had cell phones, to look out their windows and report what they saw. The information started pouring in. They began to plot not only the hot spots of the violence but also the cold spots, since it was important to know where people were running to, so they could be protected. They then began to develop strategies for each spot, with the help of trusted local leaders, to work out together how they could stop the killing without using force. Almost miraculously, in less than three weeks, with the help of community, youth, and church leaders; sports personalities; the police; and the media, these strategies brought the violence under control.

When Kofi Annan arrived to mediate between the rival leaders, Kibaki and Odinga, it was possible to secure a peace agreement based on a mix of official and local methodologies—exactly in the way advocated by Dekha and her colleagues."[2]

She saw only too clearly the fragility of peace, saying that peace needs to be nurtured as carefully as an egg. Dekha found deep fulfillment in enabling others to develop their full potential as leaders for peace and justice, never seeking the limelight for herself. She died at age forty-six on July 14, 2011, from injuries sustained in a car accident. The loss of her as a person and as a peace builder remains almost unbearable to me and to those who have been touched by her.

Doing What Means Most to You—
ELLEN MacARTHUR

Photo: Liot Vapillon/DPPI/ Offshore Challenge

Nothing mattered more to Ellen MacArthur than the sea, unless it was being the fastest person on its surface. It was her element, her great obsession from childhood. She had a kind of symbiotic union with the boats that took her round the world. They worked as one. In 2005, she established a round-the-world solo record, an experience so savage that it's a wonder she came back.

Then, something changed: "I still felt as much in love with the sea as ever, but something inside me had grown to eclipse that passion. . . . Persuading people that to rethink the way we do things is the biggest challenge I've ever faced, a Herculean task. . . . We have to design a way of not using things up."[3]

In her autobiography, Ellen says:

All of a sudden, the big picture came into focus; in fact, it hit me like a ton of bricks. The very framework in which we live is broken—the structure of our boat is fundamentally flawed. Rather than plugging holes in a sinking ship, should we not be aiming to build a new one that can sail for ever? . . . It wasn't about the world being a mechanical system that we can control, but rather an intricate web of systems from which we can harness power and resources. One of the rules is that we put back what we take.[4]

This was her leap in consciousness. For the next three years, she tirelessly toured factories, mines, and power stations in the United Kingdom, talking to government and business about the necessity of changing our addiction to exploiting finite resources. "This became something I just couldn't ignore. Sailing, by comparison, seemed incredibly selfish. It was all about me. This is different. It's about trying to find out how my voice can be the most useful. It really matters."[5]

She has since launched the Ellen MacArthur Foundation (motto: "rethink the future"), a charity that works to give young people the vision to design a sustainable future. Ellen realized that the linear "take, make, dispose" way that we currently live our lives relies on large quantities of easily accessible resources and energy, and as such, it is increasingly unfit for the reality of the earth today. Working toward efficiency—a reduction of resources and fossil energy consumed per unit of manufacturing output—will not alter the finite nature of their stocks but can only delay the inevitable. Ellen saw that a change of the entire operating system was necessary.[6]

The Ellen MacArthur Foundation has adopted the concept of the circular economy—an industrial economy that is restorative by intention; one that aims to rely on renewable energy; one that minimizes, tracks, and intends to eliminate the use of toxic chemicals and eradicate waste through careful design. The concept of the circular economy is grounded in the study of living systems that naturally recycle.

Ellen is a wonderful example of how to listen inside oneself, allowing imagination and creativity to flourish, and then following your passion and becoming a pragmatic visionary in the process. She says, "It is the best decision I have made in my life. . . . This beats everything I've ever done."[7]

Risking Your Life to Free Child Soldiers—
HENRI BURA LADYI

Photo: Fiona Lloyd-Davies, courtesy of Peace Direct

Over five million people have died as a result of war in the Democratic Republic of Congo since 1998. Whole communities have been torn apart as neighbor turns on neighbor, law and order disintegrates, and development grinds to a halt. Boys as young as seven are abducted in rebel militias, their mothers and sisters raped, their fathers murdered. The tragedy seems overwhelming. Henri Ladyi has first-hand experience: "I grew up in war and, like many boys from my community, I thought about joining the local militia to protect my family."

Twice he has been abducted by militia and tortured with sticks forced under his fingernails. The last time, he fled for his life with his wife and child, walking for days through dank jungle, in fear of trigger-happy militia at every moment. Such profound experiences, together with his

Christian faith, made him decide to dedicate himself to working full-time to build peace, and he became the director of the local organization Céntre Resolution Conflits (CRC). This shift in consciousness has enabled him to work in the thick of the war, mediating in violent flashpoints, building relationships between the United Nations and the militias, and training people from different tribes to live together peacefully, prevent violence, unite communities, and save lives.

Fiona Lloyd-Davies wrote a play about Henri and his work, entitled *The Peace Builder,* which was performed by Mark Rylance on Broadway in 2012. She writes:

> Tens of thousands of kids have been kidnapped or enticed into armed militias, with false promises of a "better life" and "meat everyday." They're made into killing machines, all the more tragic because at the age of 9 or 10, they're so eager to please—so they kill to please, usually after being drugged. . . .
>
> I first met Henri in 2009, when I was researching stories for a BBC film. What struck me was Henri's outward calm. He comes across as deeply thoughtful. He doesn't rush to answer—you can really see him thinking about things. And he has to be the politest person I've ever met.
>
> Maybe this is what makes him so good at his job. He has a veneer of total unflappability, but as I learnt after hours of listening to him, this often masks an inner fear—because he's experienced what can happen, what can go wrong at a moment's notice. Each time he goes into the forest to meet the militia groups, he knows he may never come back. This is what I call real bravery.[8]

In just two years in the eastern Democratic Republic of Congo, Henri and the CRC convinced 4,532 militia fighters to put down their weapons and leave the bush. They did this by sitting down to dialogue with them and offering an alternative. Their success is not only in convincing fighters to give up their guns; they put each ex-combatant through an extensive program to prepare them for a life outside the bush. The men are trained in farming, animal husbandry, or building roads. They are helped to form working cooperatives, so they can pool their resources for the benefit of the whole community.[9] Without means to support themselves, many former militia would drift back to their ranks.

Henri is the best example I know of having the courage to acknowledge your terror and then walk *toward* what most terrifies you. In doing this, not just once, but repeatedly, he has developed an inner calm that is evident as soon as you meet him.

Whenever I have a problem, I remember Henri and the work he does. Whatever my problem is, it immediately shrinks.

How the Cultivation of Inner Calmness Can Save Lives— AUNG SAN SUU KYI

Photo: Christopher Lunch

She was leading students in a protest in Rangoon in Burma when they rounded a corner and suddenly came face to face with a line of machine guns. She realized instantly that the soldiers—who had their fingers on the triggers—were as scared as the students. So she told the students to sit down, and she walked steadily on. She heard the order given: "Release safety catches, prepare to fire!"

Aung San Suu Kyi walked quietly forward, a tiny figure emanating complete calm. She walked up to the first gun and slowly put out her hand to lower the barrel. Nobody got killed.

How was she able to do this?

Her father was a revered general. He had died when she was only two years old, but even so, she knew a bit about the military. Though she grew up in Burma, Aung San Suu Kyi never intended to become the leader of the opposition to the military junta. She was married to an academic in Oxford and had two growing sons. But on a visit to see her mother, she became involved in the pro-democracy movement that her father had been a part of and eventually became the leader of the National League for Democracy.

She was passionately devoted to the people of her country, so much so that when the Burmese authorities refused to guarantee her safe return to Burma if she went back to the United Kingdom, in the end she made the agonizing decision to put her people before her family. The personal cost to her has been unimaginable—being unable to support her beloved husband when he was dying or see her sons grow up.

While she was under house arrest—off and on for fifteen years—she practiced meditation. She says that it is meditation that gives her inner power. She has steadily developed ways to deal with a ruthless military regime, growing her consciousness of the intricate workings of her own mind and her own inner attitudes. By becoming calmly present in herself, she has the ability to be absolutely focused in the moment when violence strikes. Since she was released from house arrest she has been elected to Parliament, and things in Burma are beginning to change. In May 2014, along with thousands of party supporters and leaders of prominent student activist groups, she called for constitutional amendments ahead of the general election in 2015, saying that the current constitution needs to be amended in order for elections to be free and fair.

In 1995 she wrote, "In societies where men are truly confident of their own worth, women are not merely tolerated but valued."[10] She's a magnificent example of how the masculine and feminine energies can be fused in one person, and of the gentle, unshakable power born from that fusion. When she visited the United Kingdom in 2013, television audiences marveled at this delicate figure with roses in her hair talking with sharp, analytical clarity about governance, strategy, and political power.

Aung San Suu Kyi is radiant—evidence of the state of inner peace she has attained. She says that anyone can develop the inner calm that fuels her. And that it can be the deciding factor in a conflict, whether you're faced with a line of machine guns, a fight on the high street, or a row in the kitchen.

No Cosmic Sofa Needed—
THOMAS HÜBL

Photo: Markus Heinbach

We already met Thomas Hübl in chapter 2, but I want to come back to him now, as he is a good example of what happens when a person shifts consciousness and learns how to serve—how to move from "I" to "we."

Although only in his early forties now, it's been an intense journey for him. As a twenty-six-year-old medical student in Austria, he felt a strong inner calling to abandon his medical studies. He listened and acted upon this inner voice and spent the next four years in a retreat in the Czech Republic. During this time, he did almost nothing except meditate and explore the spaces of inner consciousness. Looking back on this time, he talks about a "fundamental opening" that took place. This was his leap in consciousness.

After returning to Vienna, he started offering spiritual guidance. His ability to touch people very deeply—and to encourage them to take a look beyond what they usually see—soon led to invitations to lead larger workshops. His popularity grew, and he began to be known internationally. Since 2004 he has been active worldwide, organizing talks, workshops, trainings, and the annual Celebrate Life Festival near Bremen, which draws a thousand people to camp for ten days round a lake and meditate, learn, and sing.[11]

Thomas is fun to be around, full of original ideas, and not saintly at all. His workshops and trainings invite people to become profoundly authentic, to experience a deeper dimension of self-awareness and individual responsibility. He founded the Academy of Inner Science in 2008, creating a space for the exploration of contemporary mysticism, which directly contributes to a "waking culture." The programs of the academy focus not only on personal transcendence but also on an active commitment to respond to the challenges of the human condition in today's postmodern world.[12]

For years, Thomas has led what he calls "Healing Events," which have brought thousands of Germans together with many Israelis to acknowledge, face, and heal the cultural shadow left by the Holocaust. In April 2010, the fourth Healing Event, called "Truth Heals," took place in Berlin. Dealing with the Holocaust and with Germany's role in World War II, the event was attended by a thousand people who wanted to direct their attention toward healing this collective shadow, which can otherwise be handed down from generation to generation.

The result was felt to be so powerful that the German group was then invited to Israel, and those whose parents had been in concentration camps were able to talk on a one-to-one basis with Germans who recognized and accepted responsibility for the acts of previous generations.

In February 2013, Thomas partnered with the Shift Network in the United States to offer an easy way to engage with his work. He guides participants through the fundamentals and practices of how to authentically awaken spiritual potential while engaged in the rigors of everyday life.[13] The number of his students is increasing fast, evidence of the powerful ripple effect of his "fundamental opening" that took place in Austria twenty years ago. He has a unique way of presenting clear, simple guidelines to people who want to deepen their spiritual practice.

> We don't need any form of paradise or cosmic sofa at the end of the exhausting path—rather, we walk the path because we love walking it. The moment you start loving your path, you don't need to finish it. . . .
>
> The moment you don't need to arrive in some perfect place in the future, the more you will enjoy walking your path—so much so that you will fall in love even with the challenges that come. This is because your love and your unconditional embrace of what you are experiencing is getting so strong that you will develop a very high level of clarity even in very difficult situations. You know you are not supposed to be in a perfect world without difficulties. The perfection is in the beauty and in the difficulty. . . .
>
> Then it doesn't matter where life sends you, or what life presents to you: this is where you are supposed to be. And there is no doubt about this. Then your ability to be with very difficult situations and with very beautiful situations is immense.[14]

Picking Yourself Up When Things Fall Apart— PEMA CHÖDRÖN

After she had been a housewife for a number of years, one day Deirdre Blomfield-Brown heard her husband's car drive up and the door bang shut. "Then he walked around the corner, and without warning he told me that he was having an affair and he wanted a divorce. I remember the sky and how huge it was. I remember the sound of the river and the steam rising up from my tea. There was no time, no thought, there was nothing—just the light and a profound, limitless stillness."[15]

She describes this as her initial experience of awakening, and it was the first indication of a leap in consciousness that gave her the courage to persist in self-knowledge. She describes her eventual spiritual path as learning how to die. For her, the fear of death—and the fear of ground-lessness, insecurity, and not being in control—are the most fundamental blocks to following the path of inner peace and thus are the most common emotions to deal with. This was what inspired her to pursue the spiritual path she has followed.

When diagnosed with chronic fatigue and immune dysfunction, she spent a year undergoing healing therapy and simplifying her life. This gave her a sense of compassion for all people going through similar ordeals.

After years of study, she was ordained as a Buddhist monk, became known as Pema Chödrön, and is now resident teacher at Gampo Abbey, the first Tibetan Buddhist monastery in North America. Her retreats are overflowing, and her books have become bestsellers. She learned through trial and error some of the ways to a life of inner peace.

A central theme of her teachings is *shenpa,* the Tibetan word for "attachment," which she interprets as the moment you are hooked into a cycle of habitual negative or self-destructive actions and thought. Shenpa—getting hooked—occurs as a response to a comment, situation, or other stimulus that is similar or related to past experiences. Often, the past experiences are negative, leading to a pattern of self-destructive thought and behaviors, such as excessive eating or drinking or angry outbursts. "Somebody says a mean word to you and then something in you tightens—that's the shenpa. Then it starts to spiral into low self-esteem, or blaming them, or anger at them, denigrating yourself. And maybe if you have strong addictions, you just go right for your addiction to cover over the bad feeling that arose when that person said that mean word to you. This is a mean word that gets you, hooks you. . . . That's a shenpa."[16]

When harsh and difficult emotions arise, like anger, fear, jealousy, or hatred, Pema teaches that—instead of flinching and drawing away from the pain and tension of these emotions—we can "lean in" to them. We can take the troubling emotion right into our heart and simply hold it there, in the heart, and watch what happens. What happens is that the emotion gradually changes and transforms—of its own accord—just by being held. She likens this process to what a child needs when he or she is overwhelmed—just to be held.

This life lesson is not simple; it has to be practiced many times. But when we have learned it, we possess a secret of transformation that is invaluable almost every day. This secret is especially useful in facing the challenges that all pioneers of the future tend to experience.

Dealing with Bullies, without Becoming a Thug Yourself—
DESMOND TUTU

Photo: Rosie Houldsworth

Because he's so extraordinary, perhaps it's best to describe Archbishop Desmond Tutu in the words of Pieter-Dirk Uys, South African satirist and social activist: "I put him in my show, wrapping his joyful purple-ness around the immortal phrase: *Love your enemy; it will ruin his reputation.* Shockingly, most of my audience had never thought of this man as an ally and a patriot, as a man of God and a man of the people. They accepted the official version that this Tutu was too-too . . . liberal? anti-white? pro-black? Cheeky?"[17]

Tutu's father was a teacher; his mother was a cook. During his youth, like all black South Africans, he had to struggle during with the insults, harshness, and cruelty of the apartheid regime. How did he turn that humiliation into the humor that sparkles out of his merry eyes today?

It was through a long apprenticeship: noticing human rights abuse, working out how to counter it without getting killed, and teaching. He found that nonviolence was the most effective method of "dealing with a bully, without becoming a thug yourself." This is not easy, but once it is learned, it can be a life gift, available in an instant to transform any threatening situation.

Tutu became a teacher and was then ordained as an Anglican priest and became the first black general secretary of the South African Council of Churches. From this platform, he began to speak out about the evils of apartheid, and for the next twenty years promoted nonviolent resistance to the apartheid regime—even getting beaten up for protesting on whites-only beaches. It was this training in nonviolence that consolidated his inner peace, a peace that cannot be destroyed by brutality, and that led to the level of consciousness that enables him to radiate love in the darkest hours.

Tutu is remarkable for his alertness. He notices everything around him, even the mood of people entering a room—and he instantly acts on it, sometimes comforting and sometimes challenging. This is a man for whom activism, rooted in spirit, is vital. He knows that activism must be free of ego—that is, it must have 100 percent integrity. This is the reason he gets up at four in the morning to pray for two hours. The strength that he has derived from his deep inner work has sustained him in his tireless willingness to champion a long list of unpopular and unfashionable causes.

He became the first black archbishop of Capetown and won the Nobel Peace Prize in 1984. After the elections ten years later, he was named by

Nelson Mandela to be chair of the Truth and Reconciliation Commission, set up to help heal the traumas inflicted during the apartheid regime. What shocked the world was his understanding, not only for the victims of torture and abuse and for their families, but also for their tormentors. This is compassion in action. He knew this would be a better way of addressing the trauma—and the guilt—than a series of witch-hunts and trials that could have taken place after the change of government in South Africa. "Forgiveness is my ability to know that you are more than the act you committed."

At the core of Tutu's vision for the work of the Truth and Reconciliation Commission was a sentence from the new South African constitution: "There is a need for understanding but not for vengeance, a need for reparation but not for retaliation, a need for *ubuntu* but not for victimization." Ubuntu is a key to the essence of the archbishop, who explained it for the predominantly white readers of a Johannesburg daily as follows:

> It referred to what ultimately distinguished us from the animals— the quality of being human and also humane. . . . The person who had ubuntu was known to be compassionate and gentle, who used his strength on behalf of the weak, who did not take advantage of others—in short he cared, treating others as what they were, human beings. . . .
>
> Without this quality a prosperous man, even though he might be a chief, was regarded as someone deserving of pity and sometimes even contempt. . . . If you lacked ubuntu, . . . you lacked an indispensable ingredient to being human. You might have much of the world's goods, and you might have position and authority, but if you did not have ubuntu, you did not amount to much.[18]

In the Truth and Reconciliation Commission, Tutu advocated "restorative justice" which he described as characteristic of traditional African jurisprudence: "Here the central concern is not retribution or punishment but, in the spirit of ubuntu, the healing of breaches, the redressing of imbalances, the restoration of broken relationships. This kind of justice seeks to rehabilitate both the victim and the perpetrator, who should be given the opportunity to be re-integrated into the community he or she has injured by his or her offence."[19]

In this respect, one of the most powerful experiences of the commission was in 1996 in Cape Town. Being questioned was a man had betrayed seven antiapartheid activists—previously his colleagues—to the security forces, and these men had been ambushed and shot in cold blood in March 1986. The photographic evidence was chilling and horrific for the men's mothers, who were sitting in the front row. At the end of the hearing, the man was asked what he wanted to say. He said he regretted what he had done. Just that. Nothing much happened.

Then a very perceptive commissioner asked him if there was anything else he wanted to say. He thought for a long time and then said, "Yes. I'm willing to go into a room alone with the mother of each of the men whose deaths I caused and hear what she has to say to me."[20] The entire room shivered. The mothers cried. An energetic transformation had happened, and everyone knew it instantly.

"Do Not Disappoint Your Soul"— ANUPAM JALOTE

Photo: Shrey Jalote

It's quite curious to hear a graduate of the world's leading business schools enthusing about cow dung, deeply proud of the fine blue flame that it can produce. This pale flame is almost invisible, yet it can cook food for hundreds of hungry people.

I'm standing on a hill in Rajasthan, India, overlooking a slurry pit and listening to Anupam Jalote. He's an innovator in producing renewable energy from organic and farming waste in a unique, low-cost anaerobic digester. This is a process by which microorganisms break down biodegradable material in the absence of oxygen, producing both fuel and compost.

Anupam has quiet authority. An MBA from Purdue University, a graduate of Lucknow University and courses from INSEAD and Michigan University, he has over twenty-five years of leadership and techno-commercial experience with Bharti Airtel, Escotel Mobile, and Tata Communications. Among other achievements, he introduced Global Positioning Systems (GPS) in India as early as 1999 and introduced the use of high-gain antennas and low-loss cables to boost signals in black spots and fringe coverage areas. So what made him quit a lucrative career at India's largest telecom service provider?

He had been practicing meditation as a daily ritual for several years. One day, in a quiet moment, he heard a clear voice—so clear that it could not be ignored: "Do not disappoint your soul." This was the moment when his consciousness made a leap.

Anupam learned to listen to what he needed to do and where he needed to go. He discovered that he needed to use his skills and experience to bring more meaning and deeper satisfaction to his otherwise extremely successful life.

"All our lives, we walk on roads built by others. Perhaps I too can build a small footpath that will help others over a particularly rocky stretch," he says. He sees India as having two parts—the urban centers, which attract all the resources and manpower needed to develop and grow, and the vast rural areas, which are starved for resources and high-quality manpower, languishing far behind. Development of the country should not be left solely to the Government and administrators. "If educated people like me can embed ourselves in the rural hinterland, and make a profitable enterprise there, lasting improvement will be an automatic outcome."

He found that his passion lay in converting organic and farming waste to energy. The rural areas of India are desperately in need of cheap energy, not only to prevent the use of wood in industry and domestic use, but also to lower carbon dioxide emissions. So Anupam set up GreenOil Energy Sciences, with three aims:

- *To democratize power* by developing a technology that can be used in small farms to enable people to generate their own electricity with waste and organic matter they have themselves grown.
- *To create a large-scale design* that can lower the cost of power plants by as much as 30 percent, eventually producing the cheapest bio-methane in the world.
- *To make an enriched organic fertilizer*—through the bacterial augmentation of post-digestion slurry—that can offer farmers a replacement for chemical fertilizers.

"It's not easy," Anupam says, "listening to the song in your heart. There are long periods of doubt and uncertainty when you are not even sure if you are doing the right thing. Fortunately for me, my wife Mamta is a pillar of strength, pushing me ahead in these moments of self-doubt."

With a mischievous glint in his eyes, he says, "Don't laugh, but in real life, the orchestra never plays a powerful toccata in the background, letting you know that you have made the right decision."

It took well over three years, but eventually his expertise in strategic management and process reengineering—not to mention sheer determination—has enabled him to

- increase methane production in anaerobic gas digesters by almost 30 percent,
- enhance the potency of organic fertilizers by slurry augmentation,
- produce a range of enriched organic fertilizers that local farmers love,
- organize tribal farmers into cooperative societies for reforesting their waste lands.

More than 50 percent of GreenOil's revenues go back to the local community, and the use of chemical fertilizers has been reduced on over two thousand acres of vegetable farming.[21] This makes Anupam feel fulfilled, and it energizes him for the long slog that still lies before him. And he continues to meditate daily.

Becoming the Hub of a Village—
SARAH INGAMELLS and YVONNE BLANKLEY

My village fought hard to keep our local post office when the Labour Government proposed sweeping closures in 2008, but we lost. Everyone in the village missed what has been a staple of British life. In Britain, a village post office is more than just a post office—and more than a place for people to collect benefits or pay their car taxes and for the kids to buy sweets—it is crucially a meeting place where the fabric of village life is sustained.

For the next two years, if we wanted to mail a parcel, we had to get in our cars—or wait for a once-a-week bus—to get to a neighboring town, which had a post office. Then suddenly a note plopped through our mail-boxes. Signed by "Yvonne and Sarah," it said: "if we were to re-open the shop, what would you like to buy?" Not having a clue who Yvonne and Sarah might be, villagers quickly filled in the little questionnaire.

The next thing we knew, carpenters and painters were erecting shelves, large freezers arrived, and a shiny new sign went up outside the old shop. And finally we were greeted by the dazzling smiles of our new shopkeepers. Both refugees from inner-city Manchester, they were thrilled to be buried deep in the countryside, bringing a heart-opening eagerness to serve the community. From the word go, their friendliness was so real that it was irresistible; even the most curmudgeonly of us warmed to their straightforward, no-nonsense, "let's get on with it" attitude.

And that's what they did—they got on with it. Taking on the shop was a big risk for them. They had each had left a well-paid job—one in local government and one in business. They had become disillusioned with bureaucracy and shortsighted management. Taking on the shop meant putting all their savings on the line, every penny. But they felt strongly guided that this was the right thing to do.

The day before they opened, they sat in the shop and cried for an hour, because of crushing doubts about what they had taken on, their bank balances depleting rapidly, and missing home and family. They looked at each other and said, "We're here for a reason, we've got to have trust." That was the moment that has inspired all that has happened since. So they had a cup of tea—which they call the fuel of giants—and didn't sleep much for a week.

Buying a gleaming Italian coffee machine was a leap in the dark for them, but within days, more cappuccinos were being consumed in this hamlet of three hundred people than for miles around. Mothers dropping their children at the primary school across the road took to meeting in the shop for a morning gossip. Farmers came in at lunchtime for a sandwich. After school, the kids would be playing Scrabble on one of three tables squeezed into the tiny interior.

Who would have believed what a tiny village shop could stock? Suddenly, only a short walk away, along with soap and toilet paper, we could buy six different local cheeses. Would all this delicatessen be too grand, to expensive to be viable? How they kept the prices as low as they did we shall never know, but I worked out that it was cheaper for me to shop with them than drive fifteen miles to the nearest supermarket. And a great deal more fun, because in the shop there are always familiar faces, the latest news, and a sense of belonging. In her gorgeous Mancunian accent Yvonne will always shout "Allo Scilla!"—and so brighten the darkest morning.

Make no mistake, what Yvonne and Sarah do is hard, grueling work. They have to unload stores, stock the shelves, and ring up purchases, as well as make hot drinks and meals, run back and forth to serve tables, and wash the dishes, and then, late at night, order supplies and balance the books. And although they are often exhausted, I have never—in four years—known them to have anything but wide-open hearts. What they do every day amounts to love, actually, in action.

Where do they get their inner strength and stamina to keep going? Sarah says: being able to help people. "If someone has a bad day, we can listen and have a chat, and hope they'll leave with a smile on their face. Nowadays in a supermarket you can't speak to a person. Both of us come from a strong line of women, both of our mothers were pioneers. Even now my grandma, who's ninety-one, doesn't let anyone tell her what to do."

Now the village has its core back—and more. The neighboring town's post office sends a mobile service to our village twice a week—a person perching on one of the café tables with machines and computers—so we can draw our pensions again and post parcels. There are tables outside all summer, and walkers design their day's outing to include lunch or coffee at the shop. They even won the Cotswold Life's Independent Retailer of the Year Award in 2013.

People don't come to the village shop just to shop. They come because of the warmth that Sarah and Yvonne constantly give out, to everyone. But more than that, these two women radiate care and compassion. And everyone who goes there knows it.

Postscript

Anyone who is an idealist or visionary—as well as being a realist—will probably be trying to bridge the gulf in understanding between the hard realities of politics and what might erroneously be called the "soft" disciplines of psychology and self-awareness. Anyone who is a pioneer of new ideas, like all the people profiled here, will encounter cynicism—that's part of the job description. But the question is, how best to deal with it?

Some giants like Archbishop Tutu will simply laugh, while throwing the cynic a glance of such piercing, twinkling intelligence that the bubble of aggressiveness bursts. Others will have developed what is now recognized as "presence." Presence is a *solidity of being* that results from having one's feet firmly planted on the ground while the mind is free and fast and the heart is wide open. A person with presence is not someone that a cynic will be drawn to attack, because presence is its own subtle protection, an invisible bodyguard. Think of Nelson Mandela or Aung San Suu Kyi. In their cases, of course, their presence is enhanced enormously by their reputations, but there are many little-known people who have extraordinary natural presence.[22] My experience is that those who have pure *presence* are automatically perceived as *authentic,* and the *influence (or personal power)* that they have is *in direct relation to the degree of that authenticity.*

Others simply ignore cynicism and get on with the job. But it can get to you, even if you don't show it at the time. Imagine the scene. You've just poured your all into a presentation of the ideas and possibilities that are close to your heart, which is pounding with the excitement of exposing your vision to the world. And someone—a person with extremely raised eyebrows—gets up to say: "You're not *seriously* suggesting that . . ." (followed by a parody of what you're trying to say, geared to get a laugh from the audience). What then?

I find that, buried in the lip curl of the cynic's comments, there is often something valuable hidden. But before I can find it, I first have to get past my own inner saboteur, who may be saying, "SEE? I told you it's a silly idea. I told you it wouldn't fly . . ." I have to be quick to catch the saboteur and not dissolve into a puddle of doubt. Then if I can listen to what the cynic is saying, I can find what is hidden. It's possible that the cynic lost her hope some time ago, and somewhere deep inside her, she longs to feel that hope again. I am unlikely to be able to touch that secret place in public, but in a private conversation, it may emerge. In public, it is best to reply straight, saying something like, "Well, let me rephrase. What I am suggesting is . . ." (and repeat what I actually said or wanted to say).

If all else fails, it cheers me up to remember what Oscar Wilde said: "A cynic is a man who knows the price of everything, and the value of nothing." British comedian John Oliver has another take: cynicism gets easier with practice, he says. "You get better at it. You kill the thing inside that's holding you back. . . . You flick a switch and turn off the human side of you." He laughs nervously. "And then you just hope you can flick it back on again afterwards."

One of the scariest aspects of Western culture is its prevailing tone of nihilistic irony and cynicism, posing as sophistication. Cynicism is a crazy pose to adopt when faced with annihilation.

In the Oxford Research Group, we dedicated ourselves to finding out how the decisions about nuclear weapons were made in all the nuclear nations in order to render those decisions accountable and bring production to a halt. We learned gradually—by making countless mistakes—how to engage in real dialogue with nuclear policy makers, getting to know them well enough to invite them to spend two days in a medieval manor house near Oxford talking confidentially with their counterparts from other nuclear nations, as well as with their most knowledgeable critics. Eventually they rolled up their sleeves to thrash out possible terms of treaties.

To do this we had to create a very safe environment. At the time we began organizing these meetings, I had begun to understand the value of meditation and had become a Quaker. Moreover, I had had the opportunity to know a number of extremely wise people, including my beloved mentor, Professor Adam Curle, who *really* knew how to meditate. I invited some of them to be "Standing Stones" for the meetings, meditating all day in the library underneath the room where the talks were taking place.

One day one of the US State Department negotiators said to me, "This is a very special room."

"Yes, it was built in 1360."

"No, it's *really* special."

"I agree. It may be because many good things have happened in this room."

"No, I mean there's *something coming up through the floor boards.*"

I explained that the meeting was being supported by meditation, taking place in the library below. He looked as if I had slapped him. He said,

"You *have* to be kidding. . . ." He was aghast—so shocked that I knew our reputation was at stake. So the only thing was to refer him to the source. "You know those older people who serve you your lunch? Ask them. They sit in the library meditating while we are in here."

Compared to the mockery and vilification—and worse—that social activists in conflict zones have to undergo, most of us have an easy time. Around the world, many activists risk their lives—and some lose them— for their beliefs and their willingness to stand up for the truth. Knowing this should make it easier to stand the blast of a little cynicism.

Cynicism can, in fact, be a pragmatic visionary's secret ally. It can compel us to hone our arguments, to become crystal clear in our presentation, to invent new strategies to reach people where they are and not where we would like them to be. If we understand cynicism to be deeply rooted in fear, disappointment, and exhaustion of the soul, then we can make space for its healing in ourselves and others.

> Nobody grows old living a number of years, people grow old only by deserting their ideals. Years wrinkle the skin, but to give up enthusiasm wrinkles the soul. Worry, doubt, distrust, fear and despair . . . these are the long, long years that bow the head and turn the growing spirit back to dust. Whether seventy or sixteen, there is in every being's heart the love of wonder, the sweet amazement of the stars and starlike things and thoughts, the undaunted challenge of events, the unfailing childlike appetite for what is next, and the joy and game of life.[23]

A question for you:
How do you deal with cynicism—your own and that of others?

CHAPTER 4

CHANGING THE VALUES THAT UNDERLIE OUR DECISIONS

A secure and satisfying future for all of humanity is possible, but only if there is a leap in human consciousness. Only such a leap can create the shift in paradigm that will allow for the necessary actions to resolve the problems we have created. In earlier chapters, we examined what this leap in consciousness might be and investigated what some great world changers have achieved by developing their awareness, harnessing their inner power, and shifting their consciousness.

Now we must take a clear, hard look at current beliefs and value systems, as well as the decisions they produce. One of the main causes of the fragile state of the planet today is the value systems or norms that underpin most current decision making and make it hard to implement profound change.

Norms or values are important precisely because they're invisible, often unexamined, and almost never stated openly or explicitly. They can have an overwhelming effect on what governments do and what people put up with, without ever being discussed or agreed upon. What are essentially historical constructs have come to be enshrined as perennial truths. From this arises a kind of mission creep—they become the unquestioned bedrock on which large institutions, corporations, and governments make the kind of decisions that are destroying the planet.

I have compiled a basic set of eleven norms. There are, of course, many more, but I see these as the essential ones. In each case I offer examples of the kind of reality the application of these norms produces. These eleven norms are as follows:

1. "The earth is ours"—humans have the right to do as we like with the earth.
2. "In the image of God"—humanity is separate from and superior to other creatures.
3. "Nature is a soulless mechanism"—science and the rational mind rule.
4. "Maximize profits"—endless economic growth is essential.
5. "Survival of the fittest"—competition is the engine of the economy.
6. "Good fences make good neighbors"—the compulsion to defend against exterior threats.
7. "Might makes right"—armed force trumps ethics.
8. "Short-termism is fine"—and damn the consequences.
9. "The technical fix"—something will always be invented in time to resolve serious problems.
10. "Women should not have authority"—they are too emotional to deal with the real issues of business and world affairs.
11. "Consuming is our right"—we always need more and better.

"The Earth Is Ours"—Humans Have the Right to Do As We Like with the Earth

This notion—possibly derived from the first book of Genesis—has, over time, come to be interpreted to mean that human beings can impose their will on nature to serve their needs. In modern Western thinking, this has often been extended to imply that the earth—and even the universe—is accidental and unintelligent, and anything that human beings may do to it has no consequences. If interpreted crudely, this entitles humans to mine its minerals, dredge its seas, pollute its waters, and foul its air, because it is inert and not part of a living system.

To give just one example: the rate at which we are destroying tropical rainforests and woodlands is *increasing* every year, and has done since at least 1700. Today we do this to grow crops for biofuels for industrial expansion and to clear land for cattle for our rising demand for meat consumption. Plans to halt this loss have failed and continue to fail. According to the UN Food and Agriculture Organization, overall tropical deforestation rates this decade are 8.5 percent higher than during the 1990s. Most experts agree that we are losing upward of eighty thousand acres of tropical rainforest *daily*, as well as some 135 plant, animal, and insect species *daily*—or some fifty thousand species a year—as the forests fall.[1]

In our headlong rush to "modernize," we tear apart the fabric of the earth. There are thousands of examples worldwide, but here's one example from Uttarakhand in India, conveyed to me by India's famous environmentalist Dr. Vandana Shiva:

> Uttarakhand is the source of the sacred river Ganges and its tributaries. Mass pilgrimage tourism has led to construction on the fragile banks of the rivers and an attempt to make four-lane highways in the mountains. Reckless blasting with dynamite for the construction of dams and tunnels has triggered thousands of landslides. When the first rain comes, these landslides fill the riverbed with rubble. There is no space for the water to flow, and the rivers flood more easily. Floods in June 2013 led to an estimated five thousand deaths and the disappearance of nearly one hundred thousand people.
>
> The disaster was clearly manmade, not a natural disaster, due to ignorance of local culture and the ecological fragility of the Himalaya. The entire catchment of the Ganges system needs to be protected as a cultural heritage and a sensitive ecosystem. Disaster preparedness needs honest and robust ecological science, and equally honest and robust participatory democracy.[2]

SEEDS

In 1998, the World Bank's structural adjustment policies forced India to open up its seed sector to global corporations like Cargill, Monsanto, and Syngenta. Seeds traditionally saved by farmers were replaced by corporate seeds, which need fertilizers and pesticides and are engineered so that the plants that grow from them do not themselves produce viable seed, forcing the farmer to buy new seed every year. This new expense increases poverty and leads to indebtedness and thousands of farmer suicides.[3] In 2009, Dr. Shiva wrote that Indian farmers who had previously paid as little as 7 rupees per kilo for seed were now paying up to 17,000 rupees per kilo after switching to Monsanto's BT cotton.

"In the Image of God"—Humanity Is Separate from and Superior to Other Creatures

This norm seems to date back to Genesis 1:26: "And God said, 'Let us make man in our image, after our likeness: and let them have dominion over the fish of the sea, and over the fowl of the air, and over the cattle, and over all the earth, and over every creeping thing that creepeth upon the earth.'"

This Old Testament verse is deeply embedded in the human psyche in many parts of the world. While this may not have been intended, it has been interpreted to permit us to play god with other creatures, treat them badly, deprive them of their natural habitat, and often hunt them to extinction.

David Attenborough said in 2000 that the (then) impact of humanity on the biodiversity of the planet could be compared to the impact of a ten-mile-wide meteor on earth.[4] Reputable scientists believe that earth's creatures are on the brink of a sixth mass extinction. A study published in 2011 calculates that three-quarters of today's animal species could vanish within three hundred years. "Earth has already endured five mass extinctions, including the asteroid that wiped out dinosaurs and other creatures 65 million years ago. Conservationists have warned for years that we are in the midst of a sixth, human-caused extinction, with species from frogs to birds to tigers threatened by climate change, disease, loss of habitat, and competition for resources with non-native species."[5]

One consequence of this way of thinking is that in order to satisfy the rapid increase in the demand for meat, the number of land animals killed each year for food has exceeded sixty-five billion, according to conservative UN Food and Agriculture Organization figures. By 2050 nearly twice as much meat will be produced as is today.[6] Factory farms now account for 72 percent of poultry production, 43 percent of egg production, and 55 percent of pork production worldwide.[7] These facilities rely on commercial breeds of livestock that have been bred to gain weight quickly on high-protein feeds. Factory farms are extremely crowded, confining animals closely together; many of the world's seventeen billion chickens that are raised for eggs or meat each live in an area that is less than the size of a sheet of paper.

"Nature Is a Soulless Mechanism"— Science and the Rational Mind Rule

In her recent book *The Dream of the Cosmos*, Anne Baring writes that until the time of Copernicus, Kepler, and Galileo (basically in the sixteenth and early seventeenth centuries), "science believed it was working in harmony with the laws of the cosmos and had no conflict with religion. The universe was regarded as a sentient organism governed by those laws."

As a result of their discoveries, she continues, "there was a fundamental shift of focus from religion to science, from faith to knowledge, from confinement within a rigid, controlling orthodoxy to release into the passionate exploration of the material world. However, as science drew away from the oppressive control of religion and turned to the observation of nature, it was a nature that increasingly came to be regarded as a soul-less mechanism and as something completely separate from both man and the cosmos."[8]

Commenting on this situation, the philosopher Joseph Milne says that science became an ideology—a belief system—regarding nature as something to be mastered, manipulated, and controlled for the benefit of humanity.[9] He places the onus for this change in the attitude to nature on the writings of the philosopher, scientist, and statesman Francis Bacon (1561–1626), who declared that the object of knowledge was the control of nature and that nature, in itself, had no purpose.

Later, Anne Baring continues, science rejected the concepts of spirit and soul altogether "because it could find no evidence of either in the fields of its exploration: the idea of God was deemed irrelevant; the concept of soul an outgrown superstition. It concluded that the universe had come into being by chance and that consciousness, emerging out of matter, was a product of the neurology and biochemistry of the physical brain—a conclusion it has presented as irrefutable fact."[10]

This way of thinking about consciousness, intuition, and the soul has prevailed until the present day, with Richard Dawkins asserting that we are "robot vehicles blindly programmed to preserve the selfish molecules known as genes."[11] The popularity of this nihilistic reductionism is not only alarming but bizarre in the face of the astonishing discoveries of quantum physics, which have opened up for us the reality of a most mysterious and magical universe.

There is absolutely no argument about the value of scientific discoveries for the well-being and advancement of humankind. This is not in question here. What is in question is the consequence of dismissing the concept of soul as an outgrown superstition. It affects almost everything we do—how children are educated, how research resources are allocated, how forests and oceans are exploited, how animals are treated, and particularly how women are viewed, since for millennia women have been associated with nature, intuition, and the soul. While modernity freed us from much dogma, our current narrative of a purposeless universe with humanity in it by chance may well turn out to be the most destructive dogma of all.

It was Einstein who said, "The rational mind is a faithful servant. The intuitive mind is a sacred gift. We have created a society that honors the servant and has forgotten the gift."

Sally Dearman Cummings, who for eleven years was a Royal Air Force fighter controller and the first woman to pilot their fastest jets, says:

> We have become accustomed to living bent out of our natural shape as clear, resonant bells with a left-brain perfectly designed to complement and support a magnificent right brain. We have lost balance. Our left-brain is now so dominant in our social structure that its landscape is taken as the only, or superior, reality. We fail to acknowledge just how much it is informed by the right brain. Without the right brain, the left brain would have very little to analyse or present. It is a brilliant, clinical, zeros and ones pattern-recognition device that is complementary to our right brain. We feel—resonate with—truth

and the amplified field with our right brain and use our left to notice its effects and make logical deductions that can be verbally expressed and written down. Neither task can be performed by the other.

At first, opening to truth beyond our conditioned range of acceptance can feel uncomfortable. We have spent so much time in left brain-dominated reality, ignoring right brain signals, that heeding non-linear over linear language can be a scary enterprise. With learning and practice, the opposite develops. Non-truth becomes intolerable to feel, whatever our left brain may say about it. Our right brain is ideally developed to read complex, non-linear, non-verbal signals beneath the linear landscape and present that information to us in its own language of emotional, energetic and physical feelings of coherency as previously described. The right brain is a richly equipped, reliable and accurate tool for discerning truth. It requires commitment and the support of others, however, to learn to use it well.[12]

"Maximize Profits"—Endless Economic Growth Is Essential

There is no doubt that economic growth has brought hundreds of millions out of poverty and has relieved untold suffering across the planet. The question is whether this most sacred cow of contemporary economics—one that now dominates world culture—can be sustained. Western nations that already have a high standard of living naturally want to keep it, and developing nations—some of which are in survival mode—dream of one day being able to be emulate the West. Nevertheless, it is clear that the planet's resources—particularly water—simply cannot support endless economic growth.

Some economists are now saying that measures of growth are deeply flawed in that they are purely measures of activity in the monetized economy. Expanded use of cigarettes and alcohol, for example, increases economic output both through sales and because of the related increase in health-care needs. The need to clean up oil spills generates economic activity. Gun sales to minors generate economic activity. A divorce generates both lawyers' fees and the need to buy or rent and outfit a new home. Yet it is now well documented that in the United States and a number of other countries, the quality of life of ordinary people has been declining as aggregate economic output increases.

The extravagant promises of the advocates of the global economy are based on a number of assumptions that have become so deeply embedded in Western industrial culture that they are rarely questioned. These assumptions are that

- growth in GNP is a valid measure of human well-being and progress;
- free, unregulated markets efficiently allocate a society's resources;
- growth in trade benefits ordinary people;
- economic globalization is inevitable;
- global corporations are benevolent institutions that, if freed from governmental interference, will provide a clean environment for all and good jobs for the poor;
- absentee investors create local prosperity;
- wealth automatically trickles down and benefits everyone.

These assumptions have remained unquestioned and become even more powerful after the demise of socialist economies, and as a result, the power of global corporations has begun to eclipse the power of the state. Every one of us needs to be aware of the power that large transnational companies have accumulated. This power is now sufficient for them to negotiate punitive, internationally binding trade agreements, which, in turn, lead governments to develop policies that not only benefit the giant oil, drug, weapons, and gene corporations but also promote the deregulation of environmental protections, which leads to the degradation of our land, air, and water.

There are so many examples to quote to illustrate this that I have opted to describe just one in some detail, because I was completely ignorant of it, and it shocked me. Maude Barlow, national chair of the Council of Canadians, describes a process known as *investor-state*—now included in most bilateral and regional trade and investment deals in the world.

Investor-state gives corporations from one country the right to sue the government of another country if that government imposes new environmental, health, or safety rules that cause the company to potentially lose money. For example, Sweden's *Vattenfall* is suing the German government for 3.5 billion euros because Germany is phasing out nuclear power.

> Investment treaties give foreign corporations "investor-state" rights, allowing them to bypass their own governments and directly sue the government of another country if they believe their "right to profit" has been affected by a law or practice in that country. Investor-state rights first appeared in the 1995 North American Free Trade Agreement and have exploded since. There are almost 3,000 bilateral deals between governments, most giving corporations these extraordinary rights, and many of them are used to gain access to the commons resources of other countries, putting the world's forests, fish, minerals, land, air and water supplies under direct control of transnational corporations. . . .
>
> Yet in spite of the profoundly undemocratic nature of the notion that corporations can hold foreign countries hostage in this way, both investor state treaties and disputes are exploding in number. An April 2013 report by the South-North Development Monitor on the rise of international investment disputes found that there were 62 new cases of corporations challenging governments for compensation in 2012, the highest number of known treaty-based cases ever filed in one year. This brings the overall number of known cases to 518. . . . The strong majority of cases are filed by corporations from wealthy countries against countries in the developing world. This clearly demonstrates that the process works to favour powerful corporations and countries. As well, there are a growing number of disputes challenging environmental rules around the world, a dangerous development that threatens the rights of governments to protect vital water sources from corporate control.[13]

These assumptions, however, are at last beginning to be questioned. Several countries (including Australia and Brazil) have implemented the "best practice" of saying no to investor-state and many others are thinking about it.[14]

"Survival of the Fittest"—Competition Is the Engine of the Economy

It goes without saying that competition can be a great spur to improvement, can stimulate activity and creativity, and can help modify behavior. As the echoes of Darwin become louder, spreading across the entire planet, most people live their lives in the bland acceptance that competition is essential for economic growth and prosperity.

Nevertheless, in recent decades, competition has grown to become like a towering giant wielding a massive club and driving hundreds of millions of humans to run full speed over a cliff. Listen objectively to the news for a week and count how many times reference is made to the unquestioned force of "the market," the importance of share prices, the necessity of economic competitiveness, and the requirement for growth. Economist Hazel Henderson talks of "the poverty-exacerbating global casino, the speculation in oil and commodities which drive up fuel and food prices, leading to deprivation and hunger."[15]

THE GAP BETWEEN RICH AND POOR

Put in global economic terms, today the richest three hundred people on earth have more wealth than the poorest three billion (that's almost half of the world's population).[16] Actually the situation is even more serious: the richest two hundred people have about $2.7 trillion, which is more than the poorest three and a half billion people, who have only $2.2 trillion combined. It is very difficult to wrap one's mind around such extreme figures.[17]

The film *Into the Shadows* shows just how bad things are—this short film won the 2013 first prize in the World Press Photo multimedia award. It describes what happens to migrants fleeing political brutality in Zimbabwe. They find themselves in Johannesburg with no shelter, no family, no job, and no money—totally alone. They are "desecrated so comprehensively that in the end there's nothing left."[18]

This situation has been getting progressively worse. The UK-based charity Oxfam says in a report published in January 2013 that the income of the world's richest one percent has increased by 60 percent in the last twenty years. The report says the world's one hundred richest people earned enough in 2012 to end extreme poverty four times over.[19]

A remarkable video called *Global Wealth Inequality—What You Never Knew You Never Knew* shows how this widening disparity operates between countries. [20] During the colonial period, the gap between the richest countries and the poorest widened from 3:1 to 35:1, in part because European powers extracted so much wealth from the Global South in the form of resources and labor. Since then, that gap has grown to almost 80:1. Such a tragic gap is a recipe for class warfare, violence, and terrorism on a massive scale.

THE PRISONER'S DILEMMA

We are walking past a playground. [21] Behind the fence, a fight is underway between a group of hungry children. Their prize? A plate of sandwiches: a special lunchtime bounty. Each child is in it to win it—no one willing to back down. The potential outcome of success is obvious—fend off the others and get a belly full of the best sandwiches ever served. But weaken for even a second, and you risk losing everything. As the pint-sized fight continues to get out of hand, the plate gets closer and closer to being overturned, the sandwiches ruined, the object of their furious competition lost.

The predicament of our hypothetical children is not unfamiliar. In Game Theory, the "Prisoner's Dilemma" describes a situation where competitiveness risks driving two jailbirds to betray each other (one goes free, the other to receive life in prison), even though cooperation might ease the sentence for both. [22] In both the playground and the prison, it is the risk of losing out to someone else that propels destructive competition.

We all recognize that particular form of destructive competition— blinkered, single minded, short term. Not the kind that inspires us to feats of Olympic athleticism, but the kind that compromises our ethics and isolates our worldview—upturns the sandwiches. It is just such destructive competition that has come to not only define our global problems but also keep us from solving them.

FEAR OF LOSING IT ALL

Anyone with an eye on the headlines will know that "losing it all" is not journalistic hyperbole. The real and potentially catastrophic nature of today's global problems—from climate change to the crises of global financial markets—make the phrase "losing it all" alarmingly appropriate.

In the face of such calamity, it is the destructive aspect of competition that prevents us from taking charge of our global future. Like the children lost in their fight, our global leaders are caught in an inescapable struggle for national gain. But unlike the case of our hypothetical children, their battle is not defined by single-minded immaturity, but by a more *systemic* form of competition from which no individual nation can break free.

Any successful national economy is determined by its ability to attract and retain capital, investment, and the contribution and jobs provided by multinational corporations. It is why we measure global progress on such metrics as gross domestic product and why gaining a high position on the World Economic Forum's annual "Global Competitiveness Index" matters.[23] It is not by accident that we refer to this as a nation's "competitiveness"—their individual ability to compete for economic symbols of success.

But here's the rub: national policies that aim to solve global problems —that is, policies that would increase social or environmental protection— would only increase business costs, thus inviting capital, corporations, and investment to move elsewhere. Such a move would therefore endanger a nation's economic competitiveness. Is it any wonder that progress on challenges like climate change or financial regulation suffer international stalemate? Which nation could risk moving to save the planet if it means losing out to a market competitor and damaging its very economic future?

Such destructive international competition doesn't just paralyze nations from changing the world, it also drastically undermines the ethics of multinational corporations. Would we be seeing the collapse of Bangladeshi factories favored by Western retail giants if not for the destructive competition to keep costs low? And would Starbucks or Amazon really be exploiting the law to avoid taxation if they weren't competing with their peers to keep profits and share prices up? By the same token, would governments be so slow to address this tax avoidance if they didn't fear the multinationals moving elsewhere? It is not that those institutions or organizations lack ethics per se, it is that they exist in a destructively competitive global economy that makes it difficult and often impossible for them to act otherwise.

Bunzl observes acidly that maintaining *national* competitiveness is fundamentally incompatible with solving *global* problems.[24] "Be it climate change, global poverty, workers rights, corporate accountability or financial market instability, they all remain unaddressed and/or exacerbated by essentially the same vicious circle. . . . That is, any nation that moves first to more tightly regulate or tax corporations or financial markets would be punished by capital, corporations or investment moving elsewhere to avoid such regulations. Any nation that moved significantly to do the right thing would lose out."

Bunzl calls this *destructive international competition*, which may be the key phenomenon underlying current global problems.

> The factors that determine national economic success or failure—capital, corporations and investment—today move freely across national borders. Governments therefore have no choice but to implement only those policies that attract or retain capital, corporations and investment. Policies to solve global problems—those that increase social or environmental protection and would thus increase business costs—are this effectively excluded or diluted because they would inevitably endanger a nation's economic competitiveness and increase unemployment. Governments therefore find themselves unable to act substantively on global problems. And with governments fearing to tax and regulate business adequately, corporations and banks can only continue to compete destructively with their peers to the detriment of society and the environment."[25]

"Good Fences Make Good Neighbors"— The Compulsion to Defend against Exterior Threats

Overall, the volume of international transfers of major conventional weapons grew by 17 percent between 2003 and 2007 and between 2008 and 2012.[26] I find this decidedly odd, because it is happening precisely at the same time that major wars and episodes of mass violence worldwide have become less frequent and less deadly. Gareth Evans, former foreign minister of Australia, wrote in December 2012: "After a high point in the late 1980s and very early 1990s, there has been a decline of well over

50% in the number of major conflicts both between and within states; in the number of genocidal and other mass atrocities; and in the number of people killed as a result of them."[27]

Why then is the arms trade growing when conflict has fallen by half? This links to the previous point about employment: governments have found that support for defense manufacturing is easy to justify on two grounds—national security and jobs. They can keep giving subsidies and export-credit guarantees to prop up the defense industry by proclaiming that the jobs provided are vital to the national economy, never mind studies showing that investment in socially useful manufacture would produce more jobs.[28] Competition for arms export deals now involves not just arms manufacturers selling weapons, but prime ministers and even royalty.[29]

Wealthy regimes with bad human rights records accumulate vast arsenals of fighter jets, missiles, cluster bombs, and attack helicopters in a deadly global competition to be armed with the latest and most lethal weapons. Military leaders are encouraged by the industry to use the weapons, so that manufacturers' catalogues can then list them as "battle proven." Arms fairs promote weapons sales by offering arms dealers— deep pocketed and studiously amoral—the chance to meet military delegations, ministers, and government officials. Defence Systems and Equipment International is one of the largest arms fairs in the world, held biannually at the ExCel Centre in London's docklands.

One consequence of huge arsenals is the consumption of oil and emission of carbon dioxide by the military. The Pentagon, for example, is the single largest institutional user of petroleum products and energy in the world.[30] Yet the Pentagon has a blanket exemption in all international climate agreements. At the time of the Kyoto Accords negotiations, the United States demanded as a provision of signing that all of its military operations worldwide and all operations it participates in with the United Nations and/or NATO be completely exempted from measurement or reductions. After securing this gigantic concession, the Bush administration then refused to sign the accords. This information is not well known, because military emissions abroad are exempt from national reporting requirements under US law and the United Nations Framework Convention on Climate Change.[31]

Barry Sanders has received a Fulbright Senior Scholar Grant and has been nominated twice for the Pulitzer Prize. In his book *The Green Zone: The Environmental Costs of Militarism*, he says, "the greatest single assault on the environment, on all of us around the globe, comes from one agency . . . the Armed Forces of the United States."[32]

DECLINE IN MAJOR CONFLICTS

It is to the immense credit of diplomats, negotiators, and all the thousands of local peace builders worldwide that there has been such a marked decline in the number of wars in recent years, as reported above. Many of these people risk their lives daily to prevent or resolve conflicts.[33] Put simply, the decline is also because anyone—soldier or refugee—who has seen the horror of war, the devastation and the agony, wants peace.

Certainly there is a case to be made for good fences between neighbors—humans have a fundamental instinct for territory, and that space can need defending. In an increasingly digitalized world, however, the notion of good fences is fast becoming outdated, as attacks in cyberspace become the strategy of choice.

On the hidden battlefields of history's first known cyberwar, the casualties are piling up. In the United States, many banks have been hit and the telecommunications industry seriously damaged, likely in retaliation for several major attacks on Iran. Washington and Tehran are ramping up their cyber-arsenals, built on a black-market digital arms bazaar, enmeshing such high-tech giants as Microsoft, Google, and Apple. This story gives a flavor of what to expect.[34]

Their eyeballs felt it first. A wall of 104-degree air hit the cyber-security analysts as they descended from the jets that had fetched them, on a few hours' notice, from Europe and the United States. They were in Dhahran, in eastern Saudi Arabia, a small, isolated city that is the headquarters of the world's largest oil company, Saudi Aramco. The group included representatives of Oracle, IBM, Crowd-Strike, Red Hat, McAfee, Microsoft, and several smaller private firms—a SWAT dream team for the virtual realm. They came to investigate a computer-network attack that had occurred on August 15, 2012, on the eve of a Muslim holy day called Lailat al Qadr, "the

Night of Power." Technically the attack was crude, but its geopoliti-
cal implications would soon become alarming.

The data on three-quarters of the machines on the main computer network of Saudi Aramco had been destroyed. Hackers who
identified themselves as Islamic and called themselves the Cutting
Sword of Justice executed a full wipe of the hard drives of 30,000
Aramco personal computers. For good measure, as a kind of calling
card, the hackers lit up the screen of each machine they wiped with a
single image, of an American flag on fire.[35]

"Might Makes Right"—Armed Force Trumps Ethics

This concept implies that those who are the strongest will rule others and
have the power to determine right from wrong. The further implication
is that a society's view of right and wrong is determined by the victor in a
conflict or by those with the most physical power. In the same sense, it is
said that history is written by the victors—only those able to defeat their
enemies can make their idea of what is right the accepted norm.

> Naturally, the common people don't want war, but after all, it is the
> leaders of a country who determine the policy, and it is always a
> simple matter to drag people along whether it is a democracy, a fas-
> cist dictatorship, or a parliament, or a communist dictatorship. Voice
> or no voice, the people can always be brought to the bidding of the
> leaders. That is easy. All you have to do is to tell them they are being
> attacked, and denounce the pacifists for lack of patriotism and expos-
> ing the country to danger. It works the same in every country.[36]

Sixty years after that statement was made, the world is emerging from
wars in Afghanistan and Iraq. Before either invasion was undertaken, millions took to the streets to challenge the ethics of the wars, to no avail.
Now, in retrospect, thoughtful studies by diplomats with profound understanding of the psychology of war are questioning the decision-making
processes that led to both wars. "The decision to go to war is of enormous
consequence and, unless we find ways to understand the historical significance and get into the mind of the enemy when we are making these

enormous strategic calculations, we will continue to repeat the cycles of destruction that we enacted in the Iraq war."[37]

Emma Sky, who was political adviser to General Raymond Odierno, who commanded the US forces in Iraq from 2010 to 2011, is clear that "some Americans believed Iraq could become a democracy that would serve as a model for the region. Most Iraqis had not consented to this experiment, or to being occupied by foreign forces."[38]

"Might makes right" has been described as the underlying assumption of totalitarian regimes. However, in my experience in military think tanks in the West, those who think of themselves as realists in the field of international affairs take it as a norm; it's the way things work.

This idea has much to do with the attitudes of the established nuclear powers toward those countries wishing to acquire similar weapons. Retaining the nuclear option ensures that United States, United Kingdom, France, China, and Russia (known as the P5) have a place at the "top table" as permanent members of the Security Council, with the power of veto over UN resolutions. The rationales they give for possession and retention of nuclear weapons are almost identical to the rationales that India, Pakistan, Iran, and South Korea give—yet the P5 continue to wrestle with logic in insisting that it is (or was) wrong and dangerous for these countries to join the nuclear club. Put simply, those who were first to obtain the power of nuclear annihilation feel they have a right to exclude other nations.

In its daily application—in life on the street or in the home—this concept assumes that it is strength or physical might that establishes moral right. This is in the mind of those who batter, mug, or physically abuse those weaker than themselves: "I am stronger than you, therefore I have a right to your goods or to make you do what I want."

The culture of global militarism is nurtured by those for whom it seems essential to their identity and survival: monarchs whose key symbolic role is to head their subjects' armed forces; prime ministers who feel they have become true statesmen only when they have launched a war; governments that equate their nation's status and interests with its military standing and ability to dictate to others; arms manufacturers and traders who get rich by supplying the weapons and systems of death; and local and multinational business interests that are served by war.[39]

Those defending the case for military supremacy might vigorously argue that if you're not armed and dangerous, you're a sitting duck, like the Tibetans were for the Chinese invaders in 1950. They would ask what use nonviolence is in a brutal world. The response might be that it was Gandhi's insistence on nonviolence that eventually drove the most powerful empire the world has seen out of India, and Martin Luther King's similar insistence that ensured civil rights for African Americans. The Tibetan Buddhist passion for nonviolence may not have secured Tibet, but with the Dalai Lama's incandescent advocacy and example, Tibetan Buddhism and its concepts have spread over the entire planet.

"Short-Termism Is Fine"
—and Damn the Consequences

For these are all now being sacrificed in deference to short-term cost-benefit calculations, to which elected leaders have handed ultimate power, betraying their voters and peoples. They legislate to protect and increase the assets of the richest, forcing austerity on everyone else. During the Clinton presidency, 45 percent of new wealth created in the USA went to the richest 1 percent. During the pre-crisis Bush years, it was 73 percent.[40]

Forget the annual report: these days, shareholders' decisions often hinge on financial analysts' quarterly financial expectations—and, with their perks and bonuses and even their jobs at stake, more and more senior executives are unable to ignore them. Pressure to produce short-term results increased in the five years leading up to 2013, according to 63 percent of global executives who responded to a McKinsey & Company survey. Increasingly outspoken activist shareholders appear to drive today's boardroom decisions.

INSEAD research shows that—far from ensuring steady profits—"short-termism" can be destructive in the long haul.[41] But with a growing number of executive compensation packages rewarding short-termism, it takes courage and willpower to keep the future in focus. Jakob Von Uexkull, founder of the World Future Council, says that the gap between short-term thinking and long-term consequences has never been wider.

The problems inherent in the market system are reflected in political systems. Western governments appear to be influenced more by opinion polls than by the likely effect of their policies on future generations. While informed political leaders agree that transition to a green economy is essential to sustainability, their actions rarely reflect this knowledge. The British coalition government's decisions to abolish the Sustainable Development Commission, the Royal Commission on Environmental Pollution, and the prime minister's Strategy Unit do not inspire confidence that they are thinking much beyond the next election.

In the West, our culture has become more short-termist in its approach—a paradox in view of the fact that our scientific understanding now encompasses a far longer evolutionary timescale than our Victorian ancestors ever dreamed of. How could wise decisions—decisions that could benefit our grandchildren—be made by highly stressed politicians pursued by a frenetic media?[42]

In October 2013 the Oxford Martin Commission for Future Generations prefaced their report "Now for the Long Term" by saying: "Preparing for the future, however, seems a luxury for today's governments, who are increasingly preoccupied with the present; indeed, many governments even 'live with their eyes on the rear-view mirror, refighting ancient battles and reigniting ancient enmities.' An inability to 'look forward' characterizes much of modern politics. Government and business leaders tend to focus on the short term, which offers quicker and potentially easier payoffs at lower political cost."[43] Among their recommendations was one to invest in younger generations with social protection measures that would help reduce the "scars" of long-term unemployment and disconnection.

A way to start might be to listen to younger generations. Here are the words of Kehkashan Basu, speaking before the United Nations as the global coordinator for children and youth for the UN Environmental Program's Major Groups Facilitating Committee, when she was just twelve years old:

Honorable Ministers, distinguished delegates, ladies and gentlemen,

These are strange times indeed.

Children today are bombarded with phrases such as global warming, carbon footprint and deforestation. These scary terms were totally alien a hundred years ago, but we only have ourselves to blame for their importance now. Today . . . I stand before you and ask "What kind of future are you leaving for children and youth like me?"

Every day, every minute we are writing an epitaph for a lake, or a wetland or a forest. The mighty river Ganges which once flowed, pristine and pure, from the Himalayas to the Bay of Bengal, is now a cesspool of filth. The roaring Yangtze River has forgotten its original trail thanks to the numerous dams and barrages which it encounters. The Himalayas, shorn of their glacial cover, look like dull pieces of chalk. The historic Dodo is now rejoicing at the thought that it may soon have tigers, lions and pandas for company. The Caspian Sea is now more of a lake than a sea. Caviar may soon be just a word in the dictionary, given the rate at which sturgeons are being fished out.

Every day, while millions go hungry, we let tons of food rot in warehouses. Thousands of children walk miles in the scorching heat to collect a bucket of brackish water because the world does not take note while the rivers dry up.

The questions that arise are: by the time my child goes to school, how many more such species, lakes, forests, rivers will disappear? What kind of environment will the future generations inherit? Isn't now time to institute ombudspersons for our future generations so that we can prevent repeats of such environmental disasters? The question that we ask is when, instead of why.

In the words of Robert Swan, "The Greatest Threat to Our Planet Is the Belief That Someone Else Will Save It." I implore you to take action and turn back the clock before it is too late. We urge you not to ignore us. Listen to us, involve us, allow us to help you in framing the policies that will deliver the future we want.[44]

"The Technical Fix"—Something Will Always Be Invented in Time to Resolve Serious Problems

Technocentrics, as they are known, firmly believing that humans have control over nature, have absolute faith that all environmental problems can be solved though science and technology. Technology has indeed brought untold benefits to humankind—everything from the wheel, the reflecting telescope, the toothbrush, the spinning frame, the light bulb, the electrical motor, the sewage system, the telephone, the bicycle, vacuum cleaners, photography, stainless steel, the glider, microscopes, penicillin, television, hip replacement, cash dispensers, carbon fiber, computers, the worldwide web—the list is extensive.

This has given us such confidence in science and technology that we have found it easy to forget cases of "advancements" that have proved disastrous, such as the drug thalidomide, which was to help pregnant women with the effects of morning sickness and was sold from 1957 until 1962, when it was found to cause many forms of birth defects.

The Soviet Union did not immediately report the Chernobyl disaster of 1986 (Sweden reported the radiation leak two days after the accident), and children living in the area were not given potassium iodide tablets to protect them against the cloud of radioactive Iodine 131. Over two hundred have developed thyroid cancer to date. One study carried out in 2010 by Alexey Yablokov, president of the Russian Center for Environmental Policy, predicts an excess mortality close to one million worldwide due to the global radioactive fallout, a figure vigorously denied by the International Atomic Energy Agency. The Chernobyl reactor core was eventually sealed inside a massive concrete sarcophagus. However, this is known to be structurally unsound and has now begun to degrade on account of water penetration.

The Fukushima Daiichi disaster in Japan in 2011 has left ten million people living in highly radioactive areas, and ultrasounds have shown that around fifty thousand children have thyroid nodules. The meltdown at Fukushima was three times worse than Chernobyl, and radioactive waste was still pouring into the sea in October 2013. There remains the likelihood of further meltdown if there is another explosive release of hydrogen gas or more seismic activity. There is no way to decommission either Chernobyl or Fukushima. Both will remain intensely radioactive for millennia.[45]

Rupert Wingfield-Hayes made a second trip inside the crippled plant at Fukushima in October 2013 and reported for the BBC that Fukushima was not an unavoidable natural disaster. Prof. Kiyoshi Kurokawa, who chaired the Japanese parliamentary inquiry into the Fukushima disaster, told the BBC that it was "Man-made, and made in Japan." When the earthquake and tsunami hit on March 11, 2011, there was no plan for how to deal with such a large and complex disaster. Prof. Kurokawa blamed what he called "regulatory capture," a process by which the nuclear power industry "captured" the bureaucracy that was supposed to regulate it.[46]

In October 2013 there were three concurrent on-going meltdowns at Fukushima that no one knew how to halt. At the damaged Unit 4, there were 1,500 radioactive fuel rods in a cooling pond on the upper floor of a severely damaged building that is tilting and sinking because the tanks storing the radioactive cooling water for Units 1, 2, and 3 are leaking and have saturated the ground supporting Unit 4. Together, the fuel rods weigh four hundred tons, and if they catch fire as a result of loss of cooling water, they will emit radioactive fallout many times greater than that produced by the Hiroshima bomb.

As former ambassador Mitsuhei Murata has put it, full-scale releases from Fukushima "would destroy the world environment and our civilization. This is not rocket science, nor does it connect to the pugilistic debate over nuclear power plants. This is an issue of human survival."[47] This reminds me of what Einstein said, years ago, "The unleashed power of the atom has changed everything save our modes of thinking, and thus we drift toward unparalleled catastrophe."

A statement issued in October 2013 reflects the wisdom of the Spiritual People of the Earth, of North and South America:

> Powerful technologies are out of control and are threatening the future of all life. The Fukushima nuclear crisis alone is a threat to the future of humanity. Yet, our concern goes far beyond this single threat. Our concern is with the cumulative and compounding devastation that is being wrought by the actions of human beings around the world. It is the combination of resource extraction, genetically modified organisms, moral failures, pollution, introduction of invasive species and much more that are threatening the future of life on Earth. The compounding of bad decisions and their corresponding actions are extremely short sighted. They do not consider the future generations and they do not respect or honor the Creator's Natural Law. We strongly urge for the governmental authorities to respond

with an open invitation to work and consult with us to solve the world's problems, without war. We must stop waging war against Mother Earth, and ourselves.[48]

Even the air we breathe has, without our knowledge, for many years been impacted. The high atmosphere of our planet has been seeded with nanoparticles of chemicals distributed from airplanes by aerosols—ostensibly to mitigate the effects of global warming by creating artificial cloud cover. As a result, tons of highly toxic chemicals such as aluminum oxide, barium, and strontium have entered the air we breathe, the soil, the oceans, and the food chain, affecting plants, fish, and animals—including humans.[49] Rainfall tested in Australia has showed high levels of neuro-toxic heavy metals including aluminum (3,000 times the safe limit of exposure), manganese (1,700 times the safe limit) and boron (5,000 times the safe limit).

This seeding of the atmosphere with chemicals is a method of what is called Solar Radiation Management that seeks to reduce the amount of sunlight hitting the earth by increasing the planet's reflectivity—thus reflecting solar radiation back into space. Many geo-engineers prefer Solar Radiation Management to carbon dioxide removal as a much cheaper and quicker method of fighting global warming. The International Risk Governance Council notes that Solar Radiation Management is "cheap, fast and imperfect. . . . Significant problems with [Solar Radiation Management] as a form of geo-engineering include the major effects on the global hydrological cycle that include increases in acid rain globally."[50]

This geo-engineering technology not only poses a serious danger to human health and the biosphere of the planet as a whole but also is an astonishing infringement of our human rights—as well as those of future generations. It can create extreme fluctuations in weather patterns, increasing drought and floods that, in turn, impact food production and food prices worldwide. The chemicals involved lead to an increase of asthma, rickets, and dementia, as well as cancer and autoimmune diseases.

Were reason to prevail, we would capture solar energy, not block it; we would shun fossil fuels, not wage ecocidal wars to seize the remaining supplies. In today's world, however, policymakers have diverted billions of dollars into blocking the sun.

Hubris is an ancient Greek word meaning extreme arrogance. Wisdom is cautionary good sense. Hubris is at the heart of Greek tragedy—the arrogant belief that one's power is unassailable. Wisdom counsels that no human power is impregnable.[51]

The arrogance of thinking we can control nature makes me gasp. Try making a pact with a hurricane, try stopping a volcanic eruption or an earthquake, try arranging a deal with a tsunami so that it won't flood your nuclear plant.

When the oceans begin to rise faster, what will happen to the populations of the world's coastal cities? More than a billion people—most of them in Asia—live in low-lying coastal regions. More than two hundred million people worldwide live along coastlines less than sixteen feet above sea level.[52] How will technology handle this level of human migration?

"Our times are driven by the inestimable energies of the mechanical mind; its achievements derive from its singular focus, linear direction, and force. When it dominates, the habit of gentleness dies out. We become blind: nature is rifled, politics eschews vision and becomes the obsessive servant of economics, and religion opts for the mathematics of system and forgets its mystical flame."[53]

"Women Should Not Have Authority"— They Are Too Emotional to Deal with the Real Issues of Business and World Affairs

To understand attitudes toward women today, it's useful to look into Old and New Testament texts that have influenced fundamentalist thinking, both in and far beyond religion.

In Genesis 3 we find the story of our expulsion from a divine world and our Fall—a Fall that was brought about by a woman, Eve, who disobeyed the command of God, tempted Adam to taste the fruit of the Tree of Knowledge, and brought sin, suffering, and death into being.

A bride who is not a virgin deserves death: "If no proof of the girl's virginity can be found, she shall be brought to the door of

her father's house and there the men of her town shall stone her to death."
—Deuteronomy 22:20–21

Women, but only virgins, are to be taken as spoils of war: "Now kill all the boys. And kill every woman who has slept with a man, but save for yourselves every girl who has never slept with a man."
—Numbers 31:17–18

Menstruating women are spiritually unclean: "When a woman has her regular flow of blood, the impurity of her monthly period will last seven days, and anyone who touches her will be unclean till evening. Anything she lies on during her period will be unclean, and anything she sits on will be unclean. Anyone who touches her bed will be unclean; they must wash their clothes and bathe with water, and they will be unclean till evening."
—Leviticus 15:19–31

"Women should remain silent in the churches. They are not allowed to speak, but must be in submission, as the law says."
—1 Corinthians 14:34

"Wives, submit yourselves to your own husbands as you do to the Lord. For the husband is the head of the wife as Christ is the head of the church, his body, of which he is the Savior. Now as the church submits to Christ, so also wives should submit to their husbands in everything."
—Ephesians 5:22–24

"I do not permit a woman to teach or to assume authority over a man; she must be quiet. For Adam was formed first, then Eve."
—1 Timothy 2:11–15

"A man ought not to cover his head, since he is the image and glory of God; but woman is the glory of man. For man did not come from woman, but woman from man; neither was man created for woman, but woman for man."
—1 Corinthians 11:2–10

After thousands of years, the results of this way of thinking are that:

- Women work two-thirds of the world's working hours, yet earn only 10 percent of the world's income.
- Women are responsible for producing 60 to 80 percent of the world's food, yet hold only 10 percent of the world's wealth and own 1 percent of the world's land.[54]
- Just 7 percent of executive directors in FTSE 100 companies are female.
- The only national parliament that has more women than men is Rwanda's, with 56 percent. The United Kingdom ranks fifty-sixth, with 22.5 percent female MPs, and the United States seventy-seventh, with 17.7 percent of Congress being female.[55]

How might men feel if, for the past three thousand years, they had been educated to understand that god was a woman and that her laws were to be obeyed? This meant that men had to entirely repress their sexuality yet be available for sex on demand, walk three paces behind their wives, hide any sign of their attractiveness, do most of the manual work, have no say in lawmaking or government, and own no property.

Despite adopting scores of pious resolutions on gender empowerment since 1946, the 193-member UN General Assembly has failed to practice what it has vigorously preached to the outside world. So far, the United Nation's highest policy-making body has elected only three women as its president; there has never been a female UN secretary-general.

For thousands of years, the potential creativity and contribution of half the population of the world has been crushed by the experience of violence. Violence literally handicaps women and girls and keeps them down, whether it's sexual abuse of children in the home, rape in marriage, female children deprived of food, sexual slavery, trafficking, honor killings, genital cutting, forced marriage, kidnapping, or systematic use of rape as a weapon of war.

Mass rape is becoming a preferred tactic in civil war. Militias have discovered that the most cost-effective way to terrorize civilian populations is to conduct rapes of terrible brutality, raping women with broken bottles, knives, or bayonets, or firing their guns into women's vaginas. In reported cases in eastern Congo, soldiers rape children as young as three years old. A rape counselor in Goma, Congo, says, "In other places, there is rape because the soldiers want a woman. Here, it's that but it's also a viciousness, a mentality of hatred, and it's women who pay the price."[56]

Even today, the World Health Organization indicates that 35 percent of women worldwide have experienced sexual violence in their lifetime, either from an intimate partner or a non-partner. On average, 30 percent of women who have been in a relationship report that they have experienced some form of physical or sexual violence by their partner.[57]

FROM PAKISTAN . . .

A Pakistani woman of awe-inspiring courage, Mukhtaran Bibi, is bringing about a change in tribal attitudes toward women in her country. As a result of a feud between families and a demand for reparation, she was gang-raped on the order of a local village council and was made to walk home, nearly naked, between jeering ranks of villagers. As a victim of rape, it was expected that she would kill herself, but instead she took her attackers to court and has become a figurehead in the struggle for women's rights in Pakistan. Only recently has she been allowed to leave Pakistan and visit America, where she was welcomed as a heroine.

In Pakistan, Bibi is still followed by intelligence agents, who open or confiscate her letters and feed lies about her to the Pakistani press. She has received death threats. But she also received money ($8,300) in compensation from the court that prosecuted her attackers, and with this she started a small school in her village. As her story became known in the West, money flooded in to help her—more than $130,000—and with this she has improved schools in her area, endowing them with cows to generate income to pay for expenses.

Bibi has also bought an ambulance for her wider community, set up a police station to provide security, and is now preparing to build a school for older children, as well as a clinic and a woman's shelter. As Nicholas Kristof comments, "She is a woman simultaneously ordinary and extraordinary, who transcended her role and started a broad movement for justice."[58] From such humble beginnings in the lives of individual women who are courageous enough to overcome their fear, great events can unfold that can change the condition of women from one of virtual slavery to self-respecting freedom of action.

. . . TO WALL STREET

One of the most shocking effects of centuries of oppression is how some women have begun to deny their feminine sense in order to be considered as competent as men. I heard recently about a senior executive in a Wall Street international banking firm who, three weeks after she had given birth, accepted a three-month assignment in another country, leaving the baby behind. What part of herself did she have to cut in order to do that?

During these centuries of denial of the feminine aspects of humanity, men have certainly also suffered grievously. They have been forced to fight in wars when they chose not to; they have been physically or psychologically maimed in war, returning home to find themselves uncared for by the government that sent them to fight. They have been crushed by authoritarian regimes and held in jail for years without trial. They have become economic migrants desperate to find a way to work and feed their families. They have been sexually abused as children by priests in whom they placed trust. They have experienced trauma—usually of a more subtle kind—at the hands of women, sometimes their mothers. It's time for both men and women to release themselves from the norms that have afflicted them.

"Consuming Is Our Right"— We Always Need More and Better

We have become a society of instant gratification. We expect our desires to be fulfilled. Are we now living like addicts looking for our next fix? Are we hooked by a mainstream culture of consumption leading to excessive materialism? Incessantly we seem to be urged by governments to shop, in ever more desperate attempts to make the economy grow. Governments are enthusiastically assisted in this by the advertising industry, using every psychological trick to play on our insecurity and convince us that a car or a holiday or new clothes will make us the person we aspire to be.

It was not so long ago that we enjoyed an enforced day of rest when, on Sundays, shops were closed. Now we have everything 24/7: cash from ATMs and shopping on the internet or even on Main Street. Shopping has filled our leisure time.

US advertisers spend more than $400 billion every year trying to convince you that without their products, you are a complete and total loser. The ad shill's entire reason for being is to make you and me dissatisfied with what we have and who we are. And the average American sees between 1,500 and 3,000 of such commercials per day.[59]

And, like all powerful drugs, purchases do make us feel better for a little while. But then we have withdrawal symptoms—when we face again the lack of a more meaningful narrative or of belief in a higher purpose. Have our values become so thin? To transform this, we would have first to admit our addiction to consumerism, and governments would have to wean themselves off the imperative for economic growth. Until that happens, it will be hard to change. We can, of course, propose inquests into why business behaves badly, why banks are corrupt, why corporations are deceitful. But this may not change the root causes until we recognize the degree of our addiction to the consumerist worldview, which we have raised to an unquestioned reality.[60]

"The consumer society is the shop window of secular technology. It promises happiness but the best it can give is pleasure and when the excitement of the latest "must-have" is over, the need for the next one takes its place. Compulsive pleasure-seeking has the same root cause as much alcohol and substance misuse—warding off feelings of emptiness and futility. It arises as the consequence of growing up without an appreciation of spiritual values such as the pleasure in helping others; a sense of kinship; the lightness that comes with honesty and openness; appreciation of the gift of life; and the confidence to speak from the heart. These attributes of the soul are awakened by loving relationships, for which no machine or electronic device can compensate. The less time that is found for face-to-face human intimacy, the more impoverished the child and the greater the handicap for the adult-to-be."[61]

The final film in the "Story of Stuff" series asks, "What if the goal of our economy wasn't more, but better—better health, better jobs, and a better chance to survive on the planet?" This fantastic nine-minute video is one that kids seem to absorb quickly.[62]

One consequence of both consumerism and advertising is the effect on families and children. A US study showed that children spend three and a half "meaningful" minutes a *week* talking with their parents and an average of four hours a *night* watching television. By the age of eighteen, a young person will have seen 360,000 commercials and at least 60,000 murders on television. Two-thirds of families now watch television while eating dinner, and by the age of sixty-five a person will, on average, have spent *nine years* in front of the screen. Another US study finds that the average young person, by the age of twenty-one, has spent ten thousand hours playing video games, the same length of time it takes to become a concert pianist or a world-class athlete.[63]

Underneath the modern story of never-ending progress and growth are concealed—usually hidden from our conscious minds—our own experiences and perceptions of a fragile world. We notice big changes in our local weather patterns but brush them under the carpet. We read about the dangers of fracking and forget them in the rationale that we must not let the lights go out. We can't resist an offer of a cheap flight to a sunny vacation spot, though we know that flying produces levels of carbon dioxide that are unsustainable. I personally do all these things, and I try to pretend that I don't. We have elevated increased consumer choice to be our highest goal. Yet this goal is increasingly in conflict with maintaining a livable planet.

When I absorb the facts and statistics in this chapter, I am overwhelmed by sadness. I see a woman fleeing from warlords in Somalia, having to bury one child—who has died of starvation—by the side of the road while she battles to save the other two; I see the last snow leopard, hunted for its fur in the wilds of the Himalaya; I see hills strip mined, oceans empty of fish, and air so polluted that humans wear masks; I see a child searching rubbish dumps in the Philippines, his feet bleeding from broken bottles; I see men in masks and paramilitary fatigues shooting down naked indigenous peoples in an Amazon clearing.

How do we deal with such sadness? We go deep within and then we act.

Dark and cold we may be, but this
Is no winter now. The frozen misery
Of centuries breaks, cracks, begins to move;
The thunder is the thunder of the floes,
The thaw, the flood, the upstart Spring.
Thank God our time is now when wrong
Comes up to face us everywhere,
Never to leave us till we take
The longest stride of soul we ever took.
Affairs are now soul size.
The enterprise
Is exploration into god.
Where are you making for? It takes
So many thousand years to wake,
But will you wake for pity's sake!

     —Christopher Fry, "A Sleep of Prisoners"

CHAPTER 5

THE SHIFT TO DIFFERENT NORMS

Throughout the ages, people have said that the world is in the midst of big change. But the level and degree of global change that we face today is far more profound than at any other period in my adult lifetime. I call this period the Great Transition. . . . I believe we face a unique opportunity. Because the changes we face are so profound—the decisions we make will have a deeper and more lasting impact than perhaps any other set of decisions in recent decades. We have no time to lose.[1]

—UN Secretary-General Ban Ki-Moon

Albert Einstein said, "Humanity is going to require a substantially new way of thinking if it is to survive." In this chapter we shall investigate the underlying shifts in values that could create this new way of thinking and explore whether humanity can make such shifts. The questions that we need to investigate, I believe, are the following:

1. How can humans become responsible stewards of the earth, in order to preserve its beauty and diversity?
2. Can we recognize that humanity, other creatures, and nature are integral parts of the same whole?
3. Is it the case that the human body, mind, feelings, soul, and spirit are all one, interacting constantly—and that the entire package is what we experience as consciousness?

4. Is growth in consciousness now urgent?
5. Can emphasis be shifted from individual competition to cooperation aimed at the greater good?
6. Could building trust between groups and nations be a more effective and less costly form of security?
7. Would common security be safer and cheaper than an international system based on weapons and superior power?
8. How could our decisions take account of future generations, as the oldest indigenous traditions advise us to do?
9. Is the divine—or "greater intelligence"—not only available to us here and now but also infinitely more powerful than human intelligence?
10. Are the capacities of the deep feminine and the deep masculine—in both men and women—vital for human survival on the planet?
11. How can we satisfy the human need for meaning and beauty?

How Can Humans Become Responsible Stewards of the Earth in Order to Preserve Its Beauty and Diversity?

Treat the earth well: it was not given to you by your parents, it was loaned to you by your children.

—Ancient Indian Proverb

Indigenous elders have long said that we live in a web of interconnections spanning the world—the Unified Field or Amplified Field discussed in chapter 2—and this is increasingly supported by laboratory science. In the new scientific paradigm, it's clear that consciousness can no longer be explained away as a side effect of the brain. Each of us matters more than we thought.[2]

What if we saw ourselves as entrusted with the care of an unbelievably valuable gift, a complex system of inestimable worth, a precious inheritance that must be passed on intact? What then? How might we act?

I believe that there is an even greater challenge. It took billions of years to produce the beauty and abundance around us, but in the past few decades, we humans have desecrated and harmed the planet's systems to such an extent that our responsibility is now *repair*. While *sustainability* may be a current buzzword, the need is far greater than that—the need is for *regeneration*. Our job now is to support the earth's recovery systems so that the balance of delicate ecosystems can be restored.

How could a way be found for governments to stop dragging their feet, to work in concert to outwit the pressures of multinational corporations and make agreements to stop the destruction of virgin forest, coral reefs, and fish stocks?

What if the production of carbon dioxide and the release of methane could be brought under control?

Why use a third of the world's arable land to grow soybeans and other cereals to feed farm animals, when they could graze in fields?

Why waste up to five tons of wild fish producing one ton of farmed fish?

What if we as the people were to wake up from our absurd sleepwalk of consuming and discarding, buying and throwing away?[3]

What if we as consumers were to insist that our energy comes only from renewable sources? This is perfectly possible at a fraction of the investment currently going into drilling for oil, fracking, and the production of bio fuels. In a single *hour*, the sun beams onto the earth more than enough energy to satisfy global energy needs for an *entire year*.

Seeing ourselves as the indigenous peoples saw themselves—as stewards of the earth—would result in a subtle revolution. People who regard themselves as owners tend to operate with a top-down mentality, while people who regard themselves as stewards have a mindset of service and can work from the bottom up. This would lead to mass mobilization and empowerment; a huge growth in nonviolent protest; consumers voting with the purchasing dollar, making their wishes known to manufacturers and governments in no uncertain terms; and homeowners insulating their homes and installing solar panels.

Can We Realize That Humanity, Other Creatures, and Nature Are Integral Parts of the Same Whole?

In some parts of the world, it is explained to every child that he or she is part of a vibrant, intelligent, living planet—that it is not just the animals and insects and birds and fish that are alive, but every tiny microorganism as well. And they are not just alive, but part of a whole system; each depends on the other, and we humans depend on all of them.

This knowledge was second nature to our ancestors and is still second nature to many of the "first peoples"—indigenous cultures from around the world—who have always based their belief systems on their understanding that humanity, other creatures, and nature are integral parts of the same whole.

> The first peace, which is the most important, is that which comes within the souls of people when they realize their relationship, their oneness with the universe and all its powers, and when they realize at the center of the universe dwells the Great Spirit, and that its center is really everywhere, it is within each of us.
>
> —Black Elk

The speed of life today is such that most of us have forgotten this sense of interconnectedness. What if we remembered?

What if we taught every child about Gaia? In ancient Greece, Gaia was the great mother of all, the primal Mother Goddess, the earth itself, who gave birth to the sky and the ocean and the mountains. James Lovelock brought her to life again in 1979 in *Gaia: A New Look at Life on Earth*. Lovelock's hypothesis proposes that living organisms and inorganic material are part of a dynamic system that shapes the earth's biosphere and maintains the earth as a fit environment for life.

Children seem to have a natural sense of the interconnectedness of all life. They're fascinated by nature, by earth, air, fire, and water. Take a two-year-old out for a walk in a park or along a country lane, and it may take you an hour to progress one yard, so great is the fascination with every flower, every bird, even the pieces of a snail's shell. Children ask the kind of questions that hint that they are in touch with a deep, instinctive knowledge. "What are shadows made of?" "Why is water wet?" "Where did the first horse come from?" "Where do you go when you die?"

Schools in Europe are beginning to understand the power of children's natural connection to nature and are opening "Forest Schools," an innovative educational approach to outdoor play and learning in a woodland environment. The concept for Forest Schools was developed in Sweden in the 1950s, and it has since extended throughout the world, because this outdoor approach to learning and play can have a great effect on the natural development of children, and children love it. The kids in my local school love Monday mornings, because that's when they have Forest School. Steiner-Waldorf schools, which have a similar nature-based approach, have for decades fostered imagination and creativity as the source of ingenuity in children in many countries.[4]

What would the world be like if all children in it could be educated in this way?

Is It the Case That the Human Body, Mind, Feelings, Soul, and Spirit Are All One, Interacting Constantly—and the Entire Package What Is We Experience as Consciousness?

In chapter 2 I began to uncover the leap in consciousness now taking place. It has been compared to what happens when a caterpillar begins its transformation into a butterfly. The incredible, almost unbelievable characteristics of this "butterfly" that we are becoming are being revealed to us now by science: "Without our capacity to imagine, measure, deduce and reflect, and develop instruments to extend our power of observation, we could not know that everything we are, everything on our planet and in our solar system, has been formed from elements of the stars that have been seeded here from great galaxies millions of light years away from us."[5]

The discoveries of health professionals are now confirming what "energy medicine" has asserted for centuries, namely that the mind, body, and feelings are all interactive—each affects the other in profound ways. My own experience has borne this out: in 1974 I had a severe form of encephalitis and was unconscious for several days. There followed six years of living in a kind of brain fog, exacerbated by the most excruciating headaches, which couldn't be alleviated by anything that doctors suggested. It was only when I began to work with an acupuncturist—balancing the energy meridians in my body at the same time as working with my mind and feelings—that the headaches subsided. They have not returned.

Acupuncture was so gentle, so benign, and so powerful that I got interested in how Chinese medicine works, as a holistic system attending to causes rather than symptoms of illness. I liked this "whole body" approach so much that I have had acupuncture treatment every month since, using it as my version of health insurance. It keeps me well, and by restoring balance it provides me with energy.

Dr. Andrew Powell says that given the reductionism of so much mainstream science, we should be grateful to those physicists at the cutting edge of quantum mechanics and cosmology who are entirely at ease thinking outside the box. "The billiard ball picture of stars and planets in space is being replaced by a new perspective. We now know that only 5 percent of the universe is accessed by our sense perception. The other 95 percent, of dark matter and dark energy, weaves a single field that is thought to be infinite and timeless, in which every point in the universe is connected to every other point comprising one unbroken whole."[6]

Is Growth in Consciousness Now Urgent?

Only a leap in consciousness can provide a new paradigm from which to live—the bird's eye view—that will enable us to take the necessary actions to resolve the problems we have created. What Einstein famously said—that no problem can be solved from the consciousness that created it—was way ahead of his time and entirely correct.

This leap in human consciousness is just *starting* to happen. People seem to be feeling a sense of urgency about the state of the planet, they know that the kind of solutions proposed by political leaders are proving insufficient and often not carried through. Many feel it's time to move from the hierarchical to the horizontal—in other words, from top-down solutions to a network of people working together.

Across the planet, millions of people—young and old—are now flooding the streets to reject corruption and injustice. They're mobilizing in ways unthinkable before. Online initiatives like Avaaz (a global activist movement) are growing by well over one million people each month, tackling some of the toughest issues, and getting results. When that Bangladeshi garment factory collapsed in 2013, killing over a thousand, Avaaz joined forces with labor organizations and targeted two massive retail giants. The aim was to get them to sign an enforceable worker-safety plan that could be a model for the world. Three days later the targeted retail companies signed, prompting more than seventy-five other brands to follow.

Activist Naomi Klein was asked by Jason Mark for *Earth Island Journal* if she sees a global, grassroots response to some of the extreme weather we're experiencing. She said:[7]

> I see a people's shock happening broadly, where on lots of different fronts you have constituencies coming forward who have been fighting, for instance, for sustainable agriculture for many, many years, and now realize that it's also a climate solution. You have a lot of reframing of issues—and not in an opportunistic way, just another layer of understanding. Here in Canada, the people who oppose the tar sands most forcefully are Indigenous people living downstream from the tar sands. They are not opposing it because of climate change—they are opposing it because it poisons their bodies. But the fact that it's also ruining the planet adds another layer of urgency. And it's that layering of climate change on top of other issues that holds a huge amount of potential.

This multilayered consciousness is enabling people all over the globe to start to think what a better world could look like. They are beginning to imagine—and then to act. Like green shoots coming up through cracks in the concrete.

Have you ever dared to imagine what life *could* be like . . . if we used our skills to transform conflict, to clean up and care deeply for the environment, and to invent a financial system that is fair and just? How it would be if we set up systems for wise governance, if we kicked out the cynics and gave medals to people who outlaw corruption? What would life be like if we were to bring feminine attributes into balance with masculine, to free the creativity of children, to produce healthy food and water? What if we were able to have a pace of life that honored our natural rhythms?

For much of my life, I have worked with people in some of the most desperate situations on earth, the most violent, as well as some of the most privileged. That half-century of experience has shown me that a secure and satisfying future for all of humanity is possible. This is not a utopia. It's happening, as you will see in the next chapter. There are examples all over the world, but not in clear view—they are under the radar, in the streets—and you might well miss the movement. The media certainly has.

Isn't this an issue of personal responsibility—a call to engage in this patient, loving work oneself? It seems to me that it has to be done person by person until critical mass is reached. For me, it becomes more and more rewarding and exciting as I go farther along this path. You may notice how you yourself begin to see the world differently as you go through the steps suggested in chapter 7.

Can We Shift the Emphasis from Individual Competition to Cooperation for the Greater Good?

Nature itself, long thought to be based solely on brute competition, has revealed artful kinds of synergy, cooperation, and cocreation woven into its deepest levels.

> Animal societies, in which collective action emerges from cooperation among individuals, represent extreme social complexity. Such societies are not only common in insects, mammals, and birds, but exist even in simple species like amoebas. Animal societies vary in structure from eusocial insect colonies with a single reproductive female supported by hundreds, thousands, or even millions of nonbreeding workers, to cooperatively breeding groups of vertebrates with one or more breeders and a small number of non-breeding helpers.[8]

Research with non-ordinary states of consciousness is beginning to reveal that humans have the ability to connect with other humans—as well as with nonhuman animals and even plants—in surprising ways, through telepathy, nonlocal sensing, and meditation.[9] This means that humans can help one another and enlarge the Golden Rule from "Do unto others as you would have them do unto you," to "Be compassionate toward all creatures, because, in some sense, they *are* you."[10]

One example would be the kind of cooperation that is possible in addressing the global food problem. There is already enough food in the world to feed everyone adequately if we who have enough, or plenty, used our skills to take care of those foodstuffs for others who are starving. "The total amount of grain produced in the world around the year 2000 could keep eight billion people alive at subsistence level, if it were evenly distributed, not fed to animals, and not lost to pests or allowed to rot between harvest and consumption."[11]

The Limits to Growth team, who in 1972 compared computer modeling of exponential economic and population growth with finite resource supplies, gave extensive figures on the physical resources necessary to support human biological and industrial activity, making the distinction between those resources that are finite and limited and those that are renewable. They say in their thirty-year update: "Even if the earth's physical systems are capable of supporting a much larger, more industrially developed population, the actual growth of the economy and the population will depend on such factors as peace and social stability, equity and personal security, honest and far-sighted leaders, education and openness to new ideas, willingness to admit mistakes and to experiment."[12]

Since the global population is growing fast, and all of us are increasingly dependent on nonrenewable resources such as fossil fuels, high-grade mineral ores, and deep ground water, it is essential that we learn to work cooperatively. The simple fact is that *we can no longer afford competition;* it costs the human race—not to mention the rest of life on earth—too much.

Cooperation, of course, can be difficult. If it were easy, we would not have become so competitive. We have seen see how cooperation is possible in urgent, stressful situations, such as war or a moon launch, when the motivation is high enough. What will it take for the human race to wake up to the fact that we're now in a global situation worse than any war, demanding the most urgent action? Why is it that we can mobilize massive forces to kill one another, yet remain paralyzed and in numb denial before the greatest evolutionary challenge of human history?

Frightening though the situation is, we need to stay steady and take the responsibility to awaken ourselves, so that when we act, we will act wisely and effectively. History shows that great changes start in small ways, with small groups of people coming together. Think of the how the movement for the abolition of the British slave trade began meeting in 1789 in a coffee house in Parliament Street with a group of less than a dozen people. Even the greatest changes have to start one person at a time. Given the enormity of the challenges facing us, this may seem derisory; but that's because we're judging the situation from our rational minds, not understanding how, through the interaction of the Unified Field, one person waking up can have an improbably contagious effect. Like leaven in bread, the awakening of a few individuals can raise the whole loaf.

Here's a very local example of cooperation for the greater good, one that is spreading fast. Mumbai is a city of twenty million people, of whom more than half live in "informal settlements." These settlements are made of tottering corrugated-iron shacks piled on top of one another or dismal eight-story cement-block apartment buildings with no elevators. Alleyways with open sewers thread their way through the buildings. Nine out of every ten women in the settlements experience domestic violence, but groups of them are now pioneering an innovative method of putting an end to this violence.

Sangita Kamble and Sujata Lavhande are two grassroots leaders from CORO, the Community of Resource Organizations.[13] They work in Ashoknagr, in the eastern part of the city, where the average worker makes $1.50 per day and people have to pay a fifth of that for water. They are empowering other women who have developed a community system for the protection of victims of domestic violence. When a woman in the neighborhood reports violence in her home, two or more other women from the community go with her to discuss the incident with the perpetrator. If the violence continues, more women come to confront him. Usually this is sufficient to convince him to stop—because by now his acts are becoming known to the community. If not, the women lodge a complaint against the perpetrator with the police, and the police either come to the home or call the perpetrator to the station.

This is a brilliant example of cooperation and the power of nonviolent dialogue, which resolves rather than escalates a brutal situation. I met the women involved and was stunned—not first of all by their courage—but by their beauty and their energy. Before they even spoke, their glowing skin and their confidence spoke volumes about how they feel about what they're doing.

The jewel colors of their saris shone as they talked and joked in a tiny home off a narrow alleyway, and I began to realize the extent of their courage, facing the physical and sexual abuse that is endemic, extending to teenaged girls and even young children. While we talked, a drunk man tried to intervene in the conversation and was instantly hissed at; he disappeared fast. Had I not been there and listened to them and witnessed the tangible evidence of their confidence, I could not have believed these women were victims of violence. I could detect no trace of victimhood. The method they have developed is now being copied and is spreading fast in other parts of the state of Maharashtra, through the fellowship program organized by Leaders' Quest.[14] Leaders' Quest is a social enterprise committed to improving the quality and impact of leaders around the world.

Could Building Trust Between Groups and Nations Be a More Effective and Less Costly Form of Security?

> Love and compassion are necessities, not luxuries.
> Without them, humanity cannot survive.
>
> —His Holiness the Dalai Lama

Building trust *sounds* like a good idea, but how do you actually do it? Does it work to help build national security, and if so, what does it cost? In my experience the basic methods apply whether it's an issue of mistrust in a family, suspicion in a community, or a conflict between nations. And like anything entrepreneurial, it requires investment.

BUILDING TRUST AND TRANSFORMING CONFLICT

First, it's a good idea to get a broad perspective of the issue, a bird's eye view. Peer into the future, picture the consequences of the conflict escalating, and imagine the lasting damage it could do in people's lives. Then make the effort to speak person to person with those involved in the issue, because email or letters will cause problems. Create a safe and confidential space where a conversation can be take place off the record.

Explain that you're really interested in understanding their point of view, and ask them to speak only in the first person and say what they feel and what they need. The key at this point is to give them your absolute full attention—to listen so well that you could, if necessary, repeat back not only their words but also the feelings you sense behind the words.

When it's your turn to speak, do the same thing: express the facts or the situation without allowing yourself to accuse, blame, or judge. When both parties do this, it becomes possible to move from your entrenched positions—basically "I'm right and you're wrong"—to begin to discover what your mutual interests might be. See where these interests coincide and build on them, so you can begin to construct an agreement on what each party will do and say. Then fix a time to revisit that agreement.

FROM THE PERSONAL TO THE POLITICAL

In the 1990s I witnessed a striking change: for the first time, more wars ended by negotiated settlement (forty-two) than by military victory (twenty-three). This started a trend that accelerated in the new millennium. Between 2000 and 2005, seventeen conflicts ended in negotiated settlements; just four ended in military victory.[15]

Astonishing research compared the outcomes of 285 nonviolent and violent campaigns to resist dictatorship in the twentieth century and found that "major non-violent campaigns have achieved success 55 percent of the time, compared to 28.4 percent for violent resistance campaigns."[16] Why does our media obsession with violence—and our addiction to melodrama—prevent us from seeing that nonviolence is profoundly effective, even in seemingly intractable situations?

The cost of effective intervention to end violence is ridiculously low. It cost only $350,000 for the initiative by the Community de Saint Egidio to successfully end the Mozambique civil war in 1992. It cost only $200,000 for the networking of private citizens that complemented Kofi Annan's efforts to end the postelection crisis in Kenya in 2008. It cost only $1.3 million for the weapons collection program in El Salvador that ended the hijacking of trucks after the civil war.

The costs of preventing conflict at a local level are even lower. From 1998 to 2000, the OTPOR student campaign to monitor elections in

Serbia—which ultimately deposed Slobodan Milosevic—cost an estimated $5 per student (to be trained and deployed), of whom there were about twenty thousand. In 1995, the Committee for the Protection of People's Dignity (COPPED) was formed to galvanize the youth of Nigeria to retract its threat of violence and instead require oil exploration companies to undertake proper consultation with local communities. The annual budget of COPPED is $100,000.[17]

In his 2006 UN Secretary General's Report on Conflict Prevention, Kofi Annan said, "Too often the international community spends vast sums of money to fight fires that, in hindsight, we might more easily have extinguished with timely preventive action before so many lives were lost or turned upside down. Over the last five years, we have spent over $18 billion on United Nations peacekeeping that was necessary partly because of inadequate preventive measures. A fraction of that investment in preventive action would surely have saved both lives and money."[18]

How does effective prevention work? My colleague Gabrielle Rifkind, who is engaged in mediating conflicts in the Middle East with the Oxford Research Group, cautions: "The role of a small group of mediators can only have real impact if governments are better prepared and more ready to understand the importance of bringing the enemy in from the cold. This requires a shift in mindset in which the mediators would have the responsibility to be familiar with the local narratives. . . . They would need to be trained in the skills of. . . . listening, and have training in understanding the complexity of the human mind."[19]

It's worth pointing out the vital difference between mediation and negotiation, since this difference affects the long-term success of agreements reached. Negotiators, be they diplomats, merchant bankers, or CEOs, have a large constituency sitting on their shoulders during talks. That constituency may be government leaders, clients, or shareholders, all of whom require results in their favor in a zero-sum game. Mediators, by contrast, are usually third parties, whose main interest is in enabling the parties in dispute to move from their set positions and discover where their mutual interests might lie.

Independent organizations in the United States and United Kingdom have been designing security policies that could effectively replace government plans. In 2013 the American Friends Service Committee, deeply respected for its consistently pragmatic proposals over many years, published a new vision of shared security as the foundation for an ethical and effective US engagement with the world.[20]

Most conflict and violence is rooted in mistrust stemming from humiliation of some kind. The antidote for humiliation is respect. So in mediation, it is important to demonstrate your respect for the other person. Here's a true story:

> In 2003, shortly after the invasion of Iraq, US Lieutenant Colonel Chris Hughes was leading his men down a street in Najaf, when suddenly people came pouring out of the houses that lined the street and surrounded the troops. They were furiously angry, screaming, and waving their fists. The soldiers, who were mainly about nineteen years old and spoke no Arabic, had no idea what was happening and were terrified.
>
> Chris Hughes strode into the middle of it, raised his rifle above his head—pointing the barrel at the ground—and said to his men "KNEEL." The bewildered troops, burdened by their heavy body armor, wobbled to the ground and also pointed their rifles downward. The crowd quieted in disbelief, and there was absolute stillness for some two minutes. And then the crowd dispersed.[21]

This gesture of respect averted a bloodbath; no weapons were needed; no shots were fired; no expense was incurred.

Would Common Security Be Safer and Cheaper Than an International System Based on Weapons and Superior Power?

David Miliband, former British foreign secretary, wrote wise words in July 2012: "Good politics starts with empathy, proceeds with analysis, then sets out norms and establishes the vision, before getting to the nitty gritty of policy solutions."[22]

Some Western governments tend to be lost in a paradigm that takes no account of the belief systems and ethos of those with whom it goes to war. We ignore Miliband's four prerequisites and rush to "solutions."

These solutions, as seen in Iraq and Afghanistan, not only are obscenely expensive and ignorant of the psychology of people in the region but also leave fundamental problems unsolved, as well as a legacy of violence and hatred that is likely to last several generations.

An arsenal of weapons does not make us safer, and traditionally it has simply made our enemies more fearful and keen to build up their own arsenal. During the Cold War, each move made by the Soviet Union or the United States simply made the other ratchet up its own nuclear arsenal.

I'm not sure that the superpowers have yet left that Cold War mentality behind. In December 2013, British defense secretary Philip Hammond published his annual update on the Trident nuclear weapons replacement program, announcing two further contracts would increase the total spent on replacing Trident to more than £800 million since 2011.[23] Analysis by the Royal United Service Institute shows that spending on the Trident replacement program is expected to consume one-third of the United Kingdom's military equipment budget for most of the 2020s—and beyond.[24] I know I am not alone in finding such decisions astonishing when, in an increasingly digitalized world, no amount of nuclear weaponry can protect against cyberattacks or terrorism.

Instead, imagine what could be done if even a fraction of the current global annual spending on defense—$1,582,800,000,000[25]—were shifted gradually, through a series of global treaties, to fund environmental, food, and water security; efforts to build trust; and the protection of the common heritage of humankind (oceans, atmosphere, and outer space).[26] This would enhance common security by orders of magnitude. *Common security* is the concept that a state can best maintain its own security by ensuring the security of others. Shifting some of the global defense budget to efforts that would increase common security would narrow the disastrous global inequality of wealth noted earlier in this chapter.

Negotiating global treaties to reduce spending on defense will depend on achieving agreement based on simultaneous action. Why? Because no national government wants to be the first to disarm or even decrease their arsenal. This is more likely to happen against a backdrop of worsening circumstances in which the common interest to cooperate to solve larger problems is in the self-interest of each competitor. Cooperation, paradoxically, becomes not about *self-sacrifice* but about *self-interest*. Or, to put it another way, the more intense and damaging competition becomes at one level, the greater is the drive toward fruitful cooperation at the next.[27] This idea is explored in detail in the chapter 6.

I would add that this process is more likely to succeed if it is driven from the bottom up. This campaign would begin with people talking about it, imagining how it could work, and then organizing massive, international social-media campaigns to demonstrate public support for it. Government ministers have frequently told me that without public protest, they cannot justify changing policy. Pressure might then be put—simultaneously—on governments in all the major defense-spending regions, namely the United States (which spends 41 percent of the total), Asia (20 percent), Europe (18 percent), Middle East and North Africa (11 percent).[28]

Building common security begins at home; it begins at school.

> For nonviolent people power to displace violence, as the recognized means of delivering human security, it would need to be taken seriously by the powers that be. Then there would be an ongoing program of research and training for nonviolence, which would be recognized as an essential part of citizenship education, a guarantor of democracy. At present, we live in a world where violence gets the money and attention; where it is regarded as normal for army personnel to go into schools to promote the central role of the military and "warm up" potential recruits, and where peace activists are seen as unruly troublemakers.[29]

Can you imagine a world in which children were taught the basic skills of how to prevent and resolve conflicts?

How Could Our Decisions Take Account of Future Generations, As the Oldest Indigenous Traditions Advise Us to Do?

The Kogi people of the Sierra Nevada de Santa Marta, whose civilization has continued since the pre-Columbian era, base their lifestyle on their belief in Aluna, "The Great Mother"—their creator figure—whom they believe is the force behind nature. The Kogi understand the earth to be a living being and see humanity as her children. They say that our actions of exploitation, devastation, and plundering for resources is weakening the Great Mother and leading to our destruction.

Today, vast factory trawlers are vacuuming every living thing off the floor of the oceans. Toxic wastes are being dumped in poor communities while governments turn a blind eye. Millions of acres of primeval forest are being burned every day to make way for cattle ranches. These are crimes against the future—crimes that are happening today, in large numbers, all over the world. These crimes will not only injure future generations but destroy any future at all for millions of people. And today there is, in most countries, no institution or person whose job is to defend the rights of those future generations.

What if there was a basic requirement that every corporation, government and world body installed a department specifically empowered to stand up for future generations?

The World Future Council is calling for the establishment of Guardians for Future Generations.[30] These would be tough, experienced policy experts appointed at local, national, and global levels, whose job would be to safeguard environmental and social conditions by speaking up authoritatively for future generations in all areas of policy-making. This has already become a reality in some countries. The redoubtable Sándor Fülöp filled such a post in Hungary and managed, with support from community groups, to protect major environmental sites in his nation. The Israeli Knesset appointed a judge as Commissioner for Future Generations; New Zealand established a Parliamentary Commissioner for the Environment; and the Welsh Assembly recently appointed a Commissioner for Sustainable Futures.

Given that we humans already live well beyond the carrying capacity of the earth, an environmentally restorative change is essential if lives and livelihoods are to be maintained and cultivated. Translating the interests of future generations into policies and actions means choosing more sustainable solutions today—everywhere.

Industrialized countries, with ecological footprints in most cases exceeding five times their bio-capacity, urgently require robust institutional mechanisms not just to help reorient their economies toward sustainable futures but also to take measures to regenerate what has been depleted or destroyed.

On retirement, political leaders often voice their regret that they had no time to think, no time to reflect on the consequences of their decisions, particularly with respect to the state of the world they are leaving to their grandchildren. The appointment of Guardians for the Future, by whatever name, would not only remove the reason for such regrets, it could leave behind a legacy that future generations would honor.

Developing countries—and their negotiating groups—could take credit for and ownership of such an initiative to protect future generations, since it arises in large part from the wisdom of traditional cultures that have flourished in harmony with nature for thousands of years.

Judge Weeramantry, former vice president of the International Court of Justice, says of this initiative for Guardians for Future Generations:

> A significant omission in most legal systems is their lack of adequate concepts, procedures and institutions to protect the rights of future generations. Concentration on the rights of the present obscures their view of the rights of those who are unable to stand up for themselves when their rights are being denigrated. The present generation is damaging their rights irretrievably, as no other generation has done, and is doing so on a scale unmatched in human history.
>
> Every culture and religion stresses the importance of protecting our children. This is a primary duty and it extends a fortiori to the protection of our children's children. If we fail to do so, we are betraying the most solemn and sacred trust that lies upon us as human beings and trustees for future generations.[31]

As former US president Jimmy Carter says, "Putting aside the short-term political advantages in favor of serving the broader interests of humanity takes enormous courage."[32]

Perhaps this courage is not only required of political leaders; it's also required of us as parents, in taking account of our future generations and what they know of life on earth today. Lindsay Levin is the founder of Leaders' Quest; she spends her long working days taking corporate executives to some of the poorest neighborhoods, allowing them to experience what life is like at the other end of the spectrum. Then she and her husband, David, decided to take their two boys to India to introduce them to some of the people who made the country so special for them.

> So it was, as 2010 came to a close, that we found ourselves in the narrow alleys of Rafi Nagar, in the vast slum of Govandi, home to Mumbai's largest rubbish dump. . . .
>
> We were looking out over a sea of hunter gatherers, some as young as nine or ten, sifting through the wet of animal and vegetable decay. Small bare feet, thick-skinned and chapped, which navigated shards of broken glass, crushed plastic bottles and twisted scraps of metal buried in the mound. Every day, thousands of men, women and children, with sacks on their backs, came here to tramp from dawn to dusk across seething dunes of discarded life, to pick and sort amongst the waste and salvage what they could sell. These were some of the people known as rag pickers.

If you read Lindsay's book, you'll find out what happened on this particular Christmas holiday and how the two boys responded and became fascinated with the issues faced by the rag pickers.[33] Imagine if parents all over the world took care—as Lindsay and David did—to introduce their children to how other people live, and they began to instill early the necessity for compassion and action for a better world.

Is the Divine—or "Greater Intelligence"—Not Only Available to Us Here and Now but Also Infinitely More Powerful Than Human Intelligence?

Grappling with the overwhelming challenges of the future often reduces even competent, clever people to a numb silence. The problems we have caused—and only recently become aware of—are so vast, so multidimensional, that they can paralyze the rational mind. Most of us would, frankly, rather think about something else. The frown lines appear, the eyes narrow, people begin to shake their heads a little and say something like "I just can't get my mind around this."

It takes a certain degree of self-awareness to realize that they shouldn't expect the mind to manage that trick. It is not within the capacity of the human mind to grasp the full complexity of what faces us, given the interactions between the physical world and the human response, the emotional reactivity of humans, the geo-physical sequences that have been set in train, and so on. That is why climate-change predictions, for example, are so confusing and problematic. The unintended consequences of what we have done—and are doing—can bewilder even systems thinkers with their brilliant feedback loops.

This is the point where humility is essential. If we can abandon, just for a while, the natural human tendency to want to sort things out, to find a solution, to fix the problem, then—and only then—can there open up the possibility of something new and fresh that we have never imagined. This requires being willing to sit in the uncomfortable seat of "not knowing" for as long as required for transformation to take place.

Psychologist Shelley Reciniello says that women have a lot to teach men about getting comfortable with the feeling of not knowing. Women's very biology entails times of waiting, and the waiting requires not knowing, being patient, and being able to tolerate frustration. "It is in the 'not knowing' that men are most threatened. It violates their need to appear sure of themselves and confident, and therefore, not weak. It feels passive because they do not understand that receptivity can be active and empowering. But what is hopeful is that men and women can learn and do learn from each other."[34]

Being in a state of not knowing means letting go not only of relying on my own capacities and my own intelligence but also my ego; and then opening up to being receptive to what I can only call a "greater intelligence." This type of intelligence was well known to our ancestors and to those who have developed the mystical side of the Abrahamic religions. It is inherent in the cultures of the indigenous peoples of the world—in Tibet, in Ladakh, among the Kogi in Colombia, the Aboriginal peoples of Australia, and the Maori of Aotearoa. Some North and South American Indian peoples refer to it as the "great mysterious."

The intellectual sophistication of the philosophical traditions of China and India is extraordinary. There is no lack of intellect here in the West. But it's service to a much richer concept of development that is needed. The next stage of human development is certainly not industrialization, technology and all that—but somehow this next stage is about bringing back the interior to be in balance to the exterior. I think that has to come from China or India and maybe to some degree from the indigenous peoples.[35]

This "greater intelligence" is not available to a noisy mind; it requires stillness. And stillness, as anyone who has meditated knows, is not usually available at the drop of a hat. It requires practice; sitting quietly—or walking quietly—in a quiet place on a regular basis. And being willing to surrender.

Surrender for all of us is hard. We have used our will to get where we are, and it's hard to imagine dedicating it to an intelligence greater than ourselves. We in the West are schooled, daily and methodically, to believe that being in control is essential. The alternative to being in control is consciously to surrender—to give up our personal mind to the guidance of a higher intelligence. Giving up is not weakness; in fact, it requires repeatedly summoning up great courage.

Perhaps it's easiest first to think of surrender as trust. Imagine you're on one side of a huge field that you know is planted with land mines, the kind that explode at the slightest touch. But you have to get to the other side, and there's no way round. A Buddhist nun offers to guide you through the minefield. You know she has done it a hundred times before and knows the minefield like the back of her hand. You have no alternative but to trust her.

You start out. With every step, your trust grows. By the middle, you are entirely in her hands, and you would do exactly as she told you. You have surrendered. By the time you reach the other side, you are overwhelmed with gratitude.[36]

Stillness, trust, and surrender are the path to a quiet mind. It's quite a relief, really, inhabiting an empty place. And into the empty mind drop small wisps of ideas. If that mind can stay still a little longer, those wisps form into shapes, and the shapes take on color, and before long, there is something like a concept. It might even become a vision.

This is one of the ways in which the "greater intelligence" works, experienced by wise people in every corner of the earth—and certainly by the nuns in the minefields. They say not only that it is available to us here and now but also that it is infinitely more powerful than human intelligence.

Charles Steinmetz was a mathematician and electrical engineer who pioneered the development of alternating current. He was a confirmed agnostic. When asked about future discoveries, he said:

> The greatest discovery and development of the coming years will be along spiritual lines. Here is a force which history clearly teaches has been the greatest power in the development of man and history, and yet we have been merely playing with it and have never seriously studied it as we have physical forces. Some day people will learn that material things do not bring happiness and are of little use in making men and women creative and powerful. Then the scientists of the world will turn their laboratories over to the study of God and the spiritual forces. When this day comes, the world will see more advancement in one generation than it has in the past four.[37]

Are the Capacities of the Deep Feminine and the Deep Masculine—in Both Men and Women— Vital for Human Survival on the Planet?

The world is starting to grasp that there is no policy more effective in promoting development, health and education than the empowerment of women and girls. And I would venture that no policy is more important in preventing conflict, or in achieving reconciliation after a conflict has ended.

—Kofi Annan

A recent UN report states that women are natural peacemakers.[38] This may be because under stress women produce oxytocin, which is called the "bonding" hormone, rather than testosterone, the fight-or-flight hormone. (Of course, men produce oxytocin too.) Women's hormones generally have received bad press and are blamed for women's mood swings and worse—but maybe they could also be the key to a more harmonious world. The report states: "Women reduce stress by sharing perceptions, feelings and strategies, which is called the 'tend and befriend' oxytocin response and which is enhanced by estrogen. This hormonal response supports dialogue, collaboration and peaceful resolution of conflicts, in contrast to men's 'fight or flight' physiological adrenaline and testosterone response to stress, which increases aggression and competitiveness. . . . For peace and sustainability, political decisions and budgets need to be more oxytocin-influenced and less testosterone-driven."

The conclusions are clear. In order to have wise leadership, we need women in positions of power in significant numbers, and men need to cultivate a more oxytocin-based leadership style. This is not a male versus female position—everyone benefits when women have a voice in decisions.[39]

Kofi Annan and the UN report, however, were talking about gender, and while it is vitally important to bring more women into leadership positions, that is not quite what is of interest here. What I'm interested in is actually the *yin/yang* balance in *both* men and women—how both genders develop and use both their masculine and their feminine qualities. Put in very simple terms, these qualities may appear as follows:

Compete	Cooperate
Organize	Collaborate
Focus	Feel
Plan	Intuit
Discover	Ground
Achieve	Include
Solve	Transform
Question	Empathize
Specialize	Assemble and communicate

If you would be willing to go one step deeper, it is possible to unearth the profound power of the feminine, which has largely been lost for three thousand years or more but is now reemerging. This "deep feminine" is powerful because it is rooted in the earth, in absolute respect and reverence for Gaia—the planet that provides abundance—and her interconnected systems that sustain beauty and life.

The deep feminine is available equally to men as it is to women. It is powerful because it takes its time, it digests ideas and takes them from the mind into the gut, allowing them to sit in the belly before taking action; it considers and discriminates. Words may be few. Being sensitive to the atmosphere in a room, the deep feminine will calibrate its response so that the tone used can expand and deepen the level of listening. It is self-contained, complete; it has no neediness, resting on the self-knowledge of the person who carries it. When you're around someone who has this quality, there is no need for someone or some achievement to fill that sense of lack.

But the deep feminine is not always quiet. When roused, it is fiery, as consuming and as unstoppable as lava pouring from a volcano. The deep feminine roars like a lioness in the protection of children, of the defenseless, of the natural world that is being desecrated. It can be as powerful as a massive serpent or a mysterious current that sweeps all with it. It is powerful because it comes from the heart.

The deep feminine speaks of the future in words that may be difficult to understand. It is attuned to the seasons and the phases of the moon. It rests on ritual. It is familiar with darkness; some people say it's like "black light." It knows and has not forgotten our original and eternal identity. It responds equally to the monstrous and the exquisitely beautiful.

Having spent five decades with the nuts and bolts of politics, I conclude that using the deep feminine is the most powerful tool now at our disposal to ensure a safe and inclusive future. It's a question of balance. This is the time for the deep feminine to emerge as cocreator of the future with the deep masculine, the masculine that has so brilliantly given us insight and invention and the power to create and to destroy.

The deep masculine is the archetypal protector, he who wields the sword of discrimination, distinguishing between right and wrong. This is the glorious ability to focus, to question, to find out, to be precise, to get things done. It is the pioneering spirit that's willing to go out and take risks and explore. It invests selflessly in the protection and support of nature, of women, of children, of the feminine. The deep masculine is the courage in the heart of every one of us, able fearlessly to confront the challenges facing the planet.

All men hold the essence of the true masculine, an essence so deep and powerful, so pure and protective, that it envelops the whole of the earth in the safety of its arms. It is the quality that has been written of, from ancient times, in all myths throughout the ages—it the essence of the hero.

This hero is a human man, with no superpowers, except for his pure heart, his integrity, his wisdom and bravery, and the code of honor etched into his very being. When a man lives from this place, all of existence conspires to support him, all the powers and energy of Life Force itself stands by his side—and he is invincible in the deepest sense of the word. . . .

Masculine strength also means the courage to surrender to love, to embrace, to tenderness, to the feminine, to the soft whispers of Mother Earth and all her wisdom. To relax into the heart. A true hero is vulnerable, his heart is open like a child, he listens to love, and is guided by the power of life. He is ready to let the tender embrace of love dissolve all his manly facades into the childlike heart, and feel all his suppressed grief, hopes and pains held there. This gives him the power to overcome any enemy or obstacle no matter how insurmountable it seems. This is the hero's journey.

Often you may stumble, you may fail, and close your heart in despair. That's okay. You don't have to be perfect, or superman strong. You don't have to win every time. All you need is to love yourself enough to get up again, to keep opening to love—and to know that you are loved no matter what the outcome is. You are never unworthy. This is truly living in the heart of the masculine essence.[40]

The combination of deep feminine and deep masculine gives us the infinite creative potential to change our world through a union of mind and heart. We are cocreators in this with the greater intelligence and with the earth.

When feminine and masculine principles are out of balance there is oppression. Not oppression just of the feminine, but oppression of the masculine as well because you cannot oppress one without distorting both. Oppression does not discriminate. It oppresses all. Its invisible and pervasive force constricts the heart, suppresses the spirit and censors expressions. When the focus of our attention lives in stillness and animates balance and renewal, there is an endless breadth of possibilities that nourish heart, spirit and creativity.[41]

How Can We Satisfy the Human Need for Meaning and Beauty?

When I go into a shopping mall, I feel dry and tetchy; I pick up a sort of frenzy around me. Babies are screaming in their strollers, young children are whining for things they want, teenagers look dazed and disorientated, and adults look driven and stressed.

I understand why people go shopping, why retail therapy is such great business. It's quite true that when I buy new clothes, I like the crackle of the tissue paper it's wrapped in and the gloss of the carrier bag; when I get home I enjoy trying on what I've bought, and I look forward to the first occasion to wear it. But then the thrill is over. If I want more, I have to do the same things again.

What offers true meaning in our lives has more depth and color. It's the grip of a baby's fingers as they curl around mine. It's my feet hitting the exact rhythm of a beat. It's the scent of fresh flowers from somebody's garden. It's a poem that expresses exactly what I'm feeling. It's the touch of a lover's hand on my skin. It's a meeting of minds and hearts—the sudden flash of understanding that leaps from one being to another, like lightning. It's being able to tell the truth—the absolute truth of that moment—to another person, knowing that it will be received. It's the feeling of love and intimacy that can overwhelm me, like being bathed in silk.

None of these things cost any money, none of them require any marketing, yet they don't fade; we remember them. They have meaning for us. They're what people write songs about. What has meaning for people are their own values, what they care about, what they love. For some people, it's care of animals or sportsmanship. For others, the key thing is justice.

Richard Barrett, who has devoted a lifetime to studying and teaching about values, says that over time, humans have developed six ways of making decisions—instincts, subconscious beliefs, conscious beliefs, values, intuition, and inspiration. Nowadays, he says, it's normal for human beings to grow up with the ability to utilize the first three modes of decision making.

But from an evolutionary perspective, decision making based on values, intuition, and inspiration is relatively new but is increasingly being used as more and more people evolve to higher levels of consciousness. Perhaps his most profound finding is that *values unite* and *beliefs separate.*

Barrett says that one of the reasons why decision making based on values is so important at this time in our human history is that it "allows us to throw away our rule books. When a group of people espouse an agreed set of values and understand which behaviors support those values, then you no longer need to rely on bureaucratic procedures setting out what people should or should not do in specific situations. All the rules reduce to one— live the values. People can work out for themselves what they need to do, and in so doing become responsible and accountable for their behaviors."[42]

Coda

The values that could change our world cannot become mainstream— cannot become the norm—unless we, as individuals, change and take them on. Every one of us is personally invited to make the leap in consciousness that Einstein hinted at and to enjoy the freedom, wisdom, and energy that it brings. To be effective in meeting today's challenges, the first and greatest secret is to deepen our self-awareness, while at the same time becoming far more sensitive to others and their needs.

The most important lesson I've learned is that inner work and internal learning are prerequisites for outer effectiveness—they directly shape the quality of results produced. Reflection, mindfulness, and inner work are your essential tools. They will enable you—and the work you do daily—to become authentic. And the extent of your influence as a leader will be in direct proportion to the level of your authenticity.

In an online seminar, Dr. Ervin Laszlo, a philosopher of science and systems theorist, said to Dr. Stanislav Grof, a founder of transpersonal psychology, and Dr. Larry Dossey, one of the most respected pioneers of holistic medicine:

> If you think about the old mechanistic local sense world, then you act in a manipulative way, act in a way to try to explore, try to gain the upper hand of other things because we ourselves are here, the

rest of the world is there. This is a dual world. It's a manifest frag-mented world, that's a worldview that suggests, that prompts this kind of self-centered, short-term thinking because after all things are separate. What you do to yourself, you do to yourself and the rest are not directly affected.

Laszlo goes on:

The new paradigm in turn tells you something much deeper, tells you that there is something in the world that connects you; that you are not alone; that you are never in one place, you are never separate from the rest. There are no islands in this world. Everything in some sense is always connected at all times with all other things. . . .

Now this idea of things being given simultaneously is an old spiritual idea. It's an idea of timelessness. Time doesn't end here because all things are already given. But it's also an idea at the fore-front of the new physics which said that there is an underlying field, a deeper field, a unifying field, what used to be called a quantum vac-uum but now it's considered more likely to be a whole, a plenum that everything that happens in the universe, after all, is interconnected.[43]

Authentic leaders are those who work from the deepest levels of their being, connecting to this underlying unifying field. In them, a marriage takes place between the ego and the deeper self, and over time, the ego becomes the servant of the deeper self, and not its tyrannical master. Indi-vidual destiny marries the intelligence and wisdom of greater awareness, in which healing, regeneration, and transformation are possible. Truly to understand this principle of authentic leadership is, I believe, the key to a radiant future.

Now here are some questions for you:

What has most meaning for you in your life?
What are your most precious values, the ones you care about, that you love?
How might you live life, if every action you took or decision you made was in line with those values?

CHAPTER 6

STRATEGIES TO GET FROM HERE TO THERE

With the norms of our next stage in consciousness alive in us, let us now think in practical terms about strategies to get from where we are now to where we want to be—within reach of these inviting future scenarios. This chapter works out some of the steps needed now to bring into reality the world we envisage. This is the practical bit: this is where we bring in the pragmatists who know what to do in their special area, because they've tried it, tested it, and made it work. This chapter introduces living, breathing examples of what's already happening, already ahead of the curve—from a system that helps governments cooperate to align their policy making, to a bank in Indonesia where money serves people, to the organization of "people power" that is producing results all over the planet.

What follows is full of precise and gritty facts. If you really wish to be an agent of change, you have to master large quantities of information. This may seem forbidding at first, but when you understand just how much power lies in having the facts at your fingertips and how persuasive this makes you in tough situations, you will see that acquiring these facts is an invaluable investment. I've found again and again that to effect real change, an effective activist needs not only the inner power but also the outer force that comes from facts.

In this chapter we're interested not only in new systems and practical examples but also in overall concepts—global processes that help shift the blockages preventing progress to a positive future. We begin with some that work top down and then move on to others that work from the bottom up. In some cases we pose the question *"What if . . . ?"*—what if a particular idea was scaled up globally, what if a particular action was taken.

The chapter ends with my reality check about the traps and challenges that can derail this amazing energy and where we can find the power to address those darker moments.

- Simultaneous policy *What if . . . ?*
- Banking: where money serves people, not the other way around
- Business: prioritizing people and planet alongside profit *What if . . . ?*
- Fossil free
- People power: the nonviolent revolutions
- Radical efficiency in addressing social problems
- Transforming the treatment of women worldwide: educate, end violence, empower *What if . . . ?*
- What does an integrated strategy look like?
- My reality check: the shadows that can sabotage vision and action

Simultaneous Policy

In our rush to push global leaders to change the future, some are tempted to see them like the children in the playground in chapter 4, admonishing them to "grow up"!

The following was contributed by John Bunzl, author of *Global Domestic Politics.*[1]

> Maybe it's good to be aware that their decisions are often not their own; the market forces at work overwhelm the individual. Listen to former Greek prime minister George Papandreou recounting negotiations to organize a coordinated European response to the growing euro crisis in 2011:
>
> Picture yourselves around the table in Brussels. Negotiations are

difficult, tensions are high, progress is slow and then, at ten minutes to two a prime minister shouts out "We *have* to finish in 10 minutes." I said "Why? These are important decisions, let's deliberate a little bit longer." And then another prime minister comes in and says "No, we *have* to have an agreement now because in 10 minutes, the markets are opening up in Japan and there will be havoc in the global economy." We quickly came to a decision in those 10 minutes. This time it was not the military, but the markets that put a gun to our collective heads.[2]

In seeking to secure the future, Papandreou and the others were held to ransom by a system outside their control. There may be no morality to that system, just as there is no blame to be laid at the door of two terrified prime ministers. The traditional Western model of party politics has long shown itself insufficient to the task of escaping the competitive paradigm that threatens our future. No matter who had been elected to sit round the table with Papandreou, the market's gun would still have been there. But in seeking to define our own solutions for the future, how can we sidestep the power of that system? The answer could lie in a very simple combination of international agreement supported by public pressure, called Simpol.

Founded in 2000, the Simultaneous Policy (Simpol) is a global citizens' campaign that subverts the existing pseudo-democratic process to bring divided nations together. Its strategy is to have nations agree to implement—*simultaneously with other nations*—a range of global policies addressing our biggest global problems. Acting simultaneously is key, because if all or a sufficient number of governments act together, no one nation's economy would lose out, and the markets and multinational corporations would have no leverage to exert.

A novel kind of electoral pressure is necessary to support governments' action. In the United Kingdom, over the course of three national elections in 2001, 2005, and 2010, a tiny number of Simpol supporters succeeded in getting as many as twenty-seven members of Parliament and countless candidates from all the main political parties to sign a pledge in support of Simpol. They did this by writing both to their sitting MP or representative and to some or all of the competing parliamentary candidates in their electoral area, informing them that they'd be voting in future national elections, and saying, "I'll be giving my vote to *any* of you, within reason, who signs on to Simpol, because I believe strongly that only global cooperation can now defeat destructive international competition." Politicians who fail to sign the pledge risk losing their seats to those who do. This electoral incentive is what distinguishes Simpol from ordinary international treaties. It's the difference that makes citizens—not politicians—the driving force.

The by-product of this simple yet powerful voting mechanism is that many candidates, irrespective of party, agree to the same principle—the principle of cooperation—to ensure they don't lose the Simpol voting block. In doing so, they commit to working together with citizens on a set of policies to address the full range of global problems, and they seek to implement them simultaneously. While the voting mechanism used by Simpol is in itself remarkable (a lobbying campaign that works *within* the political framework to effect change), what matters most is the idea at its root—a future built on cooperation.

Why is cooperation so important to the future? As we've seen, whether it is national governments, international corporations, or children fighting over sandwiches, we have created systems that make it impossible for politicians to act beneficially without losing out. The playground fight can only end if all nations drop their fists simultaneously, otherwise someone loses, and we all lose. Cooperation gives everyone a chance to gain, giving us the perspective needed to take a look at the landscape and work out what needs to be done.

Such cooperation at the global level would, of course, be more complex than sharing sandwiches. The process of policy formation that Simpol proposes takes that complexity into account—proposing a system that would allow nations to collaborate on two or more problems at once. That way, a nation that might lose on one policy can gain on another. The cost of reducing carbon emissions could, for example, be compensated through the revenues raised from a currency transactions tax. Simpol offers a vision of the future wherein all global problems are up for discussion and everyone can gain by working them out together.

When seeking to solve global problems, some look to institutions or groups like the G8 nations or the United Nations to show us the way by negotiating treaties or agreements. But such institutions are not always successful at coming to agreements that actually get implemented. Why? Because—gun-toting markets aside—the G8 already sets an exclusive table, undermining its decision-making power by including the contribution of only a select number of participants. Furthermore, individual governments are lobbied by interest groups (or threatened, as is clear from investor-states in chapter 4) to water down or eliminate implementation of their commitments.

As a campaign, Simpol has already seen some success within the United Kingdom, but it is by no means confined to that country alone. Members of the European, Australian, and other parliaments have signed up alongside their UK colleagues, and Simpol already has supporters in over one hundred countries and endorsements from many leading statesmen and women, economists and ecologists."[3]

My take on Simpol is that, like many powerful new ideas, it demands a mind-shift to really get your head around it. It also depends on a growing interdisciplinary and international community of supporters using their votes to achieve global cooperation. It needs NGOs around the world to participate in this effort, and it needs funds to design a brilliant information campaign to demonstrate how it works—how simple it is to use our votes in this way. That's what could make Simpol a powerful voice for the future of global change.

It's clear to me that cooperative ideas are spreading. For example, the Climate Parliament has teamed up with the UN Development Program to work on climate issues. They are creating cross-party networks of legislators dedicated to making the global switch to renewable energy—eliminating two-thirds of greenhouse gas emissions at a stroke. "We already have all the technology and tools we need to fight poverty with power and fuel the global economy with green energy. We just need to build the political will."[4]

The circle of cooperation could be much wider and could involve much more cooperation between bottom-up and top-down approaches than some NGOs currently imagine. And possibly more radical:

What if all students in the United Kingdom refused to pay back their student loans until the UK government—which used to have a bold policy on renewable energy—takes the lead in engaging all other governments in simultaneous policy on environmental legislation and a global switch to renewable energy?

Banking: Where Money Serves People, Not the Other Way Around

As more becomes known about the effects that banks can have through their lending policies, banks have begun to feel pressure from the general public, NGOs, and some governments to go beyond conventional business management.

POLLUTER PAYS

Some businesses externalize costs onto the environment and society. A wood mill, for example, could dump its waste into a local river instead of paying to dispose of it properly. The cost of dealing with this waste is forced onto the public who uses this water—in the form of poor health or the work the local water treatment plant must do to purify the water.

Here's a way to create more equitable sharing of costs among consumers, the environment, and businesses: banks can raise interest rates or apply tariffs on loans given to clients with high environmental risks. This tariff differentiation by banks will stimulate the *internalization of environmental costs* in market prices. Companies would then pay more if their business causes extensive environmental damage, taking some of the cost off society as a whole. Through such price differentiation, banks have the potential to foster sustainability.

Through their intermediary role, banks could also support progress toward sustainability by society as a whole—for example, by adopting a carrot-and-stick approach, in which environmentally sound businesses would pay a lower interest rate than the market price for borrowing capital, while environmental laggards would pay a much higher rate.[5]

SOCIAL BANKING

Social banking is defined as banking that aims to have a positive impact on people and the environment. Using this definition, we find only ten to twenty truly social banks worldwide, most of which are members of the Global Alliance for Banking on Values. This alliance is a worldwide association of social banks whose "central mission is investment in a society that values human development, social cohesion and responsibility for our natural environment."[6] Members include microfinance banks in emerging markets, credit unions, community banks, and sustainable banks financing social, environmental, and cultural enterprise in Asia, Africa, Latin America, North America, and Europe.

All comply with sustainable banking principles and have a shared commitment to find global solutions to international problems—and to promote a positive, viable alternative to the current financial system. These organizations believe that we must improve the quality of life for everyone on the planet, recognizing that we are economically interdependent and responsible to current and future generations. The network's members have to meet three criteria:

- they are independent and licensed banks with a focus on retail customers
- with a minimum balance sheet of $50 million
- they should be committed to social banking and the triple bottom line of people, planet, and profit

BANK NEGARA INDONESIA

Felia Salim has used a time of crisis to lead one of the biggest banks in Indonesia out of a collapsing corporate economy and into a new era of small and medium economy, out of an environment of corruption and into one of good governance.

Unconventionally, the path along which Felia is navigating her bank has passed through remote villages and small huts all over a country with seventeen thousand islands and a population of around two hundred million people. She says, "The system that I apply in my work I have not learnt in a school of economics or from erudite books, but rather from village elders." Felia is one of the most senior figures in banking and finance in Indonesia, yet she took several years to tour Indonesia to listen to local leaders. As vice president director of the Bank Negara Indonesia, since

Photo: Desi Harahap

2008 she has—with wisdom and resolution—headed a team that is changing the entire bank.

The arena of finance is a tough one, and Felia is remarkable for achieving her goals with a soft and flexible power.[7] During this period, the bank's financial performance has improved in terms of revenue uplift, improved quality of assets, cost efficiency, and scale. Especially improved is human capital. Felia describes the process she followed:

Once given trust through a delegation of authority (decentralized governance) decisions are taken more quickly and have more immediate local relevance. This did not happen overnight of course. Despite the new roles that a Regional CEO was given, they had to go through a capability development process, partly in technical skills but more importantly the soft skills of leadership.

The most notable challenge was combining both hard and soft skills, in order to change the perspective on how to utilize the hard skill. For example: financial analysis is seen as a hard skill in the eyes of a CFO, and what is then needed is the skill of empathizing with the client's needs, thereby gaining insight in how best to serve. This learning journey takes time, as one goes from mere awareness, to understanding, accepting and ultimately commitment.

The strategy for the transformation to be sustainable is to develop a team of game changers (change agents), people in core functions, emerging leaders who will have a circle of influence in a positive way. We have developed this leadership journey with Otto Scharmer's U Theory approach[8] tailored to our bank's reality and needs. To date we have trained 800 of the 1000 middle management to be the change agents, the future leaders of the bank. It takes about 3–4 months per person for the learning journey to be effective.[9]

This took full commitment from the top management of the bank, but the effort was rewarded when the bank was acclaimed as the "Most Admired Company in ASEAN" for 2011 and 2012.

Felia explains that awareness was one thing, but pushing for execution was quite another. The key issue was to make everyone in the bank aware that the poor are not helpless—what they need is access to capability development, markets, and financing. Once the awareness was there, they had to develop a system that put the focus on local people's strength, not their weaknesses.

This means not seeing potential clients as "unbankable" but instead guiding them through various stages to becoming fully commercial. This is only possible with a community-based approach, with some hand-holding in the early stages and collaboration with capable and reliable community organizers. Thus the framework that the bank sets out necessarily takes a longer-term perspective. Felia says, "Some of the guiding principles we look at when working with communities include: local strength, local wisdom, local champions who own the work, multi-stakeholder approach, rights-based perspective, gender perspective, environmental perspective, etc. These are guiding principles still relatively unfamiliar to the corporate sector. We are still in progress of 'mainstreaming' these guiding principles throughout the bank."

One iconic program of which Felia is especially proud is the City Forrest that the Bank Negara Indonesia helped develop in Banda Aceh on the island of Sumatra, where 150,000 people were killed in the 2004 Indian Ocean tsunami. "A space that was flattened by the tsunami has been transformed into a wonderful green space where biodiversity—especially birds—has returned, and families enjoy their weekends. Other city mayors visit Banda Aceh to learn and copy. A simple idea, with a little bit of faith and a lot of collaboration with various parties, can create wonders."

When I met Felia it took a moment or two for the enormity of what she has done, which she describes with such matter-of-factness and lack of ego, to dawn on me. Then I was simply bowled over by the rugged determination of this frail figure. Her physical self seems too tiny to have taken on this massive task, yet she has actually designed and delivered a muscular model for bankers worldwide. I bow to her.

LOCAL CURRENCIES

Bernard Lietaer, the author of *The Future of Money* (which has been translated into eighteen languages), is an international expert in the design and implementation of currency systems. He has studied and worked in the monetary field for more than thirty years, and in an unusually broad range of capacities: central banker, fund manager, university professor, and consultant to governments in numerous countries, multinational corporations, and community organizations. He codesigned and implemented the convergence mechanism to the single European currency system and served as president of the Electronic Payment System at the Belgian Central Bank. He also cofounded and managed GaiaCorp, a top performing currency fund whose profits fund investments in environmental projects.

So this man is an expert on successful community currencies. He says it took him several years—and a most revealing conversation with the then president of the Bank of International Settlements in Basle (which coordinates the monetary activities of the eleven key monetary countries of the world)—to understand that "central banks exist to keep the system going as is, not to improve on it" and that, therefore, any initiatives of reform would have to come from the private sector. He has become an advocate of the creation of a more diversified money system.

> Such a system would include the creation of a global complementary currency that is nobody's national money, several mutual credit systems for businesses, and a multitude of local and specialized social-purpose currencies. . . .
>
> I often say that money is to us like water is to the fish: it is such an intrinsic part of our environment that we hardly notice it. We rarely ask how it works, even after it has collapsed on us. We even more rarely reflect upon the way it shapes our lives. I sometimes feel like a flying fish who accidentally has had the opportunity to take a "bird's eye view" of the water in which we swim, and is now trying to report back to its fellow fish what it has learned about what we usually cannot see.

Lietaer describes some of the forms that new money systems are taking:

> *Time Dollars*—whose purpose is to "reweave community"—is a currency that is now applied in several hundred communities in the United States and around the world. Time Dollars is based on an agreement to use "hours of service" as a means of payment. The system has elegant simplicity. It allows members of a community to earn credits for the time they spend helping someone else and to use those credits to obtain help from other community members.[10]
>
> *LETS money* is created as mutual credit. Each transaction is recorded as a corresponding credit and debit in the two participants' accounts. The quantity of currency issued is thus automatically sufficient and does not depend on the judgment and effort of a central authority.

Problems can arise with a local currency. If too much is issued, it will inflate or even become completely worthless; if it is under-issued, the problem that the local currency was meant to address—too little trade among people in the community—will remain. So it is not a trivial task for anybody or any group to guess the correct quantity of money to issue, because that ideal quantity will continuously vary according to the rate of acceptance of the local currency, which will change over time; and the overall state of the local economy (including the conditions of the economy in the "normal" national currency), which will also change over time). Mutual credit solves both these problems in a self-organized way.

Dr. Lietaer has coauthored books with Dr. Margrit Kennedy, a financial expert who recognized as early as 1982 that the broader application of ecological principles was inhibited by fundamental flaws in the monetary system, especially the consistent need for economic growth resulting from interest and compound interest. Through her continuous research and scrutiny, she became an expert on the subject, working on practical solutions for key problems, such as "What characterizes monetary systems that do not collapse repeatedly and that serve us rather than control us?"[11]

Business: Prioritizing People
and Planet Alongside Profit

The B Team is a nonprofit initiative that was formed in June 2013 by a group of global business leaders to create a future in which the purpose of business is to be a driving force for social, environmental, and economic benefit. The B Team brings together an initial fourteen leaders from major corporations around the world, including Virgin, Unilever, Natura, Celtel, Tata, and Kering. Their declaration states: "Business is now waking up to the reality that if we carry on using the natural resources of the world unsustainably, they'll quite simply run out. With a burgeoning population, more people are still living in poverty than ever before and inequalities are increasing in many parts of the world. . . . While there are myriad reasons we've arrived at this juncture, much of the blame rests with the principles and practices of business as usual."

Working with a global community of advisors and partners, the B Team seeks to develop and implement a Plan B for business that puts people and planet alongside profit. The B Leaders will focus on action, catalyzing and amplifying others' efforts by undertaking specific global challenges in a bid to turn business away from its fixation with short-term profits.

Paul Polman, chief executive of Unilever, has joined the B Team. He has for several years been critical of the tyranny of quarterly earnings reports and famously said he no longer wanted short-term investors to buy shares in the company.[12]

One challenge will be to accelerate a new kind of inclusive leadership underpinned by a moral compass of being fair, honest, positive, and creative. Jochen Zeitz, one of the founders of the B team, has a good record in pioneering these values at Puma, the company he led for served eighteen years as chairman and CEO.

Picture this. The scene is a monastery in Banz, south Germany. Under the ancient arches of a large refectory are the leaders of NGOs specializing in fair trade, ethical sourcing, and environmental responsibility. They are not making speeches from the rostrum but instead are separated into small groups and are deep in deliberation with the executive team of Puma. (This was two-day dialogue arranged annually by Jochen Zeitz when he was CEO of Puma, so that his team could have face-to-face conversations with their fiercest critics.) Real listening is taking place. The effects are evident on the final evening, when Zeitz (a firm believer in quantifying impacts) asks the entire gathering a question: "As CEO I am aware that—although we have done a great deal better than most—we have hardly yet scratched the surface of the actions we as a company need to take to be ethical, sustainable, and fair. Should I say this when I talk to the press?" There is urgent murmuring in the room, culminating in a consensus that yes, he should do this, even at the risk that the share price might wobble. He did. It didn't.

I can hear Zeitz's voice in the B Team statement: "Every action we take and every decision we make has a ripple effect, influencing those around us and affecting situations." If such values and practices can spread in the corporate world and become more than spin for insubstantial social responsibility policies, huge change can take place. In my experience, these changes in policy usually follow changes in the personal experiences of those at the top.

The key signal of the B Team initiative is the defection of a significant body of elite members from the prevailing groupthink, coupled with clear alternative pathways to follow. What happens when they seek alliances with pro-sustainability networks in civil society? For example, there is a growing minority in the US Republican Party willing to break ranks on climate change and mitigation policies. One strategy would lie in strengthening the position and numbers of these segments of elites so that groupthink is undermined and incentives to change are boosted. That points to a major task for civil society organizations to start talking to people they have not always been good at engaging with, for example, on the political Right and in business and religious communities.[13]

What if a representative of future generations were proposed as a member of the board of every major corporation?

WHAT WOULD LOVE "DO"? . . . A REAL STORY[14]

This is a story of Patagonia and its CEO Casey Sheehan and his wife Tara. . . . The recession of 2007 was well upon the world and companies globally were in the process of shrinking their costs (work-force). . . . Casey shared his concerns with Tara and said that the company needed to trim down their employee base to remain above water. While that would have sounded perfect to the "investor community," Tara asked him a question that was something along the lines, "Tell me Casey, is this decision originating from fear or love?" Casey replied that it was driven out of fear. Tara then asked another question, "What would love do?"

Patagonia went in for flexi-time, reduced its inventory base and weathered the storm. What is interesting is that the storm was felt on the outside while the response from within led to greater trust and a spirit of real collaboration.

LEADERS' QUEST

Leaders' Quest is a social enterprise committed to improving the quality and impact of decision makers around the world. They invite leaders— from companies at the forefront of technology, media, and financial and professional services—to experience what life is like for some of the poorest in society. The point is to integrate social purpose with company performance by mentoring high-caliber leaders from both the corporate world and NGOs. Leaders' Quest also grants fellowships to empower grassroots leaders to tackle tough problems in poor and marginalized communities.[15]

Leader's Quest can have a great impact on participants, as I have seen in journeys to the poorest areas of Mumbai and Rajasthan. Founder Lindsay Levin describes elegantly why working with companies can be a challenge: "Many struggled when it came to figuring our their purpose beyond making money, usually because their leaders had chosen to switch off their innate capacity to look beyond what could be quantified."[16]

Leaders' quest participants can have a profound experience:

When I was on the Mumbai Quest, about a dozen of us went to the charity that looks after the children of sex workers and we visited the brothel where the mothers of the children practiced their trade—a very raw experience indeed. We chatted with Priti who has been running schools for the children of prostitutes for 27 years and one question that was asked by the group was how she finds the resolve and energy to keep working in such a difficult, dark and challenging place. She looked at us with incredulity. "I love what I do"! It was a simple reply but immediately impactful and I think that we all realized how irrelevant the question was. Priti had one of those smiles that could light up the whole world and it was very clear that she was transformed and full of joy due to the positive change that she was making to the children in her care. It was clear that it was this "reward" that had sustained her for 27 years and provided the courage and commitment to be able to continue to achieve so much.[17]

Having noted some of the changes afoot in the corporate world, it's now time to examine some of the mechanisms that are currently influencing boardroom decisions globally. Possibly the most remarkable of these is the Carbon Disclosure Project.

"THE MOST POWERFUL GREEN NGO YOU'VE NEVER HEARD OF"
The Carbon Disclosure Project (CDP) uses market forces to motivate companies to disclose their impacts on the environment and natural resources and to take action to reduce them. CDP now holds the largest collection globally of primary risk information on climate change, water, and forests, and puts these insights at the heart of strategic business, investment, and policy decisions.

The Harvard Business Review blog calls them "The Most Powerful Green NGO You've Never Heard Of."

The UK nonprofit began in 2000 with a simple idea: ask the world's largest companies to publicly share information about their carbon emissions and the actions they're taking to manage them. . . . Stepping away from the old-style NGO approach to companies, the CDP and its leaders are both optimistic and relentlessly pro-business. At the core of the organization's mission is a commitment to the power of data to improve business performance, and a strong belief that for companies that tackle climate change, the opportunities far outweigh the risks.[18]

In 2013, 722 investors with $87 trillion in assets—*that's around a third of the world's invested capital*—had asked more than five thousand public companies to disclose their carbon emissions and climate change strategies through CDP. *Read that again—a third of the world's invested capital.*

More than 80 percent of the largest companies with stock exchange listings used the CDP system for climate accountability in 2012, including Siemens, Dell, Hewlett Packard, L'Oreal, PepsiCo, Cadbury Schweppes, Nestle, Procter & Gamble, Tesco, Unilever, Lloyds TSB, Amcor, and Johnson Controls. Additionally, there had been strong growth in the number of investors asking companies to submit water and forest information through CDP, further demonstrating that natural capital is increasingly understood to be of material value to the global market.

CDP already holds the biggest collection globally of self-reported corporate climate data. The Forest Footprint Disclosure Project, pioneered by the Global Canopy Program, has merged with CDP to provide companies and investors with a single source of information for the interrelated issues of climate, water, and forests, making CDP the world's most comprehensive system for natural capital disclosure.

Carbon Action, a CDP initiative to accelerate action on carbon reduction in high-emitting industries, has seen more than a fivefold increase in its investor signatories since its inception in 2011. In 2013, on behalf of 190 investors with assets of $18 trillion, CDP called on CEOs of 301 of the world's largest public companies for cost-effective management and reductions of their carbon emissions.

To me, this methodology wields a tool more powerful than legal action, protests, or even partnership, namely enabling institutional investors to put their power behind rising concerns about climate risk. The United Nations' climate secretary Christiana Figueres has said, "CDP is to the future of business what the X-ray was to the then-future of medicine—without it, we would never have seen the insides of the patient's health."

Fossil Free

Fossil Free is a campaign to urge large institutions to dump fossil fuel investments. It reached the United Kingdom in October 2013, following its success in the United States. In just a year, Fossil Free grew faster than the divestment efforts that once targeted apartheid and tobacco and arms manufacturers. It focuses attention on the £5 billion invested in coal, oil, and gas by the endowment funds of UK universities.

> "The divestment campaign will start politically to bankrupt the fossil fuel industry and throw into stronger relief that it is a rogue industry, committed to burning more carbon than any government on Earth thinks it would be safe to burn," said Bill McKibben, a prominent US climate campaigner and figurehead of the Fossil Free campaign. "One reason we are losing the battle against climate change—the most important challenge humans have faced—is the power of the fossil fuel industry to block change. . . . It is the richest industry in the history of human enterprise."
>
> The US campaign has already led to more than 40 institutions, including the city of Seattle, universities and churches, pulling out of fossil fuel investments. Addressing the political debate in the UK over rising energy bills, McKibben said: "England has been burning fossil fuels since James Watt: there is no way you get to transition [to low-carbon energy] for free. But as economist Lord Nicholas Stern has said over and over again, the cost of not doing it is orders of magnitude higher than doing it." [19]

There are now student divestment campaigns at twenty British universities, including the three with the largest investments: Cambridge, Oxford, and Edinburgh. UK universities have more than £5 billion invested in fossil fuels (that's £2,000 per student), according to student group People & Planet and the 350.org campaign, which McKibben cofounded.[20]

RENEWABLE ENERGY LEGISLATION

We know that 80 percent of our energy still comes from fossil fuels, which increase carbon dioxide emissions, trigger climate chaos, disrupt nature, and further concentrate wealth. But aren't the alternatives too slow getting off the ground—and too expensive?

My immediate response is "Feed-in Tariffs." They enable any homeowner who installs solar or wind energy production to sell surplus energy generated back to the grid at rates that will enable them to pay off their original investment quickly. It's such a no-brainer that Feed-in Tariff laws, pioneered in Germany, have now been introduced in the United Kingdom, Australia, an increasing number of US states, and in Ontario in Canada, with the support of the World Future Council.[21] I'm a councilor on the World Future Council, so I have to declare an interest, but objectively, they have done remarkable work in supporting legislation on renewables.

In establishing the Alliance for Renewable Energy, the World Future Council created a coalition to spread renewable energies and contributed to the implementation of Feed-in Tariffs in the United States. A 2013 WFC report shows that Feed-in Tariffs are a promising mechanism to unlock renewable energy development in Africa. The report provides an in-depth analysis of existing policies in thirteen African countries and a comprehensive guide for African policy makers to move to harvesting the wealth of the sun. This is already taking root in Mozambique and Ghana.

The "convenient truth" is that we can choose abundant, renewable energies to meet our needs and bring power to the people by abandoning current forms of centralized energy infrastructure and monopolies in favor of decentralized energy production from renewable sources.

The latest project of the World Future Council is the Global Policy Action Plan, which compiles the key changes required for policy to change—on a global scale and in time to avert disaster. The plan presents a coherent policy response to the interlinked global crises: climate chaos, ocean acidification, water shortages, and weapons of mass destruction.[22] There is overwhelming evidence that—with the right incentives—we can still mobilize human inventiveness and entrepreneurship to tackle them.

Today, urgent reform proposals are usually met with the claim that they are unaffordable. In response to those claims, the Global Policy Action Plan identifies the policy changes required to ensure that we can "afford" to continue living on this planet. Some are well known, but increasingly urgent, such as the progressive shifting of global military expenditures to fund human and ecological security. We also need a radical tax reform that will shift the main tax base from work (which we need) to resources (which we need to save), such as increased tax on land value. But we need to complement such (necessarily slow) redistribution with (quick) "predistribution," that is, the interest- and debt-free creation of new money by central banks to fund a crash program to ecologically modernize our production and consumption systems. As this new money will only be created to fund the production of new goods and services, it will not be inflationary.

The plan includes policies to tackle the major threats facing us, including the progressive abolition and redirection of fossil fuel subsidies while protecting the poor, legislation to maximize the use of renewable energies and provide for full-cost energy accounting. Whenever possible, the plan refers to existing successful policies—many of the policies recommended in the plan have been successfully implemented in one country or region but are unknown elsewhere. Exemplary laws to protect biodiversity, forests, and oceans (from Costa Rica, Rwanda, and Palau respectively) included in the plan have all received the WFC Future Policy Award, as have the laws to promote food security and disarmament (both nuclear and conventional).[23]

SOLAR POWER

In some regions of Africa, a single solar lantern can reduce a household's kerosene use by up to 40 percent a year, and can also save a ton of carbon dioxide emissions over its lifetime. SolarAid, the charity born in 2006 with 5 percent of British solar company Solarcentury's profits, believes it is on course to supply mass markets in Africa. In 2012, sales of solar lights by its social venture SunnyMoney were up 600 percent from the previous year. SunnyMoney aims to play the lead role in eradicating the kerosene lantern from the continent by 2020. SolarAid and SunnyMoney currently operate in four countries: Kenya, Tanzania, Zambia, and Malawi.[24]

Jeremy Leggett, founder and chairman of both Solarcentury and SolarAid, said: "This is a significant milestone in a long-running dream of mine: to create a fast-growing VC-backed cleantech company that aspires to do great good itself, but also via a fast-growing social venture of its own creation. SunnyMoney holds the potential to become a poster child as a renaissance company—one fit for purpose amid the ruins of our broken modern form of capitalism. Crowd funding at scale is just one of the innovations we hope to provide leadership on during the renaissance."[25]

Switching from kerosene to solar lighting would go a long way to alleviating poverty, improving health, and lowering carbon dioxide emissions. Local production of solar lamps would also boost employment.

What if one of the one hundred richest people in the world were to give one solar lamp to every person in Africa who currently uses a kerosene lamp?

CHINA

One frequently quoted statistic about China is that it builds a coal-fired power station each week. A much less well-known fact is that China ended 2011 with more renewable power capacity than any other nation: an estimated 282 gigawatts. In 2012 China produced more electricity from wind than from nuclear energy,[26] and the country is installing renewables at a faster rate than any other country. In 2013 the government ordered firms in heavy-polluting industries to cut their emissions of harmful gases by 30 percent within four years; this sounds impossible, but a centralized economy like China's has achieved impossible targets before. The requirement is part of a ten-point plan that is China's most aggressive antipollution drive to date. China has seen scores of protests sparked by environmental concerns in recent years; some observers say the issue is now the main cause of social unrest in China.

There are now rumors of an absolute limit over which emissions will not be allowed to rise—a so-called hard cap—in Beijing's next five-year plan, beginning in 2016. A Chinese move toward unilateral carbon reduction could make a difference to stalled UN negotiations to tackle climate change.

THE INTERNATIONAL ENERGY AGENCY

The IEA appears to be undergoing a transformation from being a cheerleader for the nuclear and fossil fuel industry toward being an advocate for renewable energy. Their 2013 report warned that the world is not on track to limit the global temperature increase to 2 degrees Celsius, and it presented four energy policies expected to significantly reduce emissions by 2020.[27]

In their 4-for-2°C Scenario, the first policy is to make the industry, buildings, and transport sector adopt stringent energy efficiency measures. The second policy is to limit or ban the construction of inefficient coal-fired power plants and to partially phase out existing ones. Minimizing the amount of methane leakage coming from oil and gas operations, transmissions, and distribution pipelines is the third suggested policy, since methane is known to be twenty-five times more potent than carbon dioxide in its global warming potential. In 2013 the IEA was still reluctant to call for a partial phase-out of fossil fuel consumption, but their fourth policy suggests phasing out fossil fuel subsidies. A more dynamic way forward would be to drop fossil fuel subsidies; this would immediately unleash the deployment of renewable energy at an unprecedented pace.

NUCLEAR POWER

Change is happening: Austria was the first country to begin a phase-out of nuclear power (in 1978), followed by Sweden (1980), Italy (1987), Belgium (1999), and Germany (2000). Austria, Switzerland, and Spain have gone as far as to enact laws prohibiting the building of new nuclear power stations. Following the March 2011 Fukushima nuclear disaster, Germany permanently shut down eight of its reactors and pledged to close the rest by 2022. The Italians voted overwhelmingly to keep their country nonnuclear. Japan's prime minster called for a dramatic reduction in Japan's reliance on nuclear power. Taiwan's president did the same. Mexico has sidelined the construction of ten reactors in favor of developing natural gas–fired plants. As of November 2011, Australia, Austria, Denmark, Greece, Ireland, Italy, Latvia, Liechtenstein, Luxembourg, Malta, Portugal, Israel, Malaysia, New Zealand, and Norway had no nuclear power reactors and remained opposed to nuclear power.

In the United States, five early reactor closures have been announced, along with nine project cancellations. Today, one hundred US reactors operate where a thousand were once promised. New orders are nonexistent. But in October 2013 UK Prime Minister Cameron welcomed his government's agreement with French-owned EDF to build the first new British nuclear power station in twenty years. And the British people, I'm ashamed to say, hardly murmured.

For decades, the nuclear industry said no commercial reactors could possibly explode. When Chernobyl blew, they blamed it on the Soviet design. Now, three General Electric reactors have exploded at Fukushima. Unfortunately, as reactors age and deteriorate, there may be more accidents to come.

"PLASTIC TO OIL—FANTASTIC!"

It's estimated that 7 percent of the world's annual oil production is used to manufacture plastic. That's more oil than is consumed by the entire African continent. Plastic is buried in landfills and is incinerated, since recycling rates are dismally low around the globe. Plastic trash is polluting our oceans, killing mammals and birds.[28]

Some countries, however, are setting an example in the fight against plastic. Rwanda enacted legislation to ban non-biodegradable polythene bags in 2008. Before that, plastic bags were a major problem in Rwanda as in other countries. They got caught in trees, lay in the fields, were pushed into the ground and impacted agricultural productivity. Today alternative packaging materials are used, many locally produced. The ban is so stringent that incoming visitors are searched at the airports on arrival and plastic bags confiscated.

Since plastic is made from oil, it has a higher energy value than anything else commonly found in the waste stream. A Japanese company called Blest has created a small, safe, and easy-to-use machine that can convert several types of plastic back into oil.[29] "If we burn the plastic, we generate toxins and a large amount of carbon dioxide. If we convert it into oil, we save carbon dioxide and at the same time increase people's awareness about the value of plastic garbage," says Akinori Ito, CEO of Blest.

Blest's conversion technology is safe, because it uses a temperature-controlling electric heater rather than flame. The machines are able to process polyethylene, polystyrene, and polypropylene, but not PET bottles. The result is a crude gas that can fuel things like generators or stoves and, when refined, can even be pumped into a car. A little over two pounds of plastic produces almost one quart of oil. To convert that amount takes about 1 kilowatt of electricity—about 20 cents' worth.

Blest makes the machines in various sizes and has sixty in place at farms, fisheries, and small factories in Japan, as well as several abroad. "To make a machine that anyone can use is my dream," Ito says, "The home is the oil field of the future." The company hopes to achieve a product "that any one can buy." Currently the smallest version costs around $12,700.[30]

"Teaching this at schools is the most important work that I do," says Ito, who visits schools where he shows children, teachers, and parents how to convert the packaging and drinking straws leftover from lunch. "If we were to use only the world's plastic waste rather than oil from oil fields, carbon dioxide emissions could be slashed dramatically," he says. "It's a waste, isn't it? This plastic is everywhere in the world, and everyone throws it away."

I have not personally seen one of Blest's machines in action, but I'm very keen to. Imagine if we had a television show on which, every week, a celebrity investigated some new invention like this one—something that potentially could alter the future for all. The inventions could be tested in real-time; some would work well, some would fail, and presumably some would explode live on television—a cross between Dragon's Den, "I'm a Celebrity Get Me Out of Here" and Emergency Ward 10.

What if the World Bank made loans to local governments in developing countries—places that have no municipal recycling of plastic—to cover the cost to purchase, install, and train people to use one of these converters? The oil produced could be sold, and the loans could be paid back within a short period of time.

Now that we have an idea of what's already ahead of the curve in government, in the world of business, energy and systemic change, we can move on to the global processes that are working *from the bottom up* to help shift the blockages preventing progress to a positive future.

People Power: The Nonviolent Revolutions

A phenomenon of the twenty-first century is the exponential rise in the influence of the public in affecting the actions taken by governments, corporations, and international decision-making bodies. Some call it "bottom up power."

Think about it first at the heavy-duty end—places where populations have been struggling with brutal oppressive regimes. Have you asked yourself how dictatorships have collapsed—in Czechoslovakia, East Germany, Estonia, Latvia, Lithuania, Madagascar, Mali, the Philippines, Poland, Serbia, Slovenia, Ukraine—and now Tunisia and (possibly) Egypt? Since 1980, dictatorships have been collapsing under the weight of . . . what? Of nonviolent opposition—the concerted political, economic, and social defiance of mobilized citizens.

While some haven't yet achieved what they set out to do, bear in mind that Gandhi took forty years to rid India of the British. Beneath the Arab Spring and many other "springs" that have been analyzed largely for their political impact, lie common themes that link the activists more closely with each other—across the globe—than with their rulers. Their activism starts from a platform of nonviolence; the changes they want can be achieved by dialogue—and this holds even when their strength is overwhelmed by armed thugs.

These revolutions haven't just happened. They have been organized by young people trained in the nonviolent strategies that can be traced back to a quiet, determined eighty-year-old man. In an old townhouse in East Boston, an elderly, stooped man is tending rare orchids in his shabby office. His Labrador Sally lies on the floor between stacks of academic papers; she watches him as he shuffles past. This is Dr. Gene Sharp, the world's foremost expert on nonviolent revolution, the man now credited with the strategy behind the toppling of oppressive governments the world over.

Sharp wrote a book called *From Dictatorship to Democracy* based on his forty-year-long study of nonviolent methods of demonstration.[31] It was originally simply handed out by the Albert Einstein Institution, where he works. Although never actively promoted, this astonishing book spread as a photocopied pamphlet to Burma, Indonesia, and Serbia, and most recently to Egypt, Tunisia, Syria, and China. It is now in its fourth edition in English and, to date, has been translated into thirty-one languages. It has slipped across borders and has been hidden from secret policemen all over the world. The how-to guide includes some "Key Steps on the Path to Revolution":

- Develop a strategy for winning freedom and a vision of the society we want.
- Overcome fear by small acts of resistance.
- Use colors and symbols to demonstrate unity of resistance.
- Learn from historical examples of the successes of nonviolent movements.
- Use nonviolent "weapons."
- Identify the dictatorship's pillars of support; develop a strategy for undermining each.

- Use oppressive or brutal acts by the regime as a recruiting tool for our movement.
- Isolate or remove from the movement people who use or advocate violence.

As Slobodan Milosevic in Serbia and Viktor Yanukovych in Ukraine fell to the color revolutions that swept across Eastern Europe, the democratic movements paid tribute to Sharp's contribution, yet he remains largely unknown to the public.

In Serbia, under the repressive regime of Milosevic, the government's attempts to stem democracy inspired a covert resistance movement known as OTPOR. Members of OTPOR were invited to a conference in Hungary, where they learned Gene Sharp's methods, which they then used to help build their movement. This movement came to a head when the elections were announced in 1998: they were ready with sixty tons of propaganda to distribute, including T-shirts. They also spread their message through graffiti and mobile phone messages. They trained twenty thousand students in election monitoring, who were sent to each election polling station. Their results made it impossible for Milosevic to manipulate the elections.[32]

OTPOR had no leader; the group opposed any form of hierarchy. The idea was that if one head was cut off, fifteen more would instantly reappear, making it impossible for the state to shut them down. This is one of the many similarities between the OTPOR movement and the protestors who took residence in Tahrir Square in Cairo to protest against the regime of Hosni Mubarak in January 2011. There is as yet no record of how these protestors became trained in Sharp's theories, though some say that Arabic translations were distributed around Tahrir Square and read by candlelight.

Nonviolence is active in China. Open Democracy reports:

In 2010, Chinese sociologist, Sun Linping estimated that the number of mass incidents across China had surpassed 180,000 that year, more than doubling from 2006. This indicates growing discontent in the world's most populous non-democracy, unrest that the regime has treated with corresponding repression. In 2013 China's internal security budget reached 124 billion dollars, exceeding military allocations. This awesome internal security spending implies the regime's trepidation about what is predominantly nonviolent resistance.

The most universal source of discontent in China is illegal demolition and eviction, a byproduct of rapid development and urbanization. Corrupt local officials profit from illegal development deals and brutally crack down on resistance; adding to widespread claims of arbitrary detention and invasion of privacy. . . . China reports more than 250 million migrant workers who leave countryside homes in search of work. They are often greeted with a litany of labor violations. Official impunity and the lack of judicial independence affords aggrieved Chinese villagers and workers minimal institutional recourse.

Chinese activists have turned to the media to publicize their grievances and voices within the media have become activists, alongside an emboldened citizen community, to challenge propaganda and make claims against censorship, coupled with discontent over the lack of freedom of expression. In January 2013, a censored message in the Southern Weekend newspaper sparked massive material and digital resistance. Such information-based grievances have slowly created activists within the previously apolitical middle class, traditionally acquiescent to economic liberalization. . . . Most recently Xu Zhiyong, who was later arrested in July 2013, called for a New Citizen's Movement.[33]

AVAAZ

One of the most effective movements of people power is Avaaz, an online activist community over thirty-five million strong in 2014 and growing by well over a million people per month. It prompts citizens to realize that the world really is ours and, while we face great challenges, what happens next depends on all of us.

Avaaz pitches in with witty, hard-hitting campaigns that use billboards, cartoons, and sheer weight of numbers to bring about positive change. For example, after more than two years of tireless campaigning, Avaaz played a key role in getting Europe to ban bee-killing pesticides—at least until 2015. This victory came from two years of flooding ministers with messages, launching a massive petition with over 2.6 million signatures, organizing media-grabbing protests with beekeepers and a sixteen-foot inflatable bee. The campaign took on mighty corporations like Bayer, and it wouldn't have been possible without the collaboration of many scientists, specialists, sympathetic officials, beekeepers, and environmental groups. Friends of the Earth said, "Avaaz's massive petition and creative campaigning helped push this over the edge."

The example of the Avaaz community underlines the point made earlier in this book, namely that government ministers often need public pressure to justify to their colleagues doing something that they feel is right anyway. I witnessed this first hand in the early days of antinuclear campaigns in the 1980s, and I agree with Sheryl Wudunn when she says, "if leaders smell votes, they will follow."[34]

Here's another Avaaz initiative:

Each year, greedy companies and wealthy individuals use tricky schemes to hide away an estimated $1 trillion, depriving governments of tax they need to fix our services and our countries. This year we spotted an opportunity to go after the missing money, built a massive petition and linked up with famous singer Baaba Maal and worked closely with Save the Children, ActionAid and other campaign groups to deliver our voices to David Cameron, G8 summit chair. Our letter signed by 21,000 business representatives helped position this as a pro-business, pro-citizen issue, and to shift the positions of Germany and Canada, resulting in an historic agreement that can get governments to work together to stop tax evasion. The "Lough Erne Declaration" was short on specifics, but gives us huge leverage in chasing governments to block shady tax schemes.[35]

In India, a twenty-three-year-old student was brutally raped on a bus and later died from her injuries. In the Maldives, a fifteen-year-old girl was sentenced to flogging for having sex outside marriage. In Somalia, a young woman was brutally gang-raped by the security forces that were supposed to protect her. In each case, Avaaz members in their millions have helped the media to pressure governments to pass stronger laws to protect women. In the Maldives, Avaaz's campaign threatening tourism made political leaders promise the girl would not be flogged, and a poll commissioned by Avaaz hit the front pages showing that citizens wanted the laws changed. In India, a big pink bus with an activist costumed as the prime minister, Manmohan Singh, was driven through the streets of Delhi, spreading the Avaaz message in a massive public-education campaign challenging outdated attitudes toward women. These actions, say Avaaz, "are just the tips of the iceberg in our fight to end misogyny."

At Davos in January 2014, Richard Branson was impressed by Jeremy Heimans, who is behind organizations like Avaaz. In his blog he wrote, "Jeremy argues they're evidence of a fundamental transformation taking place in our societies. This transformation is not a technological one—it might be enabled by technology, but it's driven by people and their changing attitudes to participation and change. Jeremy contrasts "old power" which he likens to a currency (held by a few, closed and inaccessible) with this "new power" which is more like a current (made by many, open, and peer-driven)."[36]

SOCIAL MEDIA

In chapter 2, I described the yachtsman Ivan MacFadyen, who reported seeing a severe drop in ocean life in his latest voyage. He said, "I wanted to get the word out to everybody I could reach, to tell them, the ocean is broken. We have to do something and we can't waste any more time." His story appeared in the *Newcastle Herald Weekender* magazine on Friday, October 18, 2013, and on that paper's website.[37] From that Australian platform, the story catapulted—via social media—into the global limelight.

It appeared on the front page of Reddit the following Monday, was trending in Melbourne early Monday afternoon, and was re-tweeted by, among others, Jack Dorsey, the founder and chief executive of Twitter. The story smashed Fairfax Regional Media records, registering 620,000 unique readers on the *Herald* site by Tuesday afternoon.

Social media like Twitter and Facebook are valuable tools, but to me, tweeting alone is not enough. In fact, it can leave people feeling helpless. The next step is for each tweet on a vital issue to be followed by one letting people know what they can do immediately, so that all the cyber messages result in actual change. The following sex strike story is a good example.

SEX STRIKE

In 2013 on the island of Mindanao in the Philippines, a successful sex strike brought peace to a village in the midst of a separatist rebellion. According to the United Nations High Commissioner for Refugees, the modern-day Lysistrata story unfolded in Dado village, where fighting between insurgents closed the only road between the village and outside markets. Confronted with a lack of food, supplies, and the prospect of dependency on humanitarian aid, the women of a sewing cooperative banded together to withhold sex from their husbands until they agreed to stop fighting. The goal of restoring road access to markets in other, more peaceful towns would then be attainable.

The strategy worked. The sex strike lasted just a few days before the men of both armies agreed to negotiate terms that settled the dispute. It seems that to the men of Dado, sex, like power, is most important to those who don't have it.[38]

SARVODAYA

The Sarvodaya Shramadana Movement is the largest people's organization in Sri Lanka, and it's quite a phenomenon. The word *sarvodaya* is Sanskrit for "awakening of all" and *shramadana* means "to donate effort." The movement is remarkable for its extensive reach throughout the war-torn country and the unique strides it has made in supporting fundamental change—from remote villages to urban centers, among people of all social, ethnic, and religious groupings.

Sarvodaya began fifty years ago in one village and now has impacted the life of more than 15,000 villages (out of a total of 38,000), cocreating formal associations in more than 5,000 communities throughout Sri Lanka. The organization has impacted the lives of millions of people, and the total portfolio of funded development projects is over $15,000,000.

After the 2004 Indian Ocean tsunami devastated parts of the country, Sarvodaya provided the largest volunteer support network to suffering families and made funds from foreign donation available to them. During the various civil conflicts that have rocked Sri Lanka, it stood for peace and reconciliation. During such times of conflict, Sarvodaya sponsored public meditations in which hundreds of thousands—even more than one million—Buddhists, Hindus, Muslims, and Christians meditate together on each other's welfare, using the Buddhist Brahmavihara (sublime attitude) meditations, which are acceptable within all faiths. In the aftermath of the civil war that deeply affected northern and eastern Sri Lanka, it is involved in resettlement, reconstruction, and reconciliation activities.

Sarvodaya's present focus is Deshodaya (National Reawakening), a program that promotes good governance and democracy from the local to the national level. The effort is based on Buddhist and Gandhian principles. Joanna Macy reports a young trainer telling her, "Real development is not free trade zones and mammoth hydro-electric dams, it's waking up to our own needs and our own power." She was sitting in an open-walled classroom with two-dozen Sri Lankan village workers, absorbing the principles of a movement that promised to revolutionize Third World development. "This awakening happens on different levels. It's personal and spiritual as well as economic and cultural. These aspects of our lives are all interdependent."[39]

A typical Sarvodaya program begins with an invitation from a village for discussion of what is needed and how it can be done. It proceeds in stages through creating a village council, building a school and clinic, setting up family programs, creating economic opportunity so that the village economy becomes self-sustaining, starting a village bank, and then offering help to other villages.

In my interview with Walter Link, who chairs Sarvodaya International and is a close advisor to Sarvodaya's founder, Dr. A. T. Ariyaratne, and his leadership team, I was curious about how this approach to village development reaches out to impact the whole country. He said:

> From the outset, Sarvodaya integrated the economic and social, spiritual and environmental levels of development. They understood that sustainable solutions require this integration of personal and interpersonal maturation with organizational and societal transformation into a holistic system of interaction. . . .
>
> For example, transforming the non-profit micro-lending institution SEEDS (Sarvodaya Economic Enterprises Development Services) into a fully regulated bank, the Deshodaya Development Finance Company. The challenge here is to translate the profound

Buddhist and social values of Sarvodaya into creating a bank that not only serves hundreds of thousands of poor villagers but also shows that another economy and financial system is possible. We want to be a model of how to succeed by doing things differently. For many people, ideas are not sufficient to motivate change, especially when they challenge mainstream thinking. They need to see concrete examples of how we can succeed, because we have more integrity, more social and environmental conscience. I have helped to develop such companies before, and I feel very confident that we will succeed with the DDFC. . . .

In a second project, the Deshodaya social movement we are trying to develop a new approach to civic engagement. We don't see ourselves as the "opposition," but rather as empowering people throughout the country to find their voice to support what all levels of government do well and to challenge what could be done better. This constructive form of engagement goes far beyond Sarvodaya's membership. It provides the first national platform in which individuals and members of many other civil society organizations can work together to make Sri Lanka an even better place. . . . its new projects also include the creation of an island wide network of university campuses.

When you ask specialists to critically assess change and empowerment models, they all say that Sarvodaya remains one of the world's most innovative civil society movements. It demonstrates that personal and societal development are most effective when they go hand in hand to enable sustainable change.

TRANSITION TOWNS

Transition Towns is a grassroots network of communities that are working to build local resilience in response to climate destruction, peak oil, and economic instability. It was founded in 2005 in the United Kingdom and has become remarkably effective. For instance, a Transition group in Brixton raised £130,000 to install the United Kingdom's first inner-city, community-owned power station, which has solar panels that produce eighty-two kilowatts.[40] A group in Derbyshire created a farmers' market where people can sell homegrown fruit and vegetables, creating an affordable alternative to supermarkets, and a number of Transition communities have launched local currencies. Taken on their own, these initiatives may not make a vast difference, says cofounder Rob Hopkins. "But when there are thousands of communities worldwide all weaving their bit in a larger tapestry," Hopkins says, "it adds up to something awe-inspiring and strong."

What he is arguing is that sweeping changes in history are made not only by big people doing big things but also by groups of ordinary people doing smaller things together. And that it's a mistake to overlook those small steps.

> "There is no cavalry coming to the rescue," he says. "But what happens when ordinary people decide that they are the cavalry? Between the things we can do as individuals, and the things government and business can do to respond to the challenges of our times, lies a great untapped potential. It's about what you can create with the help of the people who live in your street, your neighborhood, your town. If enough people do it, it can lead to real impact, to real jobs and real transformation of the places we live, and beyond."

Embercombe is an example of what people are doing. It's a whole valley in Devon, England, where a community has been established to champion a way of living that "inspires people to contribute towards the emergence of a socially just, environmentally sustainable and spiritually fulfilling human presence on earth." Many communities are now being set up with such high ideals, and some fail. But this one walks the talk. They not only grow their own food and take good care of the land, but they also address the substantial personal challenges of living in community and have developed a workable system of decision making. Embercombe now share their knowledge through teaching programs. These have gained sufficient reputation for companies to send their executive teams to spend five days in Devon to experience the radical shift in awareness, values, and behavior pioneered at Embercombe.[41]

THE BOY WHO PLANTS TREES

When he was nine, a German boy named Felix Finkbeiner was supposed to give a presentation at school. He says he "Googled stuff on climate change" and came across Wangari Maathai's campaign to plant trees in her native Kenya. Forty-five million trees later, she won the Nobel Peace Prize. "She achieved so much with so little," Felix says. "So I had the idea that we children could also do something."[42]

In March 2007, just over two months after his school presentation, Felix planted the first sapling of his own million-tree campaign—a crab apple. News of Felix's campaign reached other schools, and then it went viral. The next year, he attended the UN Children's Conference in Norway and was elected to the junior board of the UN Environment Program.

Felix is now an environmental superstar at the helm of a global network of child activists whose aim is to mitigate climate change by reforesting the planet. It's called Plant for the Planet, and it's up and running in 131 countries.[43] The British branch aims to plant a million trees in United Kingdom over the next few years. Individuals or groups can either pledge to plant a certain number of trees or make a cash donation—€1 buys one tree.

Earlier we asked "What if a representative of future generations were proposed as a member of the board of every major corporation?" Now imagine the sizzling energy in the room if this quality of young person brought his convictions, determination, and knowledge to the boardroom table.

Radical Efficiency in Addressing Social Problems

The skill to transform conflict is needed not only in civil war or riots; it is also needed on the streets where we live. We need laws with teeth to prevent rape. Grandmothers in the eastern Cape in South Africa are scared to go out, because so many are raped by teenagers. One elderly woman has learned to bark like a dog to scare intruders. People the world over lie in bed at night afraid of violence.

Brazil's favela shantytowns are some of the most conflict ridden and dangerous places on earth. In Rio alone, five thousand people die every year as a result of gun crimes, reflecting the huge gap in living standards between rich and poor.[44] Dominic Barter, a self-educated Restorative Justice practitioner, ignored these dangers and in the mid-1990s walked into favelas to propose a dialogue between residents, the gangs, and the police. His aim was not to convince them to change, but to explore whether there were ways to respond to conflict other than violence. Dominic's work is exactly aligned with Archbishop Tutu's approach in the Truth and Reconciliation Commission in South Africa.

Over Dominic Barter's years with these communities, a process emerged that came to be known as Restorative Circles. At its core lies an understanding of conflict as something to be engaged with and learned from, not "resolved." When he arrived in Rio, he noticed that his preconceptions and desire to help often interfered with meaningful partnership and dialogue, so he focused increasingly on following the requests of those he met or on the ideas that emerged from their conversations. This built trust. In response, the residents opened up about the tough issues they faced. Dominic says he "began to receive these stories of conflict as gifts."

He began working with the municipal government in Rio to mediate between favela residents and police, as well as between gangs. This culminated in a presentation of the principles of Restorative Circles at the World Social Forum in 2005, alongside judges and others interested in bringing restorative practices into the judicial and education systems. Following the forum, the Brazilian Ministry of Justice, with funding from the United Nations Development Program, established pilot projects in restorative justice.

Dominic was asked to apply Restorative Circles in Porto Alegre and Sao Paulo. In both cities, Dominic worked primarily with young offenders. In Sao Paolo young people who are caught breaking the law and who attend a high school close to the city's biggest favela, "Heliopolis," are immediately offered a Restorative Circle at their school, at the police station or at the courthouse. In some areas, the police have been given the authority to offer Restorative Circles as an alternative to going to the police station. These districts have seen a subsequent drop in referrals to the juvenile courts by 50 percent.

Ongoing cooperation with particular schools and families builds the trust and reputation that is pivotal to successful Restorative Circles. This kind of flexibility and scalability have seen the program spread to fourteen different countries over the last two years, including cultures as distinct as Uganda, Iran, Germany and Korea.

A survey of four hundred Restorative Circles in Sao Paulo showed that 93 percent ended in agreement. Another survey in the Campinas Municipal School District showed an impressive decrease in arrests following Restorative Circles: in 2008, there were 71 police visits ending in student arrest and subsequent court appearance; in 2009, after school-wide adoption of Restorative Circles, there was one such arrest, a drop of 98 percent.

Those are results.

"RADICAL GENEROSITY"

Vinoba Bhave (1895–1982) was a follower of Gandhi. He was deeply disturbed by the gap between rich and poor in India. Bhave's Bhoodan Yajna ("Land-Gift Movement") began when a landholder offered him some land in response to his appeal on behalf of a group of landless Dalits. He then walked from village to village, appealing to landowners to *give* one-sixth of their land to be distributed among the landless. According to Bhave, land reform should be secured by a change of heart and not by enforced government action. This became the largest peaceful transfer of land in history: five million acres changed ownership as a result of his work.

This practice of radical generosity has been picked up by Nipun Mehta[45] in present-day California. When he was in high school, his goal was to either become a tennis pro or a Himalayan yogi. However, by the third year of his Computer Science and Philosophy degree at the University of California, Berkeley, he started a software career at Sun Microsystems. Dissatisfied by the dot-com greed of the late 1990s, Nipun went to a homeless shelter with three friends to "give, with absolutely no agendas." They soon created an organization named CharityFocus (which has since been renamed ServiceSpace), a volunteer-run organization that has delivered millions of dollars of web-related services to the nonprofit world for free.

In January 2005, Nipun and Guri, his wife of six months, dropped everything to embark on an open-ended, unscripted walking pilgrimage in India to "use our hands to do random acts of kindness, use our heads to profile inspiring people, and use our hearts to cultivate truth." Living on dollar a day, eating wherever food was offered, sleeping wherever a flat surface was found, the couple walked 620 miles before ending up at a monastery, where they meditated for three months.

Today ServiceSpace has 285,000 members who incubate compassionate action in a multitude of ways, and its inspiration portals get 100 million hits a year. It has given rise to several new organizations: HelpOthers.org, DailyGood.org, KarmaTube.org, iJourney, Karma Clinic, Service-eXchange, and Karma Kitchen.

When you finish eating at Karma Kitchen, you'll get a surprise. The bill you receive reads "nothing. ooo. zero." This is because the people who ate before you have paid your bill in advance. Then you choose what you'd like to do. It works so well that between 2010 and 2013 the restaurant served twenty-six thousand meals, all on a basis of what Mehta calls "transition to trust."

Please be aware, I don't tell these stories just as a kind of "feel good" element in the book. To me, they are like signals flashing out a message of momentous change in the way we act in the world. They shift our focus. They are ideas that rumble with potential. So . . .

What if this idea of radical generosity could be picked up by the one hundred richest people in the world, who earned enough in 2012 to end extreme poverty four times over? If each gave just a quarter of what they earned, a program could be designed quickly—since all the plans are already in hand—to end poverty worldwide. The first to come forward, acting as a catalyst to others, could be asked to make a speech to the General Assembly of the United Nations, demonstrating how great wealth can be used to end great suffering.

HOW CONFLICT IS TRANSFORMED

The year 2014 marked the centenary of the start of World War I—the "war to end all wars." If you watch television news every night, you might conclude that humanity is doomed to repeat its bloodiest century. But if you watch the trends and see what's happening over time, you see a very different picture.

As we saw in chapter 4, in a brilliant article in December 2012 former Australian foreign minister Gareth Evans spelled out the facts: "Over the last two decades, major wars and episodes of mass violence worldwide have become much less frequent and deadly. After a high point in the late 1980s and very early 1990s, there has been a decline of well over 50 percent in the number of major conflicts both between and within states; in the number of genocidal and other mass atrocities; and in the number of people killed as a result of them."[46]

It's true, he continues, that there has been a resurgence since 2004 of what statisticians would call "minor armed conflicts." But in the case of "high-intensity" conflicts or wars (defined as entailing one thousand or more battle deaths in a year), he says, "the trend-line has been sloping unequivocally downward. And that goes for war-related civilian deaths as well." The conflict in Syria will alter these figures, but Evans's conclusions still stand. Evans—and others as experienced as he—conclude that this is due to "the huge upsurge in conflict prevention, conflict management, negotiated peacemaking, and post-conflict peace-building activity that has occurred over the last decade and a half—most of it spearheaded by the much-maligned UN."

Our own experience in Peace Direct would enhance this explanation by demonstrating the fast-increasing role of women in peace building. There are now 164 documented active and effective women's peace-building organizations in conflict areas worldwide, with 23 such organizations in Pakistan alone.[47]

A SIXTEEN-YEAR-OLD TAKES ON THE TALIBAN

Khyber Pakhtunkhwa is one of the most fragile provinces in Pakistan. Militant groups incite extremism and violence, increasingly among young people—most suicide bombers are under twenty-six—and Pakistani forces struggle to maintain control. For women especially, religious extremism has led to growing insecurity—many fear kidnap or worse.

At just sixteen years old, Gulalai Ismail and a group of school friends set up Aware Girls to change the lives of young women in Pakistan.[48] They began by focusing on women's rights, and as their membership has grown, they are now training young activists to become local peace builders and challenging violence and extremism. Gulalai says, "Women are not only victims of conflict, they are drivers of peace. Women's voices must be heard if peace is to last."

Gulalai is well aware that her work challenges the Taliban's power. Her fellow youth worker Malala Yousafzai was shot in the head for advocating for the education of girls. Gulalai believes passionately that building a grassroots community challenge to extremist intolerance is key to peace in the region. "I cannot accept the deeply rooted gender inequalities, and I do not want to be part of the injustices! I want to change the world for myself and other young women."

Gulalai began by working for women's rights, but she soon realized how many young men were being convinced to become jihadis. Almost every aspect of children's upbringing is affected by extremism. Even school textbooks urge children to be ready for jihad, says Gulalai, and they are bombarded by songs and films that glorify war, martyrdom, and violence. To counter this, in 2010 Gulalai set up the Youth Peace Network, which has now trained over seventy-five activists. Last year these activists reached six hundred young people vulnerable to radicalization. They identify young people in the community who might be vulnerable to militants and organize study circles to discuss the causes and consequences of conflict and the history of Talibanization.[49]

Gulalai's work is now being recognized globally, something that simply would not have happened even five years ago. In July 2013 she won an award from the National Endowment for Democracy in the US Congress, and the following August she was invited to attend the Obama Civil Society Summit in Washington, DC.

What if one of the world's billionaires gave $100,000 to each of the reliable and trusted peace activists already identified in conflict zones around the world? This is the amount that most of them say they need to reach the next level of effectiveness. The billionaire who made this decision would be taking a major step toward putting an end to violent conflict worldwide.

TIME TO MAKE THE MIDDLE EAST WMD-FREE

Jonathan Granoff is the president of the Global Security Institute and a professor of international law at Widener University School of Law. He is one of the most articulate advocates of pragmatic ways to rid the world of weapons of mass destruction (WMD). His article is reproduced here in full.[50]

Eliminating the chemical weapons stockpiles in Syria through international cooperation and bringing Syria into full compliance with the Chemical Weapons Convention would be a public good for the entire world. However, it would still leave several countries in the very volatile Middle East in possession of weapons of mass destruction (WMD), including nuclear, chemical and likely biological weapons. Ending the threat of WMD in the Middle East is critical. As long as these weapons exist, we remain only a day away from another crisis.

US leadership is indispensable and President Obama has publicly made out the case that chemical weapons are immoral and should be eliminated. If such weapons are morally unacceptable, it shouldn't matter who possesses them.

Successful leadership requires coherence in principle, policy and practice. Banning weapons of horrific indiscriminate effect such as chemical, biological and nuclear weapons is a good policy. It rests on the principle that civilization must pursue peace and security with minimum standards of civilized behavior honoring life and protecting innocent civilians. The place where coherence breaks down is in the practice of condemning immoral illegal weapons in the hands of some and condoning them in the hands of others. If the weapons themselves are unworthy of civilization, they must universally be eliminated.

One exemplary step in the process of the elimination of weapons of mass destruction has been the establishment of nuclear-weapons-free zones. There are five treaties virtually making the entire southern hemisphere WMD free, including 114 countries. Some even have beautiful names for treaties—Tlatelolco for Latin America and the Caribbean, Rarotonga for the South Pacific, Pelindaba for Africa—and then zones in Southeast and Central Asia as well.

Efforts have been made in the Middle East to establish a zone free of all weapons of mass destruction. In 1991, the Security Council adopted Resolution 687 to address the invasion of Kuwait by Iraq. Actions against Iraq were characterized as "steps towards the goal of establishing in the Middle East a zone free from weapons of mass destruction and all missiles for their delivery and the objective of a global ban on chemical weapons." Syria joined the US-led coalition against Iraq based on that resolution.

A core part of the bargain to extend, indefinitely, the nuclear Non-Proliferation Treaty (NPT), in 1995 included a commitment by all parties to pursue "the establishment of an effectively verifiable Middle East zone free of weapons of mass destruction [WMD] nuclear, chemical and biological, and their delivery systems." The treaty would commit parties not to possess, acquire, test, manufacture or use any nuclear, chemical or biological weapons or their delivery systems. The zone reaches from Libya in the west to Iran in the east, and from Syria in the north to Yemen in the south, and includes all League of Arab states, plus Iran and Israel.

In 2003, Syria, while a member of the United Nations Security Council, introduced a resolution calling for a WMD-free zone in the Middle East. Syrian Ambassador Fayssal Mekdad said such a zone "should be at the top of the agenda of the international community," and that "this is a very crucial issue in the Middle East, and I think once we achieve it, we shall have a further step in solving . . . complicated problems in a very sensitive region." The resolution did not gain the necessary support of the big players.

At the Review Conference of the NPT in 2010, the Middle East WMD-free-zone proposal gained significant traction. Over 190 States party to the NPT agreed that the United States, Russia, and the United Kingdom, working together with the UN Secretary General, would convene a regional conference in 2012 to advance the creation of a WMD-free zone in the Middle East.

The conference remains indefinitely postponed. Citing the lack of progress, Egypt walked out of an NPT meeting in Geneva in 2013.

Syria has neither nuclear weapons nor the capacity to develop them. Its immediate neighbor, Israel, is the only country in the Middle East that has such weapons. Along with Egypt, Israel is also not fully participating in both the Chemical Weapons Convention and the Biological Weapons Convention, which ban such weapons of mass destruction.

If US leadership is to be effective it must promote the principle that all WMD are unacceptable in anyone's hands and then bring that principle into practice. That would mean putting pressure on Egypt and Israel to ratify the Biological Weapons Convention. It would also mean putting pressure on the two countries to ratify the Chemical Weapons Convention. Egypt has used chemical weapons when it intervened in Yemen's civil war in the 1960s.

Such steps would begin the process of creating a WMD-free zone in the Middle East and convening the promised conference. This would require working with all regional players, including

Iran, to ensure Israel's security and end its possession of and threats to use a WMD.

Israel does not object to the principle of a WMD-free Middle East. It just requires appropriate security arrangements with its neighbors, some of which are openly hostile. That is why this moment of opportunity to change regional dynamics should be seized.

Leadership also means bringing US nuclear-weapons policy into coherence with the values the President is espousing. It is high time to take substantive steps to end reliance on the dangerous dance of nuclear deterrence. If nuclear deterrence brings security for some, it promotes nuclear weapons as valuable and thus stimulates proliferation while also prolonging an unacceptably risky status quo.

First, the United States should affirm that the sole value of a nuclear weapon, pending their elimination, is to prevent any nuclear weapon from being used. This would involve a prompt no-first-use pledge. Presently US policy is not so constrained. Second, it should start the complex multilateral process of establishing a legal prohibition that will prevent any use of a nuclear weapon. It should then begin the preliminary negotiations for a legal framework universally eliminating nuclear weapons for all time.

A commitment to negotiate the elimination of nuclear weapons is contained in the Nuclear Nonproliferation Treaty, ratified by every country in the world except North Korea, Israel, Pakistan, and India. It would be absurd to say chemical weapons are less acceptable than nuclear weapons, given the latter's indiscriminate, destructive power. For the United States or Russia to lead in establishing greater stability in the Middle East, they must demonstrate respect for minimum civilized values. The law, conscience, treaties, and reason condemn the use of all WMD no matter how righteous the perpetrator.

If the use of a WMD is illegal, surely the threat of using it is no less so. Leadership would use this moment to move the world to a much safer future where all WMD are abolished.

Transforming the Treatment of Women Worldwide: Educate, End Violence, Empower

Now we come to the one strategy that is key to all the others and without which the others won't get sufficient traction. All the future scenarios we have presented rely on one component that is fundamental—a total overhaul of attitudes toward and treatment of women, worldwide. This emerges as the sine qua non of any vision of a possible future. It has the aspects of an entire revolution.

> Matthew Arnold, the philosopher and poet, declared that if ever there would be a time when women would come together purely and simply for the benefit of mankind, it would be a power such as the world has never known. The Sufi sage Hazrat Inayat Khan said that he could see as clear as daylight that the hour was coming when women would lead humanity to a higher evolution. In 2009, the Dalai Lama astounded his audience at a conference in Vancouver by saying that the world would be saved by Western woman.
>
> There is a saying by a great Hasidic saint, the Baal Shem Tov, which goes: "When the moon shall shine as bright as the sun, the Messiah will come." Woman through her struggle to articulate the highest values of the feminine principle, will begin to make the moon shine so that it can balance the solar brightness of our present consciousness. In recognising her depression, her suffering, her longing to outgrow the subservience and powerlessness of her past and present experience, in recognising and supporting her deepest values, she may accomplish something truly heroic and extraordinary for life and the planet, something that humanity in centuries to come will celebrate. For this reason, nothing is of such importance as woman's rescue of herself.[51]

And it's happening.

FROM NGO LEADER TO WIFE OF THE PRIME MINISTER

When the Somali peace talks began in 2000, only traditional clans were recognized as legitimate units of representation. There were five clans in the war-torn country, but not one of them considered women important enough to be part of the negotiations.

The women could have sat back and accepted this as their destiny, but not when their country was falling apart in a wave of unprecedented violence. And not when a woman like Asha Hagi Elmi was around.

So the Sixth Clan was born, entirely female. And it has paid off for Somali women—who have become a driving force for peace building in Mogadishu. Through the pressure group Save Somali Women and Children, founded by Asha in 1992,[52] they gradually edged their way into the talks. When the peace agreement was signed by Somali warlords in 2004, Asha—known as "The Lioness of Somalia"—was the only woman and the only civilian to sign.

The results have been encouraging. The Federal Charter of Somalia now stipulates that at least 12 percent of the Parliament must be women. There is a Ministry for Women and the Family. Asha herself was elected to the Pan-African Parliament in Johannesburg in May 2006. She also chaired the Somalia National Committee on Female Genital Mutilation and Harmful Traditional Practices.[53]

In 2006 Asha was invited to advise those building the concept of The Elders for a week on Sir Richard Branson's island in the Caribbean. Her honest accounts of life in Somalia made a big impression on everyone, especially Archbishop Tutu.

Save Somali Women and Children now runs training workshops on conflict transformation, and it organizes an annual literacy program. In addition, they provide practical support to some of the country's most vulnerable and marginalized women through rights awareness workshops and campaigns to end genital cutting and early and forced marriage. When I asked Asha if she might get killed for doing this, she said, "I would rather die making a difference. I'm doing it for my daughters, for a new Somalia."

Asha has received many honors for her work. She has been nominated for the Nobel Peace Prize, and in 2008 she was a recipient of the Right Livelihood Award. She worked for years building her organization—with almost no financial support—and now, after her husband, Abdi Farah Shirdon, became prime minister, she finds herself at the center of decision making in Somalia. With her new position and status, she has helped Somali women make historic gains through the appointment of the first female deputy prime minister and foreign affairs minister, as well as the first deputy minister of justice and other important ministerial portfolios.

But women are usually not at the negotiating table . . .

Analysis of the results of women's work transforming conflicts has increased exponentially, with twenty-three in-depth studies over the past twelve years.[54] But while women's engagement in peace building is recognized by many international institutions as a crucial element of recovery and conflict prevention, most of these studies bemoan the fact that a full decade after United Nations Security Council passed a resolution in 2000 addressing the pivotal role women should and do play in conflict management, "the striking absence of women from formal peace negotiations reveals a troubling gap between the aspirations of countless global and regional commitments and the reality of peace processes."[55]

A UNIFEM study in 2009 found that women make up just 2.5 percent of signatories to peace agreements. A review of 31 major peace processes has showed that only 4 percent of participants were women, and that women made up only 2.4 percent of chief mediators, 3.7 percent of witnesses, and 9 percent of negotiators.[56]

In 2013/4 the Institute for Inclusive Security conducted a survey of 110 women living and working inside Syria, which indicated that the international actors responsible for coordinating the talks are not reaching active women leaders on the ground—90 percent stated that they have not been engaged at all and their voices are not being heard. This despite the fact that they have undertaken a long list of activities—from mobilization to advocacy to media outreach—to have their voices heard in the negotiations.[57]

The International Crisis Group, globally respected for its incisive and sharply focused reports, said in 2006:

> Peacebuilding cannot succeed if half the population is excluded from the process. Crisis Group's research in Sudan, Congo (DRC) and Uganda suggests that peace agreements, post-conflict reconstruction, and governance do better when women are involved. Women make a difference, in part because they adopt a more inclusive

approach toward security and address key social and economic issues that would otherwise be ignored. But in all three countries, as
different as each is, they remain marginalised in formal processes
and under-represented in the security sector as a whole. Governments and the international community must do much more to support women peace activists.[58]

It is not as though able, trained, and experienced women are not available. There are, in fact, scores of qualified women in thirty-two conflict
areas, from Iraq to Uganda—women highly trained and experienced—
who are not yet being recruited to serve in official prevention processes,
mediation, or post-conflict reconciliation. The Institute for Inclusive Security includes the Women Waging Peace Network, a network of more
than two thousand women peacemakers from conflict areas around the
world, ranging from Colombia to Congo, Lebanon to Liberia, Sri Lanka
to Sudan.[59]

Therefore, if we want to ensure that humanity is not doomed to repeat its bloodiest century, the logical move would be to mount an international campaign to see that competent women are swiftly moved into
policy-making positions in all conflict countries. This is now beginning
to happen.

Lindsay Levin asked one of the Leaders' Quest fellows why so many
of them chose to focus their work first and foremost on violence against
women. Anwari Khan, warrior queen of Mumbai's largest rubbish dump,
replied, "Because everything comes back to this issue. Everything is connected to the way women are treated and their ability to speak out. Without that, nothing can be addressed—not education nor sanitation nor
health nor water."[60]

EDUCATE WOMEN: REDUCE BIRTH RATE, IMPROVE DECISION MAKING

The United Nations Population Fund says that girls who have been educated are likely to marry later and to have smaller and healthier families.
The World Bank agrees.[61] Every year of education delays a girl's marriage and reduces the number of children she has. Girls with secondary
schooling are up to six times less likely to be married *as children* than girls

with little or no education. Girls who receive secondary and higher education beyond grade 7 have, on average, 2.2 fewer children than girls with less or no education.[62] The United Nations Population Fund reports that "the education of parents is linked to their children's educational attainment, and the mother's education is usually more influential than the father's. . . . Besides having fewer children, mothers with schooling are less likely to have mistimed or unintended births. This has implications for schooling, because poor parents often must choose which of their children to educate."[63]

Although criticisms have been made of the methodology of some studies,[64] the case for investing in girls' education is extremely strong. But building schools isn't necessarily the most effective way to do it. In *Half the Sky,* Nicholas Kristof and Sheryl Wudunn show that the best way to increase school attendance might not be glamorous, but it's cost-effective—deworm students. Increasing school attendance by building schools ends up costing $100 per year for every additional student enrolled, compared to $4 per student per year for deworming.[65] They also record the results of the Oportunidades program, which, in essence, pays poor families in Mexico to keep their children in school and take them for regular medical checkups. Now serving about one-quarter of Mexican families, it has raised high school attendance for girls by 20 percent.

Some 31 percent of households in the developing world do not get sufficient iodine from water or food. The result is brain damage. Tens of millions of children lose approximately ten IQ points each as a result of iodine deficiency when they are developing fetuses. Female fetuses are particularly prone to impaired brain development when the mother's body lacks iodine. Worldwide, iodine deficiency alone reduces humanity's collective IQ by more than one billion points. While salt iodization is one of the less photogenic forms of poverty alleviation, "development geeks rave about it."[66] By one estimate, a mere $19 million would pay for salt iodization in the countries that still desperately need it.

What if one of our billionaires were to finance the iodizing of salt?

When a woman has more control over the number of children she will have, and when her time is spent earning an income rather than having children, birthrates fall. When parents can be confident that at least two or three of their children will survive into adulthood, they will be less likely to hedge their bets by having five or six children. Having a dependable social safety net also decreases parents' anxiety about having children around to take care of them in their old age.

Since women's literacy rates are still significantly lower than men's in most developing countries, there is a huge untapped force for change here. Education helps girls and women to know their rights and to gain confidence to claim them. Studies find that educating girls and women fosters democracy and women's political activity.[67] A Bangladeshi study found educated women three times more likely to take part in political meetings than those without schooling. Educated women are more likely to resist abuses such as domestic violence, traditions like female genital cutting, and discrimination at home, in society, or the workplace.

Just as the trauma of violent conflict can take three generations to heal, so investment needs to be made in the youngest generations of societies prone to conflict. Steve Killelea, a brilliantly successful IT entrepreneur who founded of the Institute for Economics and Peace, takes this issue so seriously that he personally saw to it that every private school in Cambodia received a copy of Kerry Kennedy's "Speak Truth to Power—Human Rights Defenders Who are Changing Our World."

What Does an Integrated Strategy Look Like?

If it were possible to rise above the everyday issues and clashes of the planet and take a bird's eye view of all these strategies, what might that look like?

We would see many "stuck" areas, characterized by a thick muddy substance, in government meetings, in the United Nations, and in corporate boardrooms in every capital city. In just some of these we would observe movement, as if water was beginning to dissolve the mud and some kind of flow was becoming possible. Small green arrows—like paper airplanes—would be flying in through the windows of some of these boardrooms, trailing messages with maps of escape routes.

Meanwhile, from city squares around the world—from Cairo to

Ankara, Beijing to Barcelona, and New Delhi to New York—we would see sparks of fiery light flying up. Some would fizzle and die, others would travel quite far and land in other city squares, and some would even land in government offices and light small bonfires there. Others sparks would fall, drenched in blood.

In other parts of the world, we would see vivid green spots pulsing with life, spreading through underground runners to appear elsewhere. Some quite small areas would be infused with a deadly dark red stain. As we watched, we would see extreme weather patterns forming, great swells in the oceans, vast crashes of white ice around the poles, and we would just be able to discern alarming movements under the earth's crust, as if a massive body was moving its muscles.

But all over the planet, as it slowly revolved before us, we would begin to observe tiny points of light flickering. As we watched, these would almost imperceptibly be growing in number, until in some places they multiplied into a small, steady, radiant glow. From these glowing spots, tiny lines of light began to shoot off to connect them to other glowing spots, sometimes dipping into the mud and then moving on. Before our astonished eyes, these lines of light would spin a gossamer web around the entire globe.

THE ASPECTS OF AN ENTIRE REVOLUTION, AS BIG AS THE ABOLITION OF SLAVERY, AND IT'S HAPPENING

What if governments did hear a clear message from voters that they want action on carbon emissions, renewable energy, and resource conservation? What if they were urged to develop simultaneous policy proposals with other governments, so that shadowy corporate lobbying could be countered?

Imagine if banks understood that customers want to put their funds where money serves people, not the other way around, and prioritized that service. Picture a world where money holds its value, and companies compete to be trustworthy, because consumers insist on it. Suppose that the B Team example proved contagious, because consumers liked the model of prioritizing people and planet alongside profit.

Suppose fossil fuel subsidies were dropped and Renewable Energy

Feed-in Tariff policies were adopted worldwide to unlock renewable, decentralized energy development. Energy from the sun would be harvested so fast that southern countries become net exporters of energy, making coal-fired power stations obsolete and nuclear power unnecessary. Imagine the discarding and burning of plastic minimized as the plastic-to-oil converting machine is copied and adopted by local authorities, villages, and businesses worldwide.

On the political scene, the Arab Spring–type revolutions have discovered how to exclude the violent and bring pressure on dictatorial regimes through massive exertions of people power, supported by Avaaz campaigns. The Sarvodaya movement's community-development programs and disaster-relief schemes are copied throughout Asia. Children worldwide start planting trees.

The methods of restorative justice used in Brazil to address social problems are found to work in any culture to reduce crime and recidivism, provided they combine restorative justice with community involvement and a strong emphasis on listening.

The notion of "radical generosity" pioneered in India and California proves so contagious that people—rich and poor—start doing it all over the world. You stop to pay a road toll and discover that the person in the car pulling away from the tollbooth in front of you has already paid your fee, so you pay for the next person. A billionaire is honored in the United Nations for buying a solar lamp for every person in Africa who needs one, alleviating the drain of kerosene on household budgets and drastically cutting carbon dioxide emissions. Other billionaires are inspired to do the same for other parts of the world, and the lamps get so popular that people in developed nations buy them for themselves, cutting their own carbon footprints.

Each reliable and trusted peace activist in conflict zones around the world is funded and is able to increase their work beyond what they had dreamed possible, resulting in a dramatic drop in violent conflict worldwide. Nuclear-weapons-free zones in Latin America and the Caribbean, the South Pacific, Africa, and Southeast and Central Asia are extended to the Middle East, causing a marked lessening of tension in the region.

The treatment of women worldwide is transformed. Not just on paper, but in reality; girls have rights to full education. Violence against women is systematically made unacceptable as a result of community action. Women are not only entitled in every country to fill policy-making positions, but they can rely on popular support through online campaigns to assert their rights to equality. The values of the feminine are being sought out for their contribution to good communication in business and good decisions in the boardroom.

New energies and new methods for addressing our challenges are cooking. Dialogue is becoming a more popular word than negotiation. Boardroom tables are pondering the value of happiness. Leadership skills are less about winning and more about waking up. The technological genius of invention of the masculine can now be harnessed in what Elizabeth Whitney calls "the undoing of the damage that has been inflicted on the physical earth and the simple act of overturning our priorities that will initiate a new creative explosion of healing and restoring."

The most remarkable feature of this historical moment on Earth is not that we are on the way to destroying the world—we've actually been on the way for quite a while. It is that we are beginning to wake up, as from a millennia-long sleep, to a whole new relationship to our world, to ourselves and each other.

—Joanna Macy

My Reality Check: The Shadows That Can Sabotage Vision and Action

The ideas and energy in this chapter may well have inspired you. They are full of power and possibility. And—having done this kind of work for a while—I want, at this stage, to mention some of the issues that can, inside us and outside, derail these possibilities.

Secrecy is one of the biggest issues, because of the many decisions that are made behind closed doors without the ventilation of public debate. They are then announced when it is too late for ordinary people to organize and get things changed. Working on the decision making surrounding nuclear weapons brought us up against this issue constantly: when we knew a new weapon was in the pipeline, the answer to our questions was always "no decision has been made," and then suddenly a fait accompli was announced. The system itself, in our supposedly democratic United Kingdom, was closed to debate.

Moreover, the decision-making system was unaccountable. That's why we found it necessary to research how decisions were made and who was actually making them. When we published a book entitled *The Nuclear Weapons World—Who, Where and How* in 1988, with the names and biographies of 650 nuclear weapons policymakers worldwide, the book was banned by the Ministry of Defence and all defense personnel were forbidden to talk to us.

The key is not to be stopped by things like this. Secrecy still blankets issues that are clearly not security risks, because governments prefer that the public not know the details. The Trans-Pacific Partnership, a secretive free-trade agreement between the United States and eleven other nations, appears to be one of these.

There is disappointment also in how we as the public react when we disagree with government policy. I know that the Occupy movement worldwide has achieved much in the way of public exposure, but the lack of strategy adopted by Occupy in the United Kingdom left much frustration. As I understood it from those I worked with in Occupy London, the movement allowed itself to be split. On the one hand were the hard-core activists, some of whom believed in violence, who were less interested in policies than in expressing anger at the status quo. On the other hand were those committed to nonviolence; they cared about the squalor of the occupied spaces and ended up cooking and cleaning up after the large numbers of people who moved in just wanting shelter and food. They had little energy left for strategy. This meant that a massive communication opportunity was squandered, when original ideas, theories, and proposals could have been fed daily to a global media.

Many have written off the Arab Spring as a failure. Is this accurate? It was certainly a tragedy that the uprisings were hijacked by the violent; future revolutionaries need to be better prepared along the lines that Gene Sharp advocates—to surround and expel any thugs who may attempt to infiltrate. Violence is what the media feeds on and—through their photographs and videos—encourage. But the Spring is far from finished. If we cast our minds back to the English Revolution in the 1600s, it took decades for us to establish the beginnings of democracy—and those decades saw the beheading of the king, a civil war that caused an estimated 250,000 deaths, and the eventual restoration of a monarchy working with a more powerful Parliament.

What the activists in Tahrir and other squares—and many NGOs worldwide—see so clearly is that survival is a whole planet issue, not a continuation of the old zero-sum bargaining between nations. Given the abject failure of intervention in Iraq and Afghanistan, teenagers can see that militarism usually incubates more violence than it is capable of subduing. Many no longer see war as an effective means of resolving anything.

TURNING TO THE INSIDE . . .

What often trips up activists are our own emotions. I have seen movements and nonprofit organizations ripped apart by internal feuds when the passions driving us—often fuelled by fear or anger—overwhelm our sense of community, our respect for colleagues, and our need for cooperation. I've certainly done that.

By contrast, just observe the energy change when NGOs consciously build trust with their teams through transparency, develop the skills of internal communication, and open up spaces of dialogue where strong emotions can be aired in a safe environment. Yes, it's demanding to put aside the time to do these things. But if we don't, I believe NGOs stay in the old twentieth-century mindset of getting buried in to-do lists, targets, and deadlines, unable to rise above the daily fray to get some helicopter insight and also to get a sense of the human feelings of colleagues.

I say this because the inner, personal challenges of trying to change the world are actually substantial. We have to weather times of deep depression. We get utterly exhausted by lack of funds and support. We are driven by lists of oughts and shoulds. There is the constant specter of self-righteousness leading to superiority and alienation. We meet an enormous weight of apathy. We're stunned by the trivia of the media just when we need its support and encouragement.

It takes courage to take on some of the harshest realities of the planet, and we usually don't realize that this can leave debris or fallout inside us. For example, those who witness the brutal human casualties of war can be left with a residue of suffering that's almost unbearable. Those who are constantly seeing ecosystems trashed can endure a sense of acute loss or even heartbreak. Fury affects those who witness the results of financial decisions that rip off the poorest of the poor. When you see huge wealth being squandered, it can leave you with feelings of outrage. As we daily read about the corruption and dishonesty of some political systems, or the greed of some corporations, it can leave us feeling furious but powerless. The indifference of the media to issues we care passionately about can make us cynical. When we witness technology out of control—as, for example, in Fukushima—we are naturally filled with fear.

So it's important to give attention to this internal residue of emotion, to recognize that it will be there, and to take steps not to get stuck with it. This is quite simple to do. Usually all that's necessary is to see it, listen to it, and make space for it to transform; it will do this naturally if we just make the time and space, and give it the care it needs. There's an exercise in the appendix that takes just a few minutes.

You might compare yourself to being a doctor going into an area where there is cholera or typhoid. That doctor will need a strong immune system. Taking care of the emotions will strengthen the immune system and develop the self-awareness that is essential to doing effective work in the world.

THE SHADOWS THAT CAN SABOTAGE VISION AND ACTION

All the ruling powers of our world cast dangerous shadows—political shadows of corrupt manipulation, religious shadows of authoritarian control in the various hierarchies of the religions and guru systems, and corporate shadows of heartless exploitation.[68]

It's not only ruling powers that have shadows. We all have them and they can sabotage vision and action. In my case I have an inner critic who used to be quite vicious. He sat on my shoulder and carped at me. He was the prowling inner bully stalking and attacking my every move, muttering in my ear how I've messed up, how I've failed, how old I'm getting.

I used to hate him, because he could be extremely sarcastic whenever

I ventured into new territory, when I expressed new and unconventional ideas, whenever I put my head above the parapet, so to speak. At some crucial moments, when I wanted to speak my truth, he silenced me completely, leaving me feeling sick inside.

Now that I have faced him and changed our relationship (more on how to do this in the next chapter), I find that he can also actually be quite useful, because he makes me question my assertions. Writing about "new consciousness" can easily slip into slushy reasoning and vague opinions. Rather than a critic, he is now a skeptic and can ask the sharp questions, interrupt, argue. Sometimes he makes me laugh, sometimes he's annoying, and only rarely is he now just plain destructive.

Andrew Harvey has thought hard about the inner saboteurs and writes about them with clarity and humility. He has identified five interrelated forms of inner sabotage particularly potent in our crisis: disbelief, denial, dread, disillusion, and a death wish. We begin with a disbelief that such an immense crisis threatening everything could be possible; as the truth of the crisis starts to dawn on us, panic swerves us into denial; the more conscious we become of our denial, the more aware we become of the deep dread we have of future destruction; the more awake we become to this dread, the more assailed we are by a painful disillusion at humanity and its dark games; the more alert to these games we become (and to their potential catastrophic consequences), the more we discover in ourselves a secret death wish, a desire not to have to be here in such a desolate and bewildering time.[69]

Andrew writes compassionately too about the personal shadows that breed and feed these five saboteurs: the narcissism or self-indulgence endemic in our world; the addiction to comfort that our corporate culture institutionalizes; the use of childhood wounds to justify incessant self-absorption that modern psychology has often reinforced; the fear of standing up for truth and justice in a world that humiliates and tries to destroy whistle blowers; and what he calls the "golden shadow"—our incessant projection onto others of idealized qualities of compassion and heroism, instead of discovering and enacting them ourselves.

Andrew has worked with activist groups all over the world, and after some initial resistance he has found that almost everyone can be invited to discover this linked set of shadows in himself or herself. Coming to see this may be grueling, but facing and sharing our participation in these shadows will lead to greater compassion, self-awareness, and power.[71]

The reason that I'm so insistent about the need to attend to the inner work—as well the outer work in the world—goes right back to the theme of this book, namely that we cannot solve the problems we face from the same consciousness that produced them. For this leap in consciousness to take place, inner work is essential to reveal and evolve our extraordinary capacity for love and creativity, and to deal with our dark genius for self-destruction and sabotage.

In the words of a revered Indian educationalist:

> If we want external harmony, we must work upon ourselves to bring about harmony within. . . . If we want peace outside, we must first create peace within ourselves, and the more we are able to do this successfully within, the more we see that success mirrored in the external world.
>
> The external world is nothing but a mirror of our inner world. Create within, what you desire to have in the external world. There is no other way. Therefore self-transformation holds the key to social transformation, whether at the level of the small village or the whole world.[71]

This is why the rest of this book is devoted to the need for self-knowledge and the development of consciousness—so that activists can get the deep nourishment they deserve, feel safer in their work, feel more interconnected with the massive changes taking place globally, and find profound power to address the darker moments.

> The key leadership challenge of our time is to shift the inner place from which we operate. As individuals, as teams, as institutions, and as societies we all face the same issue: that doing "more of the same" won't fix flawed and failed systems. We have to leave behind our old tools and behaviors, and immerse ourselves in the places of most potential. We have to listen with our minds and hearts wide open,

and then connect with our deep sources of knowing and self. It's only when we pass through this eye of the needle—letting go of the old and letting come the emerging self—that we can begin to step into our real power: the power to collectively sense and create the world anew.

—Otto Scharmer, *Theory U*

A nurse recorded the most common regrets of the dying:[72]

- I wish I'd had the courage to live a life true to myself, not the life others expected of me.
- I wish I hadn't worked so hard.
- I wish I'd had the courage to express my feelings.
- I wish I had stayed in touch with my friends.
- I wish that I had let myself be happier.

So my question to you at the end of this chapter is:
If this were your last day of life, what would be your biggest regret?

CHAPTER 7

WAKING UP TO WHO WE REALLY ARE

As you will know if you've read the previous chapters, there's a transformed future possible for all of us, and a lot to do. *Doing* is one part, yes, indeed, and *being* is just as important. So this chapter sets out the skills that any person can access, in order be equipped with the inner intelligence that will allow you to BE the change you would like to see in the world. You have ample potential to make this transition, or you wouldn't be reading this.

The first step in being ready for this transformed future is for individuals to wake up to their own energetic potential. You, I, and nearly everybody else on the planet are currently using only a fraction of our potential. Remember what Daniel Siegel said in chapter 2: the brain's complexity gives us virtually infinite choices for how our brain will use its firing patterns to create itself. If we get stuck in one pattern, we are limiting our potential.

And that's just the brain. We have vastly more power to call on, in our physical self, our emotional self, our imagination, spirit, and soul. This chapter spells out nine signposts—with clues, messages, maps, and poetry—that can set you on this path to higher awareness and give you the potential to help build a positive future. This path leads to the leap in consciousness that provides the perspective—the bird's eye view—to take the necessary actions to resolve the problems we humans have created on the planet.

Ojas!

If you ask yourself: "Who do I know who's most alive, most vibrant, effective and energetic, who's also calm and generous and seems to have time for others?" Then, if you go and ask that person what their secret is, they'll be likely to tell you that they meditate, or do bodywork, or have some practice of self reflection, or like being silent in nature, or have some experience of becoming self aware.

But if they're honest they'll tell you that it's not all sweetness and light. They've probably had times of deep confusion and uncertainty, and wondered if it's all worth it. I most certainly have. I had to really work on myself and face all the lights and shadows of my being. I have stared terrified at ferocious inner demons, and often I have run away. Waking up isn't easy, because it involves not only becoming aware of our tenacious ego, but also being willing to peer into the dark parts of ourselves.

But the rewards are literally inestimable, as we become more free, more agile, less moody, and take ourselves less seriously. That's because the focus of our lives becomes less obsessed with the endless demands of the ego, and more open to the gifts that we already have, that can be so useful to the planet.

Right now you have within you talents—and power that you may not even know about yet—that are valuable for building the kind of future that will eventually have us all smiling. This can make you one of the people who are leading the wake-up call of the twenty-first century. That wake-up call is to change the daily mantra of millions—away from "what can I get?" toward a feeling of "what can I give?"

In the real world, the people I meet who have the least are often the most generous, sharing even their food and water. The people who have the most are often the most anxious to guard what they have. So what we're talking about here is not much to do with physical wealth, but an inner sense of abundance.

Nevertheless people, unless they're saints, can't give out unless they're well nourished themselves. They need a daily supply of what in India they call *ojas*, or "vital energy." *Ojas* brings with it an improved immune system, joie de vivre, and increased metabolism of all cells—as well as a glowing skin. . . .

So how do you get *ojas?* Sorry to tell you this, but it's not in a bottle or a gym. Cultivating *ojas* is really a journey to self, which culminates in knowing who you really are—no less. We've boiled it down to 13 parts, which can be done in any order, though they are probably least daunting if undertaken sequentially, so that each one can build on the previous.

1. Listening to self to gain integrity, authenticity, and personal truth
2. Developing a practice of reflection to become an observer of the mind
3. Dealing with difficult feelings
4. Increasing well-being and energy
5. Using conflict as opportunity
6. Doing nothing
7. Allowing imagination and creativity to flourish
8. Going into the shadow and the energy that comes from it
9. Learning how to serve, moving from "me" to "we"
10. Discovering the Beloved, becoming able to ask, "what can I give?"
11. Becoming a sacred activist
12. What about failure and disappointment?
13. Finding what you *really* want to do

If you think this is beginning to sound like a self-help manual, I can assure you it's not. It's just a series of vital clues—signposts posted on the side of the track by people who have walked the path before, to encourage you. Sometimes they've left diagrams, fragments of a map, riddles, apples, water, or pieces of poetry. And it's important to say that waking up is not a point or destination which is clear—it's a never-ending journey.

SIGNPOST 1: Listening to Self to Gain Integrity, Authenticity, and Personal Truth

Just six weeks after my daughter, Polly, was born, when I was thirty, I came down with a severe form of encephalitis, a brain disease, and was unconscious for several days. When the brain specialist told me he estimated that I had lost one-third of my brain cells (the only cells in the body that don't replace themselves), I burst into tears. "Don't cry," he said, "you've got a pretty face and a nice husband; you'll be all right."

It took six years to recover (not from his dumb comment, but from the encephalitis)—six years of excruciating headaches and a great deal of patience on my husband's part. During this time, my brain was foggy, and I couldn't think, beyond looking after our daughter and doing the shopping. But there was one question that went round and round in my head, *Who am I? What am I here for?*

At that time, people didn't routinely ask such questions, and it took a long time before I found my way to a Jungian analyst. Those years with her provided a richness of understanding human consciousness by way of symbol, myth, legend, and dreams, which opened my eyes to a whole inner world that I hadn't known existed. I carried around a quote from Jung: "But what if I should discover that I myself am the enemy who must be loved—what then?"[1]

Through a growing interest in holistic health systems, I was introduced to an acupuncture practitioner who works at the spiritual level as well as the emotional and physical. We've worked together regularly for thirty years, and I regard her as one of my mentors. She has taught me that it's possible—when I'm stuck in a depressing groove, and my mind goes round and round the same dense pattern—to consciously raise the energetic vibration. I came to realize that I actually have choice about what thought patterns I inhabit and that awareness of those thought patterns is the first step to freeing oneself.

The reason I feel it's vital to learn to observe our thoughts and to listen to the chatter that goes on in our heads is so that we can get a bit of distance from our mental habits. As most specialists of the mind will tell you, our emotions are heavily influenced by childhood experiences. Fear, anger, grief, or frustrations that were never processed as children can stay in the memory and suddenly overwhelm us at key moments later in life. It's vital to develop a habit of observation so that—at those key moments—we have the facility to step back and see what's going on. Many people call this the habit of *being present*, being able to distinguish those emotions that really belong to the present situation from those that are relics from the past.

Pam Grout sums this up succinctly: "If you're not really here, your mind is not available to do what you're asking it to do. It's imperative to practice conscious, moment-by-moment awareness. Otherwise, you're operating out of old encrusted beliefs, beliefs you downloaded before you were five years old. Do you really want a five-year-old running your life?"[2]

LISTENING

You probably think you're a good listener. Most of us do. But most of us are not. Why? Because most of the time, when someone else is speaking, we're thinking about whether they are right or wrong, attractive or not, or what we want to say, or what's for lunch. Our minds are full of our own opinions. That means we're not present to the other person.

Almost more importantly, we're often not listening to *ourselves*. That means we totally miss out on what is natural to us: our inner wisdom. This is so fundamental to human experience that great sages knew about it thousands of years ago:

> It is as though he listened
> And such listening as his
> Enfolds us in a silence
> In which at last
> We begin to hear
> What we are meant to be.[3]

In the appendix at the end of this book, there's a nice exploration that you can do with a close friend or partner, the Listening Exercise. It has four benefits:

- It gives you a profound deepening of your understanding of what's really going on inside you and another person.
- It helps you discover the authentic self from deep within—what you didn't know you knew.
- It helps you check your ability to give another person your full attention without "helping."
- It reveals compassion and opens the heart.

I've done this exercise with corporate leaders, top executive teams, and young social entrepreneurs from all over the world. They all found it quite tough to do at first but came out of it *astonished* at what they found—their own truths as well as their partner's.

Listening is crucially important, both politically and personally. Gro Harlem Brundtland used to be the prime minister of Norway and is now a member of The Elders. She says:

> As Elders, sometimes our most important task is to listen. The act of listening is fundamental to peace building, to ethical and inclusive leadership. Strong and stable societies are built on the understanding that everyone has the right to be listened to—and to be heard.
>
> The Elders heard from many diverse groups in Myanmar last week, in our first visit there as a group. Here is a country experiencing a formidable and daunting transition: political reforms are going ahead at a rapid pace; the government is pushing ahead with its aim to sign ceasefires with a dozen ethnic armed groups before the end of the year; and in some areas, new-found freedoms of expression are being abused by extremists.
>
> As we listened, what struck me is that the different actors are not listening to each other as much as they need to. For example, no one was more impressive than the women civil society leaders we met. I was deeply moved by their stories of suffering, and by their courage and commitment to fighting injustice and improving conditions in

Myanmar. But I wonder whether they are being heard in government, when only six per cent of elected officials in the national parliament are women—in fact, there was not a single woman among the high-level officials we met.[4]

For me, listening is the beginning of all authentic action for reconciliation and peace in the world. It is a profoundly radical action, one of the highest forms of love, and the sign of someone truly evolved.

SIGNPOST 2: Developing a Practice of Reflection to Become an Observer of the Mind

When the seventy-five members of the Stanford Graduate School of Business's advisory council were asked to recommend the most important capability for leaders to develop, their answer was nearly unanimous—self-awareness.[5] In this section, we examine why it's useful to be able to observe the antics of our own minds and what the benefits of self-awareness are that we gain from a bit of self-inspection.

Unconscious mental habits can hold us back from what we really long to do in the world. When Roopa Purushothaman was asked how she "pushed through" to become a global economist at Goldman Sachs, she said, "Something called your life's work. When I was 16, I discovered the question I would spend my life on—why are some countries rich and some poor?" She says that what holds us back are the definitions we give ourselves—"something internal in how you explain things to yourself."

Eckhart Tolle is one of the teachers who has been most helpful in getting me to begin to observe my own mind, because of the straightforward way he condenses a lifetime of deep experience into simple truths. Born in the Ruhr Valley in Germany in 1948, Tolle describes his childhood as unhappy. He felt alienated in a hostile school environment and felt depressed playing in buildings destroyed by Allied bombs during World War II. He says he was depressed until, at age twenty-nine, he underwent a profound inner transformation that radically changed the course of his life. One night in 1977 he awakened from sleep, suffering from feelings of depression that were "almost unbearable," but then he experienced a life-changing epiphany.

> I couldn't live with myself any longer. And in this a question arose without an answer: who is the "I" that cannot live with the self? What is the self? I felt drawn into a void! I didn't know at the time that what really happened was the mind-made self, with its heaviness, its problems, that lives between the unsatisfying past and the fearful future, collapsed. It dissolved. The next morning I woke up and everything was so peaceful. The peace was there because there was no self. Just a sense of presence or "being-ness," just observing and watching.[6]

Tolle spent several years wandering and unemployed, devoting himself to understanding, integrating, and deepening that transformation, which marked the beginning of an intense inward journey. Later he moved to North America, where he began writing his first book, *The Power of Now* (1997), which reached the *New York Times* best-seller list in 2000. That and his next book, *A New Earth* (2005), have each sold millions of copies. In 2008, a *New York Times* writer called Tolle "the most popular spiritual author in the United States." That same year, approximately thirty-five million people participated in a series of ten live webinars with Tolle and talk show host Oprah Winfrey.

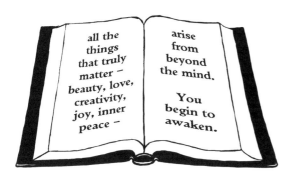

all the things that truly matter – beauty, love, creativity, joy, inner peace – arise from beyond the mind.

You begin to awaken.

Tolle is not religious, but he takes the essence of ancient spiritual practices and combines them in contemporary form. At the core of his teachings is the transformation of consciousness, the spiritual awakening that he sees as the next step in human evolution.

An essential aspect of this awakening consists in transcending our ego-based state of consciousness, and discovering our true soul purpose.

This is a prerequisite not only for personal happiness but also for the ending of violent conflict endemic on our planet.

"Watching the thinker" is what he advocates: "The beginning of freedom is the realization that you are not 'the thinker.' The moment you start watching the thinker, a higher level of consciousness becomes activated. You then begin to realize that there is a vast realm of intelligence beyond thought, that thought is only a tiny aspect of that intelligence. You also realize that all the things that truly matter—beauty, love, creativity, joy, inner peace—arise from beyond the mind. You begin to awaken."[7]

SO HOW DO PEOPLE DO IT?

Discovering inner peace is a process, the fruit of practice.
Like learning to ride a bike.
We may get frustrated at first, wobble and fall off, and feel we'll
        never get it.
Then, suddenly, we begin to find our balance.
We get the feel of it, the joy of it.
And then gradually we grow into our true potential.

This is becoming mainstream in the corporate world.

> We see leaders stumble not because they *have* undesirable thoughts and feelings—that's inevitable—but because they get *hooked* by them, like fish caught on a line. This happens in one of two ways. They buy into the thoughts, treating them like facts *(It was the same in my last job. . . . I've been a failure my whole career)*, and avoid situations that evoke them *(I'm not going to take on that new challenge)*. Or, usually at the behest of their supporters, they challenge the existence of the thoughts and try to rationalize them away *(I shouldn't have thoughts like this. . . . I know I'm not a total failure)*, and perhaps force themselves into similar situations, even when those go against their core values and goals *(Take on that new assignment—you've got to get over this)*. In either case, they are paying too much attention to their internal chatter and allowing it to sap important cognitive resources that could be put to better use.[8]

Today there are many forms of mindfulness, reflection, contemplation, meditation, and self-awareness training, as well as going on retreat. All of these practices aim to uncover the habits that inhibit our growth and help us to free ourselves and discover the core of our being. The advantages are of practical help in daily life: if we calm the mind, the space between stimulation (something that might trigger a strong emotion) and response (what I choose to do about it) becomes accessible on demand. This is the beginning of freedom. In the appendix, there are descriptions of practices that are effective. See which one attracts you and try it out.

The *New York Times* reported on the vast increase in the application of mindfulness in January 2014:

> Although pioneers like Jon Kabat-Zinn, now emeritus professor at the University of Massachusetts Medical Center, began teaching mindfulness meditation as a means of reducing stress as far back as the 1970s, all but a dozen or so of the nearly 100 randomized clinical trials have been published since 2005. And the most recent studies of mindfulness—the simple, nonjudgmental observation of a person's breath, body or just about anything else—are taking the practice in directions that might have shocked the Buddha. In addition to military fitness, scientists are now testing brief stints of mindfulness training as a means to improve scores on standardized tests and lay down new connections between brain cells.[9]

SIGNPOST 3: Dealing with Difficult Feelings

We probably all know people who are so intent on helping others or saving the world that they never look at the impatience, the anger, or the fear that drives them. And so they often unconsciously spread that anger or fear around them, projecting it onto others, who get blamed for what goes wrong.

Familiar? I've done it many, many times. After going through this mill so often, I've developed a little mantra when it comes to fear.

The things I dread
get fat on the fear I feed them.
Then they become real.

I'm sure you know what I mean. You wake up at three in the morning with cold chills about some dreaded outcome. You toss and turn for an hour, and it just gets worse, until the fear has become a monster looming above you, and you're pinned to the pillow.

When I wake up like that now, I know—having had many such sleepless nights—that it's best to get up, make a cup of tea, and deal with the fear directly. I sit in one chair (as a parent), and the fear is in the other chair (a frightened child). I talk to it and ask what it feels like. Then I sit in fear's chair and answer. The answer often surprises me, because it will speak from the depth of the feeling and reveal things I didn't know. Then I swap back—*yes, it does feel a little bit crazy*—and ask fear what it actually needs. Fear will always tell you what it needs if you're prepared to listen. Once I know what it needs—usually it includes reassurance, a reality check, and an action plan—we can agree what we need to do. And then I say, "Now we have a plan, we can go back to sleep, and in the morning, we'll do what we planned. Okay?" And we do.

The things I dread get fat on the fear I feed them. Then they become real.

Now what about anger? Anger is a powerful fuel, like gasoline. And like gasoline, if you spray it around and someone lights a match, there's an inferno. And that inferno, once lit, can burst into flames again and again over years. We know this from the grudges and revenge that erupt again and again in families.

It's anger that drives many of us who want to change the world; we're enraged by injustice, greed, and cruelty. But projecting out our anger onto "them"—the evil perpetrators of the injustice—is simply ineffective. I learned this in the early days of working to rid the world of nuclear weapons. I was driven by fury at the dangers that humanity was being exposed to, but if I spewed out my fury at the people making the decisions, it was not only entirely ineffective but also counterproductive. When attacked, people naturally defend themselves. They do not usually gasp and say, "Oh you're absolutely right!" So if you want to change the world, you need to keep your anger as fuel, well enclosed in an engine, so it can drive you forward, giving you the energy and courage you need.

I need to add a personal note here on the issue of inner violence—the critical forces within us that can crush our imagination and cripple our energy, that can shrivel our ideas and reduce us to helpless inaction. These are the forces we need to face and transmute, and it's a tough one for many people. From all I have read and heard from others, I believe most of us have these inner critics.

Finally, after decades of experimenting, I've found that when I ignore this critic or brush it off with faint reassurances to myself, it simply *gathers* force. However, when I take it in, listen to it, find out what it needs, and give it that as best I can—that's when the inner critic *loses* force.

Pema Chödrön, who is profiled in chapter 3, is an American Buddhist and the author of *When Things Fall Apart: Heart Advice for Difficult Times,* which has become a bible for living for millions of people. Her simple statements have helped me greatly:[10]

The most difficult times for many of us are the ones we give ourselves.

Rather than letting our negativity get the better of us, we could acknowledge that right now we feel like a piece of shit and not be squeamish about taking a good look.

So even if the hot loneliness is there, and for 1.6 seconds we sit with that restlessness when yesterday we couldn't sit for even one, that's the journey of the warrior.

Nothing ever goes away until it has taught us what we need to know.

If we run a hundred miles an hour to the other end of the continent in order to get away from the obstacle, we find the very same problem waiting for us when we arrive. It just keeps returning with new names, forms, manifestations until we learn whatever it has to teach us about where we are separating ourselves from reality, how we are pulling back instead of opening up, closing down instead of allowing ourselves to experience fully whatever we encounter, without hesitating or retreating into ourselves.

When I finally did this and opened up to the critic, I found I could develop a conversation with him. I asked him what he wanted. He replied impatiently that he'd been trying to get me to listen for years. He said he wanted me to be the best I could be. He wanted me to be braver, to achieve more.

I replied that he had an odd way of doing that, by constantly criticizing me! What about a bit of encouragement?

At that moment I realized that his voice was actually my father's voice. My father had an unspoken mantra: *Never mind the question, the answer is "work harder"!* During all my childhood, I tried to please my father, and it never seemed enough. And, before I could have a real conversation with him as an adult, he died, when I was eighteen. By that time, "you're not good enough!" had sunk deep into my psyche.

So in my thirties I realized it was this internalized parental message that I needed to address. Through many conversations with my image of my father, I realized that he did love me; he was simply too taken up with financial worries, depression, and the pain of heart disease to show it. Ultimately I arrived at an internal reconciliation with him. It was only then that I began to experience the positive aspects of his carping:

- His voice gets me out of bed in the morning.
- It makes me try again when I'm tired.
- It makes me do the work needed to get things done, even at midnight after a long day.

Nevertheless, I still have to watch out that he doesn't silence the feminine part of me that needs to find and trust her voice and the masculine part of me that has courage and a willingness to take risks.

SIGNPOST 4: Increasing Well-Being and Energy

When you're on a plane, the safety announcement tells you that if the oxygen masks drop down, you must put your own mask on before you help anyone else. That's pretty good advice for life. Why? Because if you want to be part of this vanguard of consciousness, you need well-being—you need to be extremely well in your being.

People can't give unless they're well nourished themselves. They need a daily supply vital energy, what in India they call *ojas*. In addition to the improved immune system and joie de vivre mentioned earlier, *ojas* brings new sources of energy, a lightness in your life, a clarity of mind, a sense of ease, and sparkling eyes.

We'd probably all like *ojas*. But the question is, how do you get it?

Well, exercise is essential. You are well able to work out what sort of exercise and what intensity level you like—though I would highlight that it's the small steps that make life beautiful, an "every moment possibility." And I'll leave it to your fitness guru to tell you what to do in a gym. Me, I like my exercise outside. Something happens when my feet touch the ground. Barefoot is best, but shoes are fine too—it's the contact with Mother Earth that matters. She nourishes us.

When I start out for a walk, my mind is usually buzzing, turning round and round some knotty problem of work or a relationship. But gradually, I become aware of color—pale yellow primroses, autumn leaves, a translucent evening sky. Then back I go into my mind to rehash the problem. But I'm interrupted by a blackbird, singing so generously that I can't help but stop and listen. Then my mind rushes back to THE PROBLEM for a while, until a scent wafts into my nose: wet earth, perhaps, or—if I'm lucky and it's July—the sweetness of a towering lime tree in blossom.

Slowly, without our hardly noticing it, the mind slows down and good sense seeps up. It does come up, out of the earth—a kind of balm that steadies us and grounds us. So that by the time an hour has passed—and it does take about an hour—we are larger.

And the problem is . . . er . . . well . . . what was the problem?

Same thing happens with growing vegetables. If you are lucky enough to have a garden or can beg, borrow, or steal a plot of earth, please grow things. Why? Because stuff you have nurtured yourself—sowed and watered and composted and harvested—tastes better than anything else on earth. And it is also better for you, because it hasn't lost 90 percent of its vitamins and minerals being flown around the world or trundled along highways.

My garden is the closest place to heaven that I know. It's an allotment in a walled garden that was built hundreds of years ago to grow fruit for the lord of the village where I live. So it's very sheltered, like a little wild oasis. When I first went there in 1996, it had been abandoned for years and was covered in brambles and nettles and docks, so I nearly wrecked my back digging and clearing every square foot that I wanted to grow things in. Thus I made the acquaintance of several cheeky blackbirds, who now come swooping down when they see the worm producer appear in her muddy boots and dirty old sweater.

Over the years, there has—I must admit—been a bit of mission creep. You might call it colonial expansion. I started with a few vegetables, and then a friend built me some raised beds—and that was a completely different thing altogether, because you don't really have to dig them. As long as you don't walk on them, the soil stays light and aerated. Then I got a beautiful curved bench as a birthday gift, which now sits at the end of the path, surrounded by old roses.

There's apple trees, pears, plums, and lots of raspberries. Currants I steal from neighboring gardeners, who have too many anyway. For a long time, I had a tattered old plastic poly tunnel, but then I invested in a little wooden greenhouse where I putter like *Peter Rabbit*'s Mr. McGregor. But we don't have rabbits, so my sadistic tendencies are reserved for slugs. I'm afraid I'm very nasty to slugs.

I have a seven-year-old boyfriend who seems to have a passion for gardening; he comes to plant seeds with me on his way back from the local primary school. He remembers absolutely everything I tell him. Often I don't remember. So when the second version is rubbish, he tells me off. We get along quite well like that.

A friend of mine says, "The information overload can be so distracting that I disconnect from my own inner self and can't read the emotions or the impulses that drive me. There is something about physicality, walking and thinking and gardening, that allows those reflections to become clear."

Working in this garden is balm for my soul. When I'm distressed or anxious, it's where I go. To have my feet in the earth simply brings me home. The wood smoke from the fire and the deep scent of the roses is what I want to breathe, when I stagger back from days of meetings in stuffy rooms in the city. I feel deeply blessed to have these times, when the chattering of my mind slowly yields to the songs of birds, and I actually notice the delight that surrounds me.

Any kind of exercise that makes you feel good is pure nourishment: yoga, dance, feasts and celebrations, martial arts, soccer, swimming, and, of course, sex. That's as long as the sexuality is really connected and not just some athletic performance or a copy of something you saw in a film.

Deep sensuality, on your own or with another person, can make you feel whole. Ancient Chinese masters said that any orgasm that may come your way can be more deeply enjoyed if directed up your spine and over your head to your third eye. In this way, it nourishes every part of you and even feeds your brain. Then you need to direct the energy back down to the lower chakras, whence it came. I think that, technically, it releases serotonin; anyway, it can make you feel astonishing. This is definitely *ojas*.

One other thing I would venture while we're on the subject of sensuality, is that *truth is erotic*. It goes like this. You and your partner are in serious disagreement about something. One of you suggests taking a half-hour off from the fight and sitting down opposite one another. Each thinks of a question he or she would like to be asked, like "What's going on in your heart?" or "What is your deepest longing right now." You ask your partner this question, thus: "Tell me, what's going on in your heart?" Your partner speaks for about five minutes, only in the first person and only about his or her deepest feelings or needs, getting to the deepest possible truth. You, meanwhile, do not respond at all, not even with nods of encouragement or grimaces; this is important, because a partner's response can subtly throw you off your truth. All you do is simply to give your partner full attention, listening carefully for the depth of feeling.

Then you change roles and do the same thing again.

People find that hearing a partner's truth—not his or her arguments or justifications—is deeply moving. No need to respond, just accept. As the process continues, you begin to see the nakedness of that person—and his or her reality. And that undefended realness cannot help but be appealing.

Now here's another kind of exercise: Write down ten things that bring you joy or that are really fun. And then do them all, as if you only had a few days to live.

I have to confess that when I was really busy saving the world, I found this almost impossible. My partner finally said to me, "You know, Scilla, you have no idea how to have a holiday." I was furious, mainly because it was true.

First, I was reluctant to plan any time off, in case I was needed for some lofty and essential task. Second, when he did manage to drag me off to a Greek island, I was preoccupied, if not actually irritable, for at least the first three days. Such are the addictions that the righteous can suffer from. Not any more. I'm a recovering workaholic, and I can't get enough holidays.

I'd like to add one more thing: love your own body. The media and the fashion world would like to keep us in a constant state of anxiety about what we look like. Models are stick-thin and anorexic and mostly seem to look arrogant, ill, or miserable. This is not a good image for any woman or man in the twenty-first century.

So I urge you to spend time every day appreciating your own self. Do it in whatever way appeals to you. Start with your best features and really go to town. Say to the mirror, "This nose is just exquisite!" or "Look how glossy my hair is today!" This can be quite a pleasant change from all the critical slaps we aim at ourselves—consistently, every day, monotonously. Just change the habit. Look for all the good stuff in yourself. Appreciate it deeply. Be grateful; it's your very own.

And you could even do what my friend Annie's ninety-four-year-old granny does every morning. She strips naked, stands in front of a full-length mirror, raises her arms, and shouts, "GOD, YOU'RE GORGEOUS!"

It works. You are.

SIGNPOST 5: Using Conflict as Opportunity

Most of us lose vast amounts of energy, not to mention sleep, by being embroiled in long-running personal conflicts—in the family or at work—that drain and exhaust us. We all know offices or organizations where vital amounts of energy go into feuds that sometimes run for weeks, draining everyone involved. Likewise, many people simply retreat from conflict because it feels overwhelming.

One of the first things to learn is that when you are facing conflict, this is precisely the time to advance rather than retreat. Moving *toward* conflict is the way into transformation. Conflict isn't good or bad; it's simply energy. As such, it does not have to be prevented or resolved, but transformed. I believe it's quite possible to imagine a world in which everyone learns to work with the energy of conflict and to use it to transform challenging situations. This is already happening in corporations and in whole countries, as we saw in the previous chapter. It's also happening in classrooms.

In a school in India, I have seen sixteen- to eighteen-year-olds fascinated to learn the simple yet profound skills of Nonviolent Communication (NVC).™[11] They learned how to listen and empathize with others, even when under pressure, and to identify the positive human needs that are longing to be fulfilled but are hidden behind hostile words or actions. This understanding, coupled with learning to express themselves without blame or judgment, enabled them to transform tricky interactions,

including some minor family feuds. Some even were able to pass on the learning to their parents! At this school, students are offered the chance to learn NVC, and the school is seeing some tangible results in the reduction of bullying and teasing.

NVC is based on the idea that all human beings have the capacity for compassion and only resort to violence or behavior that harms others when they don't recognize more effective strategies for meeting needs. The process has been steadily developed by Marshall Rosenberg since the 1960s.[12] NVC focuses on three aspects of communication:

- self-empathy—defined as a deep and compassionate awareness of one's own inner experience
- empathy—defined as listening to another with deep compassion
- honest self-expression—defined as expressing oneself authentically in a way that is likely to inspire compassion in others

In its initial development, the NVC model restructured the pupil-teacher relationship to give students greater responsibility for their learning and to allow them to make decisions related to it. The model has evolved over the years to incorporate institutional power relationships (i.e., police-civilian, boss-employee) and informal ones (i.e., man-woman, rich-poor, adult-youth, parent-child). The ultimate aim is to develop societal relationships based on a restorative paradigm of partnership and mutual respect rather than a retributive, fear-based paradigm of domination.[13]

The great thing is, it works. As we saw in chapter 6, young offenders in the favelas of Rio in Brazil, when taught NVC alongside Restorative Justice, cut their re-offending rate so dramatically that the Brazilian state juvenile justice system, as well as neighborhoods and schools, have taken up the practice.[14]

Empathy is the invisible hand. Empathy is what allows us to stretch our sensibility with another so that we can cohere in larger social units. To empathize is to civilize; to civilize is to empathies. . . . We have the technology that allows us to extend the central nervous system and to think viscerally as a family not just intellectually. When that earthquake hit Haiti, within an hour the Twitters came out and within two hours some cell phone videos, YouTube; and within three hours the entire human race was in a empathic embrace coming to the aid of Haiti. If we were, as the enlightenment philosophers suggested, materialistic, self-interested, utilitarian, pleasure seeking it couldn't account for the response to Haiti.[15]

A good way to learn empathy, which is an essential part of NVC, is through Transparent Communication.[16] When intense emotions are released in the course of dealing with another person, the responsibility remains with the speaker to lay no blame upon that person. He or she speaks only in the first person, thus accepting responsibility, not accusing, and expressing feelings and needs in a considerate and calm manner.

Transparent Communication allows the viewpoint to shift from the head ("I'm right and you're wrong") to the heart, where feelings can be sensed ("Ah, I see what this felt like for you"). A more connected, transpersonal point of view then ensues. Without this, we are bound to our own perspective and continue to view the world through our own eyes. With a transpersonal point of view, we look at things with a greater awareness. We perceive the world and ourselves not only from our narrow, personal point of view—because there is something greater that the self is aware of.[17]

The work of some of the great peace builders profiled in chapter 3 is useful here. Dekha Ibrahim Abdi learned what works and what doesn't in helping to resolve conflicts all over the world. She had a number of useful pointers:

- Humiliation is one of the main drivers of violence; the best antidote to humiliation is respect.
- Half of peace agreements fail unless peace builders follow up on the progress; it is essential that every stakeholder is engaged, even those with strong interests in keeping the conflict going.
- Listen carefully, without interrupting, to all involved in the conflict.

- Develop a personal interaction with each individual or group, in order to "feel the pain in each situation."
- When everyone feels their point of view is understood, work together with all parties to restore relations between victim and offender.
- Build local networks of trust that will be ready to activate in times of crisis.
- Draw your inner strength from trust in—and surrender to—a higher power.

Dekha also discovered that efforts to transform conflict sometimes generate brilliant technical advances. Their "cell phone + flipchart" methods to quell the 2008 post-election violence in Kenya were expanded by the brilliant *Ushahidi*—an open-source project that allows users to crowd-source crisis information sent in via cell phones.[18] This technology is now used in crisis situations all over the world.

To repeat: conflict isn't good or bad, it's simply energy. And as such, it does not have to be prevented or resolved, but transformed. In the appendix of this book, there's an exercise that enables two people in conflict to move from the head (being "right" and having a "position") to the heart (being connected and seeing what it's like to be the other person).

Nine hundred years ago, Rumi said it beautifully:

This being human is a guest house
Every morning a new arrival
A joy, a depression, a meanness,
Some momentary awareness comes as an unexpected visitor.
Welcome and entertain them all!
Even if they are a crowd of sorrows, who violently sweep your
     house empty of its furniture, still treat each guest honorably.
He may be clearing you out for some new delight.
The dark thought, the shame, the malice.
Meet them at the door laughing and invite them in.
Be grateful for whatever comes, because each has been sent as a
guide from beyond.

SIGNPOST 6: Doing Nothing

A successful, wealthy young couple went on holiday on a Caribbean island, staying in an ultra-luxe bungalow on a private jetty above a pellucid turquoise sea. By day, they kite-surfed or played tennis and swam; in the evenings, they dined on lobster and drank delicious French wines.

One day the husband strayed beyond the gates of the luxury complex and came upon a fisherman stretched out on the sand next to his boat, and they started chatting. By and by he asked the fisherman what he was doing.

"Nothing" said the fisherman.

"Are there no fish?"

"We have plenty of fish."

"You're clearly a clever man, why don't you contract with all the other fishermen to sell their fish, using your phone to get the best prices?"

"And then what?" asked the fisherman.

"Well, then you could make a lot of money and invest it."

"And then what?" asked the fisherman.

"Well, then you could buy a large house and a car and have wonderful holidays."

"What for?" asked the fisherman.

"Well, so you could relax!"

"But that's what I am doing."

The state of tension that we find normal in Western life is scarcely believable to those not hooked by our lifestyle. My own state of tension lies in a really ambitious goal, one that is deeply worthy and laudable on a global scale: *trying to beat my in-box*. As soon as I get near the bottom of it, it starts filling up again. I feel like a highly successful person if I can just empty it.

Part of my problem is the family mantra. It was never spoken, but it applied to absolutely every aspect of life: "Never mind the question, the answer is *work harder*." So I worked, and I worked. I think now there may be wiser ways to answer the question.

Taoism is a philosophical and religious tradition that emphasizes living in harmony with the Tao, which is translated as "way," "path," or "principle." Tao denotes something that is both the source and the driving force behind everything that exists. Its keystone work is the *Tao Te Ching*, a little book containing teachings attributed to Lao Tzu, who is believed to have lived in China between about 570 and 490 BCE.

One of Taoism's most important concepts is *wu wei*, which is sometimes translated as "non-doing" or "nonaction." To me, this means that instead of my attention being primarily focused on what I'm trying to achieve or do, it is focused instead on being aware of the situation I'm in, on being highly alert and conscious. On the rare occasions I manage this, it feels ultra-alive, giving me access to greater capacity for imagination and creativity.

> The gentlest thing in the world
> overcomes the hardest thing in the world.
> That which has no substance
> enters where there is no space.
> This shows the value of non-action.
>
> Teaching without words,
> performing without actions:
> that is the Master's way.[19]

I had a glimpse of this once in the Sinai Desert. The mountains there are like billowing, rounded clouds of sandstone, in ochre and peach and a soft milk-chocolate color. There are echoing, vaulted caves to shield you from the sun and the softest milk-white sand under your feet. The Bedouin in this area have such heightened senses that they can tell when someone approaches from a mile behind them. When it rains—on average once every five years—they dance.

I learned the value of spending time alone in the desert, as thousands have done before me for thousands of years. I would find a special spot—a ravine or a high ledge that simply beckoned. Spending several days there, quite alone with the stars and the occasional gerbil for company, I could let go and dream. I could forget who I think I am. If I stopped eating for a few days, I could revisit the sense of having no head, feeling full of lightness, heightened energy, and perspective.

Being alone—doing nothing—is sacred time. It's time when we can find out our own value, how much we are loved, without needing to depend on others. It's a rare chance to be just with yourself and not to be spoiled with noise and distraction. And certainly not by worrying about what other people think of you.

"One might think that an invitation to enter the stillness of nature is merely naïve romanticism that likes to indulge itself and escape from the cut and thrust of life into some narcissistic cocoon. This invitation to friendship with nature does of course entail a willingness to be alone out there. Yet this aloneness is anything but lonely. Solitude gradually clarifies the heart until a true tranquility is reached. The irony is that at the heart of that aloneness you feel intimately connected with the world. Indeed, the beauty of nature is often the wisest balm for it gently relieves and releases the caged mind."[20]

SIGNPOST 7: Allowing Imagination and Creativity to Flourish

It is when the mind goes quiet that our imagination has a chance.

That's when we can dream. That's when the visionary in us all can breathe. I imagine this visionary as powerful and alight, her right eye looking forward, over the horizon, and her left eye covered with a black patch, allowing that eye to look inward. She sees the future as a lift-off into life *as it could be*—right out of the ordinary and away from what we already know.

Google cofounder Larry Page's original inspiration for the renowned search engine came to him at age twenty-three in a dream that gave him the idea for the site-ranking feature. Says Page:

You know what it's like to wake up in the middle of the night with a vivid dream? And you know how, if you don't have a pencil and pad by the bed to write it down, it will be completely gone the next morning? Well, I had one of those dreams when I was 23. When I suddenly woke up, I was thinking: What if we could download the whole web, and just keep the links and. . . . I grabbed a pen and started writing! Sometimes it is important to wake up and stop dreaming. I spent the middle of that night scribbling out the details and convincing myself it would work. . . . Much later we happened upon a better way of ranking web pages to make a really great search engine, and Google was born. When a really great dream shows up, grab it![21]

About dreams, Jonathan Sacks, the Chief Rabbi of the United Kingdom, wrote, "Dreams are where we visit the many lands and landscapes of human possibility and discover the one where we feel at home. The great religious leaders were all dreamers. . . . One of the greatest speeches of the 20th century was Martin Luther King's 'I have a dream.' If I were to design a curriculum for happiness, dreaming would be a compulsory course."[22]

His other compulsion for life is, *follow your passion*. And I agree with him. So many people sweat away at well-paid careers to enable themselves and their families to buy whatever they want, only to find themselves feeling empty and bereft in the midst of "success." What they say they miss is meaning in their lives. By contrast, those who are clear enough about what matters to them are the ones who "follow their bliss"—they may not be as rich or famous as others, but their lives seem touched by magic.

I suppose I must have an built-in career saboteur, because at key times

I follow a hunch—something that I HAVE to do—which throws a hand grenade into my curriculum vitae. Imagine this: I start a research group that labors mightily over thirteen years to develop an excellent reputation as a reliable publisher of factual reports on security issues. I complete a serious doctorate on nuclear weapons decision making. I am trusted to host meetings where nuclear policy makers meet with critics with whom they totally disagree. And then what do I do? In 1996, write a highly personal book entitled *Power and Sex: A Book about Women,* which contains quite a lot about serpents, sexuality, and inner power. To the launch party, I invited two enormous Burmese pythons. They rather divided the party into those who have a fascination with serpents and those who do not.

Publishing this book may have—temporarily—sabotaged my reputation as a serious authority on defense issues, but the effort of thinking seriously about issues of power not only deepened my subsequent political work but also liberated my creative imagination and my sense of self. The book describes how, to be effective in the world, we need to develop inner power. And inner power comes through inner investigation—getting to know who we are, what we're like—warts and all—and what we're here for. And one of the ways to do that is through inner reflection or meditation. It can produce remarkable results in terms of outer effectiveness.

I had got an inkling of this when I was in East Mostar in the midst of the Bosnian War in 1994. More than one hundred women from all over the world had come in a convoy of buses to try to bring relief and support to the people of Sarajevo, about seventy-five miles northeast of Mostar. In order to get there, we had to get permits to go through the armies surrounding Sarajevo. To get the permits, three of us had to edge our way across a single wire cable across the Neretva River to get into East Mostar and find our way through the bombed-out city to the War Presidency. This building was guarded by soldiers with automatics, who refused entry. Because I couldn't understand what was being said by my two courageous Bosnian friends, I simply stood there.

Then I thought, *why not meditate?*

What immediately came into my mind's eye was a red rose.

Sentimental I thought.

But there it was again.

So I mentally put the rose in the heart of the hefty soldier guarding the door. At that point, his face broke into a smile, and he let us in. To this day, I do not know how much that had to do with the rose, and how much it had to do with what my Bosnian friends were saying to him. But while they went in to see the military commander, I sat in the anteroom with his secretary in silence. Suddenly she disappeared and then returned with her hand behind her back. Then she handed me three red roses. Where she got them in that devastated city, I shall never know. Then my friends came out, joyfully clutching the permits, and the convoy was able to reach Sarajevo.

SIGNPOST 8: Going into the Shadow and the Energy That Comes from It

Knowing your own darkness is the best method for dealing with the darkness of other people.

The best political, social, and spiritual work we can do is to withdraw the projection of our shadow onto others.

—Carl Jung

For the majority of people in the world today, life is a constant struggle; at the very least, it is unsatisfying and devoid of meaning. We live in dark times, times of enormous insecurity as financial systems collapse, weather patterns frighten us, violence increases, and governments appear unable to bring about the holy grail of economic growth. So, as in all great historical shifts, we are being obliged—or offered the opportunity—to change.

We can resist change—and possibly perish—or we can transform. Of key importance to the process of transformation is a willingness to enter the shadow areas, the darkest issues that are often considered "too much." This process has to start inside us, as individuals.

All of us have dark places in ourselves and in our past that we would prefer not to look at. But it is only by daring to go into those places that we can be liberated. In fact, it is in those terrifying places that we can

find the gemstone of truth—the jewel under the dragon's foot. "The cave you fear to enter holds the treasure you seek."[23]

The dragon or serpent is a key figure in myth and legend, often shown terrorizing kingdoms or being slain by a hero. There is, however, a different way of dealing with its awesome power, and that is to work with it. If we can summon the courage to approach this extraordinary force—however it manifests in our lives—and open a dialogue with it, it can become a formidable ally. The serpent is a change agent extraordinaire, a visionary, a force for the future. And a massive source of energy.

Whatever you resist, persists. Whatever you fight, you strengthen. When civilian dissent erupted in Syria in 2011, initially a nonviolent revolution similar to that in Tahrir Square in Cairo, Egypt, the government saw it as a monster and tried to kill it by force. The result was an infinitely more dangerous scenario, leading to civil war and over one hundred thousand deaths.

Andrew Harvey says that there may be a certain satisfaction in the public denunciation of corrupt corporations, what Robert Kennedy called "systems of cold evil" that keep exploiting the earth. But he says that this response has two main disadvantages in practical affairs. One, the excitement of projecting your own unacknowledged darkness onto others keeps you from seeing just how implicated you are. Secondly:

Advocating for any cause in this spirit virtually ensures your efforts will increase resistance rather than heal. Human beings will never be convinced to change their ways by other human beings who try to humiliate them. In nearly every case, such condemnation only reinforces the behavior it is trying to end. When people are accused of acts they know they are guilty of, by others who have contempt for them, they almost always retreat even further into their self-destructive behavior. If they do change, it is from fear or perhaps hypocrisy, but not from their own truth.[24]

THINGS WILL GET HOT

Many people think that the changes the world is going through are like an alchemical process. In alchemy, the vessel has to heat for the elements to change; in human terms, we have to enter the dark places in order eventually to emerge reborn.

We need not fear this. The sages of the world all say that the secret is to walk toward whatever is "too much." It might be a long-running family feud; it might be a fear of rejection; it might be illness or death; or it might be the damage being inflicted on the planet. To fend it off, avoid it, or stick our heads in the sand will simply make things worse.

> Such moments bring our world to a sudden stop. They may be terrifying, but they also constitute a great blank space that can be filled in one of two ways: by freezing and reverting to the patterns of the past, or by opening up to the highest future possibilities.[25]

All cultures know about this and have symbols to help people confront what is "too much." In India, it is the dark Kali with the skulls of children round her waist. The world's literature is filled with accounts of journeys into the depths: Dante's descent into the inferno, Odysseus's journey to the gates of Hades, Jonah's days and nights in the belly of the whale, Persephone's descent into the Underworld. Bob Dylan sang: "It's not dark yet, but it's getting there." Each of us is asked at some point to go down into the darkness, to face our fears, to acknowledge and own the darker aspects of the self—and in this way to be renewed.[26]

Go down. Face it—face despair, danger, terror—the state of blacker-than-black chaos. See what is to be learned. Come through. "We have not even to risk the adventure alone; for the heroes of all time have gone before us, the labyrinth is fully known; we have only to follow the thread of the hero-path. And where we had thought to find an abomination, we shall find a god; where we had thought to slay another, we shall slay ourselves; where we had thought to travel outward, we shall come to the centre of our own existence; where we had thought to be alone, we shall be with all the world."[27]

There is a point to darkness. Although it can be frightening when you are in it, you come out changed. You lose hubris; you gain compassion. You become more useful, because you understand more of the terrors that afflict others. You may also learn one of the great secrets of survival: *that things change*. Everything changes, all the time.

On one occasion I was asked to give a briefing on Burma to a distinguished group of political leaders. My briefing proposed that China or India could play a role in enabling a resolution to the house arrest of

Aung San Suu Kyi. This upset the Chinese minister, who raised his voice in protest.

By this time, I was meditating regularly. Having taken several delegations to China on nuclear weapons business, I had become familiar with Chinese philosophy, especially the exceptional wisdom of the *Tao Te Ching*. I had also discovered the power of Kwan Yin—the Divine Feminine within Buddhism.

I went to bed that evening paralyzed with anxiety that the Chinese would pull out of the group, that this would be an international incident, and that it would be my fault. So I meditated, deep in desperation. I called to Kwan Yin for help. She communicated that I should be calm and go to sleep and that I should take my small image of her with me to the meetings the next day.

I still remember my sigh of relief when I saw the Chinese minister take part the next day. After the meetings, I was walking up a flight of steps as he was coming down. He frowned at the sight of this troublesome woman. I walked up to him with the picture of Kwan Yin in my hand and asked him, "Do you know this lady?" He stepped back and cried out in excitement, "It's Kwan Yin! She is so dear to us in China." He then ordered an aide to take from his bag a volume of poetry that he had written and dedicated the book to me on the spot.

This experience gave me the final nudge to trust that there is a far greater intelligence than ours at work in the world. When things look black, if we can simply get quiet enough to listen to that intelligence, things fall into place in ways we could never have imagined.

The Master doesn't talk, he acts.
When his work is done,
the people say,
"Amazing: we did it,
all by ourselves!"

SIGNPOST 9: Learning How to Serve, Moving from "Me" to "We"

Why is it worth investing time in discovering ourselves?

On one level, it's simple: we can live our lives based on trust rather than fear.

We learn to believe in our dreams and instincts.

We have the freedom to experience a richer inner life.

It makes us more confident.

It enables us to be with difficult people without getting upset.

It gives us a different kind of strength.

Being peaceful inside clears the mind and makes space for inspiration.

It helps us to be clear about our values.

And furthermore, real peace lies in the realization that we are all infinitely greater than this small self whom we take ourselves to be. That self is tiny compared to who we really are.

Nelson Mandela went to jail in 1963 believing that violence was necessary to change the apartheid system in South Africa. Quite soon after he arrived on Robben Island to serve a life sentence, he realized that meeting the violence of the warders with more violence was useless and that there were other far more powerful ways to deal with injustice.

He and his colleagues began to treat their incarceration as "our university"; they taught each other subjects like mathematics, literature, and history in whispers as they worked in the quarries. After many years, they were able to get books, and later they were allowed to take correspondence courses. The warders, many of whom were barely literate, became curious. The prisoners ended up teaching the warders so they also could get a degree.

To do this required, as you can imagine, a vast transformation. What people nearly always miss when they imagine such situations is that this transformation has to happen in the inner depths of an individual. In Mandela's case, this involved a total reversal in the way he approached the oppressor.

During his twenty-seven years in prison, Mandela had hours and hours to reflect in silence. He could have become deeply depressed—and at times, naturally, he was. But as time wore on, he assembled knowledge of how the human mind works—and the human heart as well. He began to understand not only his own reactions but also those of others, as is clear from the accounts of his imprisonment.[28] By the time he left Robben Island, he had a profound knowledge of who he was and who he was meant to be.[29]

This, his personal truth, enabled him to be deeply compassionate in his understanding of others. For example, on Robben Island, the prisoners' diet was very poor. Mandela repeatedly requested a piece of land on which to grow vegetables. After many refusals, eventually he was allowed a small, stony patch of earth. He dug out the rocks, made compost to enrich the soil, and sowed seeds. The prisoners watched hungrily as the first zucchinis and tomatoes ripened. But Mandela knew what must be done with the first produce: he gave the fresh tomatoes and zucchinis to the warders.

It was this hard-learned skill of responding to negativity with generosity and compassion that gave him the mastery he needed when he was released in 1989, with the mission to lead South Africa into the difficult era of reconciliation. He insisted on negotiations, rather than confrontation, with the white government, against the wishes of those leaders of the African National Congress who had not been imprisoned. He and his colleagues from Robben Island had honed the patience, forbearance, and understanding needed to undertake the transition from one of the most oppressive and vicious governments the world has known to democratic elections—and to manage this largely without violence, avoiding the civil war that many observers had feared would slaughter millions.

So what do we learn from Mandela? What can we not learn? His greatest lesson is that when you uncover the calm magnificence of your own inner strength, there is nothing you can't accomplish.

Mandela's genius was to so transcend his own ego and pain that he could enter into the shoes of those who opposed him. It was this humane genius that inspired him, after he became president, to put on a Springbok rugby shirt during the Rugby World Cup in 1995. Rugby had always been a game reserved for whites and was despised by blacks. But in 1995 the newly democratic South Africa hosted the tournament, which is now remembered as a watershed moment in the postapartheid nation-building process. Why? Because when Mandela presented the trophy to white captain Francois Pienaar, he wore the Springbok shirt—a symbol of unity and a profound, intuitive gesture that helped to heal the bitter wounds of racial division at a deeper level than any written agreement.

FROM "ME" TO "WE"

If your consciousness is the size of a golf ball, then your perception of your world will be the size of a golf ball, and likewise the way you deal with your life. If you can expand your consciousness to a larger dimension, then your perception of your world will be larger, and the way you deal with your life, wiser.

Eckhart Tolle goes much further. He says that the ego identifies with having things, and that the thought forms of "me" and "mine," of "I want," "I need," "I must have," and "not enough" demonstrate the structure of the ego.

> As long as you don't recognize these thought forms within your-self, as long as they remain unconscious, you will believe in what they say; you will be condemned to acting out those unconscious thoughts, condemned to seeking and not finding—because when those thought forms operate, no possession, place, person or condition will ever satisfy you. No matter what you have or get, you won't be happy. You will always be looking for something else that promises greater fulfillment, that promises to make your incomplete sense of self complete and fill that sense of lack you feel within.[30]

This kind of self-awareness is the path to freedom. Not only that, but it leads to fulfillment, the feeling that you have enough and that you *are* enough. This is a crucial stage in moving from a constant state of scarcity (in which we think, *there's not enough to go round so we must grab some*) to a feeling of abundance.

The feeling that there is enough is very relaxing. The feeling that you *are* enough is pure joy. And when people relax, they are more inclined to share, which makes it possible to entertain the idea that what really matters in life is not so much "me" as "us." The consequence is that a person becomes more aware of the community and ultimately of the planet. I believe the sequence goes something like this:

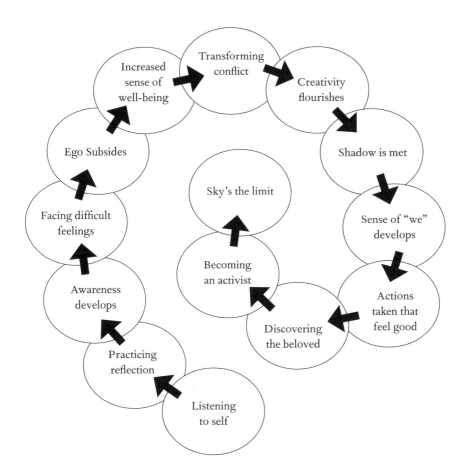

Of course, this is not linear and straightforward. It's more like the flow of a stream, with twists and turns. Some might say it's more like a spiral; you keep coming back to the same place, except at a slightly different plane.

In this need for people to move from "me" to "us" in order to become aware of the needs of the planet, I'm referring to Western culture. Most indigenous cultures have a built-in awareness of the state of the earth and feel akin to and part of the natural world. Many Eastern cultures have a far greater sense of community than we have in the West and a lesser sense of the importance of "I," but that is changing as globalization spreads Western values.

"The quality of our consciousness shapes the context of our leadership. Authentic leaders ask themselves questions to awaken wisdom and expand awareness: What is the quality of my consciousness as I create and externalize reality? Am I a victim of habitual mental patterns of perception and reactive ways of action, or am I truly open, responsive, and creative? Am I seeing and acting from fear, isolation, and urgency; or from the deep still source of clear awareness?"[31]

So it is all the more important that leading thinkers, politicians, business executives, and bloggers grow into self-awareness and, with it, a sense of global responsibility. This is one of the meanings of the term *servant leadership* that is beginning to spread. Leaders are not normally thought of as servants, so the term has a powerful resonance. From my perspective it's powerful because it replaces the sense of arrogance or superiority that can accompany the notion of a leader, and replaces it with the image of someone who is "in service to" a greater cause, having developed a sense of responsibility.

Oprah Winfrey came to believe that "each of us has a personal calling that's as unique as a fingerprint—and that the best way to succeed is to discover what you love and then find a way to offer it to others in the form of service, working hard, and also allowing the energy of the universe to lead you."

When Caroline Myss was writing *Invisible Acts of Power,* she did a mailing on her website asking people "What does the concept of service mean to you?" She received over 1,200 responses, which, she said, "broke my heart wide open." She continued, "I think it's because I had the realization for the first time of how profoundly powerful the force of love, generosity, compassion, kindness and the non-judging heart really is. . . . The more I read these stories, the more I thought: 'Do human beings have any idea what power they have at all?' . . . and then I realized that that is the soul, and we don't see that power because it is so profoundly humble."[32]

Myss investigated why people were drawn to be of service after surviving a crisis. "These people no longer wanted to take from life; they wanted to give to life. That fascinated me. Something had shifted their interior compass . . . an entirely new interior alchemy that was lying dormant before, combining gratitude for their own survival, an appreciation for the simple things of life, and a genuine awareness that the meaning and purpose they were searching for in life was to be found in improving the lives of others.[33]

The key thing is that your work is supported by a daily practice of reflection and inner listening, as investigated in signpost 2. This daily practice is as vital as training is for an athlete. Why? Because the world work that is needed from us now is as challenging as the Olympics; therefore, we need to be as fit—emotionally and spiritually—as Olympic athletes.

Servant leadership is an ancient philosophy—one that existed long before Robert Greenleaf coined the term in modern times.[34] There are passages that relate to servant leadership in the *Tao Te Ching*, attributed to Lao Tzu:

> The Master doesn't talk, he acts.
> When his work is done,
> the people say, "Amazing:
> we did it, all by ourselves!"[35]

SIGNPOST 10: Discovering the Beloved, Becoming Able to Ask, "What Can I Give?"

No one has ever become poor by giving.

—Anne Frank

Now we're coming to the culmination of the journey to self, which enables you to realize who you really are—no less. This is the juiciest part. But it's also the hardest part to write about, because it's about discovering the Beloved *within ourselves*.

In Western culture, children are often taught that it's wrong to love yourself—that you will become "big-headed," "uppity," "too full of yourself." But what we're talking about here is not about inflation or thinking you're the greatest or believing your own press releases. This is about becoming acquainted with your highest potential, about getting to know

what some people call your "Higher Self" or even your soul's purpose. It's a sacred and quite private business.

Time to call in the specialists. Deepak Chopra recognizes Barbara Marx Hubbard as "the voice for conscious evolution of our time." As president of the Foundation for Conscious Evolution, she writes that all of us, every one, has within us a deeper, wiser, all-knowing self. She calls this the "Essential Self" that is communicating with us all the time. Sometimes we hear it, sometimes we don't, but it is never really silent.

Hubbard suggests we set aside time to sit quietly every day, using any centering practice that works to quiet the mind. "I strongly advocate cultivating an inner receptivity, an inner listening and attunement to the signals of the Essential Self. These intuitions are the way the deeper self informs us and guides us."

I followed her instructions and I found a vital element of the inner world that I had not known before.[36] By putting attention on my Essential Self, focusing on it and writing about it, I established direct contact with it. "Everyone has within a deeper, wise, all-knowing self."[37] As she suggested, I started writing sentences as this inner voice and was surprised and intrigued by what emerged. I began to identify and understand the intelligence of what was available, but the wisdom that began to appear was certainly not coming from my previously existing state of consciousness.

I would often lose contact with the Essential Self, but whenever I came back into contact with it, I felt smoothed out, loving, and surprised to find I was smiling—and I breathed out sighs of relief. I felt relief was because I felt safe, as if "known"—and not always having to strive to be good enough. My body felt warm and very joyful.

I notice that I wrote that in the past tense, but that's not accurate. These feelings are just sitting there, available, all the time. We simply need to develop what Hubbard calls "the habit of a poised mind." "I know that all of us have this inner voice. It is the Higher Self, the Essential Self, within each of us—and it is communicating with us all the time."[38]

Did I experience difficulty getting into that place? Did I ever. My mind wanted to jump all over the place and think clever thoughts. But after a bit of practice, the warmth and flow came through after about twenty minutes, and then progressively I could access it more easily.

Images of the different aspects of this Essential Self became clear, and those images provided a way in. When I'm in that state, I feel authentic and forget the constant need to impress. I stop trying to "help." I have high stamina and energy. Life feels delicious, like sucking on the sweetness of a ripe peach. Hubbard again: "My sense was of a magnificent presence, far beyond my current personality or gender. What I now experienced was a full range of attractive and familiar qualities of the Beloved that had been flickering at the edges of my consciousness all these years."[39]

> The minute I heard my first love story,
> I started looking for you, not knowing
> how blind that was.
> Lovers don't finally meet somewhere,
> they're in each other all along.[40]

At this stage of the journey, you are accessing your capacity to be a visionary. This means you can be free enough from the necessities and issues of your life to have space to allow your own intuition about how the future could be.

SIGNPOST 11: Becoming a Sacred Activist

A sacred activist is someone who fuses in his or her being profound spiritual intelligence, peace, and passion with a commitment to clear, wise, radical action in the world.

Here's where the servant leader of signpost 9 meets the activist, so dear to my heart. Activists are energized, highly motivated, engaging people. They get things done. They can also be driven by a long list of musts, oughts, and shoulds—and perennially be desperate to meet the deadline of saving the world. That deadline can be, as I know full well, self-imposed.

Activists can easily climb onto the moral high ground. I know it like the back of my hand. From our anguish and fury at what others have done to the planet or its people, we can go into accuse mode, go on the attack, do battle. It feels rather gloriously "right." The ego absolutely loves it. While that approach may sometimes be a useful as a wake-up call or in rallying others to the cause, ultimately, it can be counterproductive. Why? Because those with the power to change policy tend to do that faster and more profoundly *if they see the point.*

That's where dialogue comes in—and the difference between dialogue and lobbying. *Dialogue* means learning about the responsibilities of the person making the policy you wish to see changed, then sitting down face-to-face with that person and listening.[41] It means listening to him or her with sufficient openness that you could change your own mind. This is deeply challenging but essential if you want that other person to listen to what you have to say with sufficient openness that they could change their mind.

When policy makers are engaged with their hearts as well as their heads in your proposed change, they will likely become your allies and work with you on a strategy that can be effective. They'll have energy for the change, instead of trying to subvert it.

GANDHI

Gandhi was insistent that for someone to live a sacred life, they should treat everyone else equally and not ask someone to do something they wouldn't be prepared to do themselves. He applied this to everybody in his community and every task, including cleaning the toilets. In India, with its traditional hierarchical caste system, this was revolutionary. Even today, only lower castes do the work of street cleaning, garbage collection, and cleaning public toilets.

When it came to Mrs. Gandhi's turn to clean the public toilets of the community, as a high caste Indian, she refused to do so. Their struggle of wills was difficult for both. Eventually Mrs. Gandhi agreed to clean the community toilets and ultimately even came to view the task as a sacred act. As Gandhi said, "The best way to find yourself, is to lose yourself in the service of others."

The first sentence of this chapter talked about waking up to your own energetic potential. These signposts along the path give you the potential to take part in building a positive future—to help take the necessary actions to resolve the problems we humans have created on the planet.

SIGNPOST 12: **What about Failure and Disappointment?**

When I was working with the Do School fellows in Hamburg, somebody asked me, "How do you manage to work with these topics without breaking your heart?" What I feel is that your heart does break, but does that matter? The best place to act from may be a broken heart; it's only through the cracks that the light shines in.

In the business of pioneering the possible it is inevitable that we will risk failure. That's part of the job description. Once, in a moment of despair, I made a long list of my defeats and disappointments, which included:

1. The "Peace and Security Assessment Report" completed for Fetzer Foundation; never published.
2. A series of illustrated children's stories about the deep questions children ask; not produced.
3. A detailed course developed with the Said Business School in Oxford to offer a Leadership Program for Conflict Transformation in the Middle East; turned down.
4. "The Time Is Now"—a screenplay for a drama set in the Middle East involving kidnap, terror, and the eventual convergence on Jerusalem of sacred activists, written with three dear colleagues in 2008; not accepted by any producer or scriptwriter we approached.
5. A report on "Smart Power" prepared for the International Task Force on Preventive Diplomacy; never published.
6. The "Initiative for Military Reorganization in Europe": in 2010 I persuaded a donor to loan funds to a German ex-military man to make a television program on redirecting military forces to crisis response and relief work. He never repaid her, nor paid me for any of my work on the project.
7. Outline for a television program on the potential contribution of feminine wisdom to the survival of humanity; presented to two producers, but not accepted.

8. I persuaded a donor to make a substantial bridging loan to the initiator of the World Peace Festival in Berlin. The loan was not repaid, the planned concert never materialized, and my team of eight were not paid for three months' work.

There were many more. Then I thought, *let them go.* I drank a glass of wine to them and to myself, for daring, for being willing to take risks. Pioneers take risks.

What I've learned from this is to celebrate my defeats. Can I persuade you to have a party when things go pear-shaped? There's a monster called "results" who has to be put in his place; he does *not like* celebrations of failure. You'll find that if you do celebrate the risks you took, you will be given the energy and humor to keep on trucking. You might even release yourself from the most insidious of all saboteurs—the need to have our own private agenda ratified immediately. Don't forget that Gandhi took thirty years to remove the British Empire from India.

What is quite clear to me now, after seven decades on this planet, is that anyone who looks over the horizon, who envisions possibility, and who has the nerve to act on that potential is bound to have failures. You're ahead of the curve, and you will not necessarily be welcomed with open arms and applause. The failures may be devastating at the time, but you learn from each one.

Another vital element of being a pioneer is the cultivation of radical patience. The Koran says that God is with the patient. What a pioneer needs is a paradoxical inner marriage of tremendous urgency and an equally powerful patience. For fifty years, the Dalai Lama has been working tirelessly for the freedom of his people against crushing odds. He has been defeated again and again but has never lost his persistence or his passion.

Ours is not the task of fixing the entire world all at once, but of stretching out to mend the part of the world that is within our reach. Any small, calm thing that one soul can do to help another soul, to assist some portion of this poor suffering world, will help immensely. It is not given to us to know which acts or by whom, will cause the critical mass to tip toward an enduring good.

What is needed for dramatic change is an accumulation of acts, adding, adding to, adding more, continuing. We know that it does not take everyone on Earth to bring justice and peace, but only a small, determined group who will not give up during the first, second, or hundredth gale.

One of the most calming and powerful actions you can do to intervene in a stormy world is to stand up and show your soul. Soul on deck shines like gold in dark times. The light of the soul throws sparks, can send up flares, builds signal fires, causes proper matters to catch fire. To display the lantern of soul in shadowy times like these—to be fierce and to show mercy toward others; both are acts of immense bravery and greatest necessity.[42]

SIGNPOST 13: **Find What You *Really* Want to Do**

The more you get on your true path—the route your soul has in mind for you—the more you will know the rightness of it. You'll know because your energy changes. As this happens, your fundamental orientation in life also changes. You are much less distracted or knocked off course by outer circumstances—much more fuelled by a deep inner drive, even urgency.

Things start to come to you in mysterious ways. Things flow. You're excited. It's in some sense familiar to you—and to your body too. Your bearing will change, because you will be inhabiting *all* of yourself, and people will see that. You will gradually discard the old disguises ("I'm too important for that!" "I'm not good enough." "I can't possibly do that." "Don't they know who I *am*?") and become real.

Only very few of us have this sense of self from the day they're born. Most of us have to edge our way toward it, deeper and deeper throughout our life. But as you recognize yourself and your particular challenge in this life, when you "know what you're doing," your stature will convey that. You won't have to build influence, because you will possess it. You will be authentic. And the *extent* of your influence will correlate directly with the *depth* of your authenticity and your integrity.

A QUESTION FOR YOU FROM A NOBEL LAUREATE:

Will you be at the harvest,
Among the gatherers of new fruits?

Then you must begin today to remake
Your mental and spiritual world,
And join the warriors and celebrants
Of freedom, realizers of great dreams.
You can't remake the world
Without remaking yourself.
Each new era begins within.
It is an inward event,
With unsuspected possibilities
For inner liberation.
We could use it to turn on
Our inward lights.
We could use it to use even the dark
And negative things positively.
We could use the new era
To clean our eyes,
To see the world differently,
To see ourselves more clearly.
Only free people can make a free world.
Infect the world with your light.
Help fulfill the golden prophecies.
Press forward the human genius.
Our future is greater than our past.[43]

CHAPTER 8

RECIPE FOR IMAGINING A WORLD THAT WORKS FOR YOU

Professor Sir Joseph Rotblat, the only nuclear physicist to leave the Manhattan Project on the grounds of conscience, said that "the future belongs to those who can see it."

In this chapter you will find some clues—some images of the future—that are a lift-off into life *as it could be*. They are possibilities to inspire you, some ideas to start the imaginative juices flowing. Explore the ideas that arise in you from those presented here. Allow your imagination to roam freely and shift you right out of the ordinary and what you already know.

In Martin Luther King's "I Have a Dream" speech, all the pictures he painted were doable. We are not interested in impossible wish lists, but we are very interested in your imagination. This chapter offers you a process to free your mind and heart in order to open up your own visionary capacity and imagine—in a field that interests you—a better future.

I believe that everyone has a secret visionary inside, longing to be invited out to play and dance. A visionary is a futurist who can see over the horizon and conceive what's possible. A visionary has the capacity to inspire other people, enable them to disentangle from the restrictions of everyday life, and enter the fresh world of *what could be*. One image of a visionary is someone whose right eye looks far over the horizon and whose left eye looks inward, deep into the human capacity for transformation.

You can never change things by fighting the existing reality. To change something, build a new model that makes the existing model obsolete.

—Buckminster Fuller

Childhood and Education

The current education system was designed to create a work force for jobs during the industrial revolution. Many of these jobs do not exist any more, as they have been eclipsed by robotics and computers. Being trained to arrive on time, do what you're told, believe what you hear, behave yourself, sit still for the lesson, and engage whether you're interested or not—all this has little value now.

Schooling in the future will be very different. It will not be necessary to learn facts simply to be endlessly tested, preparing desperately to pass exams in order to compete for a vanishing number of jobs. Education will involve acquiring the life skills and insight needed for a fast-changing world—and doing so in ways that intrigue children and release natural creativity.

Offering studies that encourage children's passion, putting them in a group with differing skills and ages, so that they help and are helped, will get the creative juices to flow. It can ignite the desire to learn and move the students from dependence to interdependence.[1] Learning will be about creation, performing, thinking across subjects, and exploring ideas through images, sounds, songs, dances, and artistic expression. In this way, children become "myriad minded"—conscious participants in their own unfolding.[2] Certainly they will continue to read, write, and analyze, but they will also encouraged to imagine, dream, and expand the limits of the possible.

So much of the failure in today's schools stems from boredom, which arises from the current system's failure to stimulate those *wonder areas* in a child's brain that give her so many ways of responding to the world. That boredom is what leads to teenage addictions and other problems, as seen in the epidemic of alcoholism, especially among teenage girls in the United Kingdom.

From a very early age, children understand the power of compassion, and they learn quickly how to sense when their heart is open and when it contracts. Suppose small children learned quietness or some form of reflection or mindfulness as part of their day? When children are taught meditation, their concentration increases and hyperactivity declines in line with their self-awareness. The Dalai Lama says that if all children were taught to meditate, violence would be wiped out in a generation.

Imagine if all school children were taught nonviolent communication (NVC, discussed in chapter 7) as part of their primary education. This would mean, for example, that they would immediately be able to deal with bullying in the school playground. Not only would they be able to transform conflict in the classroom and in the home, they would have invaluable skills for life, and they could—as they already do—teach their parents.

A good way for children to learn empathy, which is an essential part of NVC, is through Transparent Communication.³ Once we begin to comprehend the inner experiences of others, we make a quantum leap in our communication, because we can feel each other from the inside and know each other directly. Children are naturally open to this. If it becomes a habit early in life, it helps people discover the true cause of a conflict, looking beyond the symptoms to the root of the problem. This level of *inner*-connectedness can help to awaken our humanity and lift communication up to the next level of evolution.

One of the life skills children love to learn is how to be self-sufficient. The concept of Forest Schools has spread virally all over Europe, inspiring teachers to take kids into local woodlands to learn how to use a knife safely, how to identify birds and animals, how to build a shelter, and how to recognize the seasons. Imagine if we took these ideas further:

- At school and at home, children learn how to make compost and grow tasty vegetables and fruit, even in a tiny garden or on a balcony. They learn how good vegetables taste raw. They learn how to harvest them and store them.
- They become fascinated by building gutters and tanks to collect rainwater to use when there is drought or if the municipal supply is contaminated.
- If they want to eat fish, they learn how to set up a small fish farm in their community, sharing the daily maintenance with other children.

- If they like eggs, they learn to raise chickens, accepting the daily routines of feeding, watering, cleaning the hen house, and shutting up the hens at night so the fox doesn't get them.
- They learn how to live simply and nourish themselves and their families. This is a challenge that children thrive on, because they feel useful, and they learn how to cook, rather than relying on processed foods.

In the future there will be little formal employment as we know it today, so teenagers will develop the skills of social entrepreneurs. They will learn how to set up and run small enterprises that serve their community and provide some income for themselves and a small team. For example, in an area of London still plagued by knife crime, there is a teenager who has set up a multilingual drama group that engages gang members to develop short plays on how to resolve disputes without violence. Her work and that of her team is funded by the local council, because it cuts crime and police time.

Her friend Jacob has set up a computer literacy club in a deprived area in Nairobi; he got in touch with a redistribution center in United Kingdom that acquires high-quality secondhand computers no longer needed by companies that have upgraded their systems; this center supplied him with ten computers at no cost. Jacob teaches local at-risk youth to use email and the internet which helps them set up their own enterprises. He is funded by a Kenyan businessman who has a foundation to support youth enterprise.

But how do these young social entrepreneurs themselves get started? How do they acquire the skills they need to think through and develop a project, write a proposal, advertise it, raise funds, and learn to keep accounts? The first courses to teach these skills were the Bee School (in United Kingdom and Germany) and the Do School (in Hamburg, Germany, and New York).[4] The Do School has two thousand applicants for every one of the twenty places available in each of three courses it offers each year. Students from all over the world live together for an intense ten weeks of tuition, skill sharing, and project development, and then they return home for a year of mentoring while they apply what they have learned. These young social entrepreneurs start ventures in education, the arts, food production, sports, or conflict transformation.

Economist Dr. Hazel Henderson adds that with these kinds of programs available, overpriced universities and for-profit colleges find competition from grassroots civic education, action research, experimental problem solving, apprenticing, and internships, along with the information sharing of social media and online courses with accreditation.[5] Graduates of these programs no longer head for quick bucks on the Wall Streets of the world but pursue more useful careers in engineering, medicine, teaching, and agriculture. Many companies adopt open-source learning models and information sharing.

Dr. Monica Sharma, who worked for the United Nations for twenty-two years, now designs and facilitates programs for whole systems transformation and leadership development in both developed and developing countries. Because of her proven track record of generating measurable results at scale, she is called to advise the United Nations, governments, business, media, and civil organizations. She has spoken about the potential of these new leaders:

> Emerging new leaders understand both the visible and hidden sources of action and inaction, and the attitudes that determine them. . . . They enhance their own personal awareness, realizing that this is the most critical element of social transformation. New archetypal leaders are emerging. Largely unnoticed, they are more like midwives giving birth to other people's ideas and dreams, rather than like "stars" of the show; they foster just and sustained change for a thriving planet where everyone lives with dignity.
>
> They invest in their own spiritual (not necessarily religious) growth; they proactively inform themselves about the state of the world; they see patterns in addition to events; they have the courage to take on difficult issues; they act from a source of wisdom, courage, compassion and empathy, rather than charity and "doing good." They do not reflect the traditional sage, hero or savior archetypes. They are informed sages, wise in the ways of the world; they are courageous non-violent heroes with a cause; they are compassionate saviors, grateful to be able to serve.[6]

Reverence, Regeneration,
and Celebration for the Earth

Imagine if the earth were treated as a living system, as our mother Gaia. People all over the planet would see and feel her beauty and her vast intelligence; they would act to protect her and to help regeneration to take place. If human eyes are blind to the mystery of where they live, they cannot care. And if they don't care, they won't act.

So on television all over the world—in every language and adapted to every culture—would be shown daily the nature films that enrapture children and adults alike. Films like *Home* and like David Attenborough's nine-part *Life* series, which collectively form a comprehensive survey of all life on the planet, could be the start and could be supplemented by new series that show how the earth's weather systems are influenced by with global warming and carbon dioxide and methane emissions.[7]

Imagine such films being shown on open-air screens all over Africa, coupled with teach-ins showing how to replace gasoline and paraffin with solar energy and biogas. Films could show people how local actions can diminish global warming and could honor those global corporations that have become aware of climate issues and taken action to cut their carbon emissions.

Such films in future will be so well made, so exciting and intriguing, that children will ask to see them in school. The films will teach and inspire the children to develop their own schemes to cut carbon; the children will enter their schools' results for annual regional awards for the school most fuelled by renewable energy.

When a generation of children worldwide has understood the cycle of sustainability, there will be a natural push to cease using fossil fuels; to buy environmentally produced, fair-trade products; and to use Skype and Facetime and similar internet-based communication for visiting friends and family—instead of airline flights.

All these experiences will put a new generation in touch with the earth it walks on. Eyes will open in wonder at the way nature works. When we stand in awe, we naturally want to support, to encourage, and to give. In the United Kingdom, the largest membership organization—far larger than any political party or trade union—is the National Trust.[8] The reason it's so popular with British families from all backgrounds is that people trust the organization to look after our national heritage—our woodland, farmland, and great old houses and gardens. Just imagine if every country had its own form of organization trusted to safeguard, protect, and care for its heritage of natural beauty—not buildings and properties, but forests and deserts and oceans.

The assignment offered to the new generation would be regeneration—helping Mother Earth to heal her wounds. This process would start with ritual, meditation, and asking for help to understand what needs doing first.

Just imagine if, using Google Earth, every mine on the planet were mapped. Staring with the mines no longer in use, thousands of volunteers are invited to help fill in the pits and mine shafts, cover with topsoil, and plant trees. Mining industries are engaged in dialogue with experts about how to conserve stocks and to cease mining activities, using their own equipment to repair the damage to rock structures and underground water systems.

Integrated policies could be agreed upon and established for oceans and coasts, taking into consideration all users, stakeholders, and the threats to a given coastal or marine region. Marine Protected Areas are set up, perhaps on the model of Palau, the island state in the Pacific that is economically dependent on its oceans and coasts:

> Palau has a long history of community management of fisheries and marine resources: the Protected Areas Network Act (2003) was created to provide a framework for Palau's national and state governments to collaborate and establish a coordinated, nationwide network of marine and terrestrial protected areas. These are designed to address local resource management needs and protect national biodiversity, habitats and natural resources. To achieve this, the Palauan government has been working with local and international NGOs to devise monitoring and management protocols, based on internationally agreed standards.[9]

Major fishing enterprises and ocean researchers worldwide are consulted about how fish stocks can be replenished so that sustainable fishing can continue for centuries. Namibia's waters, fed by the Benguela Current, for example, support one of the world's most productive fishing grounds, but even here, unregulated industrial fishing drove fish populations to near collapse. Nevertheless, the government stepped in to stop and reverse the damage.

> Independence permitted the new government to start afresh, and develop a fisheries management system based on scientific evidence. A guiding principle was the sustainable use of ecological resources for the benefit of current and future generations. Namibia has developed the law and institutions, as well as the technical expertise to manage its fisheries on a more sustainable basis. The Marine Resources Act of 2000 provides the legislative framework, setting regulations to address the key drivers of degradation: bycatch and discards, illegal fishing, overcapacity from subsidies, and harmful fishing gear.[10]

When we look to the need to regenerate our forests—and the benefits of such regeneration, we should remember the story of twelve-year-old Felix Finkbeiner (discussed in chapter 6), who founded a global network of child activists whose aim is to mitigate climate change by reforesting the planet. It's called Plant for the Planet, and it's up and running in 131 countries.

Celebrations

It may seem esoteric to suggest seasonal festivals, but in fact, for centuries—and in all cultures—festivals have been the key that people have used to stay in tune with nature. A vibrant future would encourage festivals to enable more and more people to feel the changes in the seasons, so that they can live more in harmony with nature, rather than as they are now—insulated in heated or cooled boxes. There would be a memo in everyone's diary to gather four times a year to honor the seasons, as in former times. For those who live in cities, special spaces would be set aside for the local ritual to honor the seasons; in tropical climates, where seasons are less marked, the progress of the year would be marked in other traditional ways.

It is the second of February in the northern hemisphere, and pale fragile rays of the rising sun slant across the chilly landscape. A group of women,

men, and children walk up the hill to the woods, wrapped up warm, and carrying baskets and rugs. As they enter the woods, the sunlight catches patches of white flowers under the trees—the snowdrops that bloom at this time every year. The green scent of moss and clean, dark earth is everywhere. Rugs are spread under the trees and white candles are lit, for this is the ancient Celtic festival of Imbolc—"first light"—later taken up by the Christian church as the festival of Candlemas. One of the mothers explains to the children why this festival was so important to ancient peoples in the northern hemisphere, because it celebrated their survival of the darkness and hunger of winter and the birth of a new season. Hot drinks and cakes are passed around, and the children sing the song of spring that they have learned at school. A father pays respect to Mother Earth and asks her to bless the season and the seeds that will be planted as soon as the earth warms a little, so that they may germinate and provide food.

Another ritual will take place on first of May, one like the festival called Beltane by the Celts, to celebrate fertility and procreation—a festival of dancing and feasting. On the first of August the reaping of the first corn is celebrated as Lammastide, symbolized by a loaf of freshly baked bread. The first of November is the time to celebrate death and the passage to other realms, called Samhain by the Celts and All Hallows by the Christian church. In Neolithic times, burial sites, called *long barrows,* were often built in the shape of a woman's body, and the bones of the dead were deposited in the center of the barrow at Samhain, so that they could be reborn as another being through her birth passage in the spring.[11]

These markings of the year—of the cycle of birth, early growth, fertility, ripening, reaping, decay, death, and rebirth—are vital to both our psychic and our physical health, showing us that death is not final, but part of a cycle. They encourage us to allow our bodies to be in tune with the seasons—to dance all night in summer, to sleep long hours and store up energy in the winter.

They also remind us of our dependence on the planet, and the huge complexity of its systems—its atmosphere, oceans, forests, and volcanoes. Ritual enables us to pause, connect, and lose some of our hubris. It increases our respect for the delicate balances inherent in every kind of life on earth and for the unimaginably vast power of nature. Having such respect allows us to begin to regenerate what human activity has destroyed and to experience the mysterious delight of connecting with the magic of the natural world.

Touching Elephants

The first night a large bull visited us at supper
delicately stepping the narrow space between us and our
    drinks table
we sat motionless, breathless,
as he examined the mugs with his trunk
and picked seeds off the table
for the next 3 days they were a daily presence
quietly visiting each one of us
close enough for us to see the hairs on the back of their feet
their eyelashes
immense bulks reaching for leaves over our heads
close enough for us to watch the infinite gracefulness of their trunks
selecting seed pods around our chairs
and we knew a deep sense our own vulnerability
and the incredible gift we were being given
standing here at the edge
where our unquestioned control of the world is reduced to the flick
    of a trunk
our small worries of arrangements and agreements
are of nothing
in this wide wilderness of the Zambezi valley
we were told they had never been this close before
it felt as if they were learning us. . . .
what did they think
as they smelt our cups?
tasted our shoes?
do they know we are the ones
who are playing havoc with their world
bringing our fuel exhausts and plastic and bottles
invading this wild place

slowly making it into our play ground
we stand at the edge of the wilderness
both the problem and the worshiper
awed by the generosity of its sharing
and the gentleness of these wild giants.[12]

Ensuring Healthy Food and Clean Water

The enthusiasm for my work, the boundless love which fills my heart for all around me, brings forth a vision of the community: a community in which people of all nations and cultures work and learn in peace, and resonate together in harmony as a symphony; a community in which vocations from all walks of life, from all age groups, from all levels of consciousness, acknowledge, nurture and love the divine world and strive towards noble ideals; a living, ever regenerating community maintaining its dynamism by reaching towards the science of the spirit; a community pursuing truth and tolerance, generously offering its understanding in the service of the earth and man; a people where modesty and diligence prevails over vanity and comfort, and all endeavours are blessed.[13]

This is how Dr. Ibrahim Abouleish expresses his love for his vision, transformed by years of hard work into the thriving enterprise that is now inspiring people all over the planet to imitate it. Imagine that all over the planet, people could trust that their food being a source of sustenance, full of the nutrients that sustain them, and that each person had access to clean water. In Egypt this remarkable movement is happening.

On land that thirty years ago was nothing but desert, you can now walk through acres and acres of lush alfalfa, knee-deep chamomile, and the tall golden spikes of evening primrose. This is Sekem, an organic farm almost forty miles northeast of Cairo pioneered by Dr. Abouleish. As a young man, Abouleish went to study pharmacology in Austria, and then he introduced the concepts of Goethe and of Rudolf Steiner to Egypt. The encounter of East and West created a new concept of sustainable community in the Egyptian desert—a model for how the future could be.

In the midst of this farm, there's a massive processing plant where they produce phyto-pharmaceuticals, prepare hundreds of tons of organic vegetables for export, and train seven hundred Egyptian farmers in bio-dynamics. Each morning the employees gather in groups of about one hundred, and after a short prayer, each person says what they're going to do that day—an eclectic mix of German gravity and Egyptian energy. It baffles visitors, but it works.

The success of Abouleish has been built on his conviction and belief that tradition and modernity, the local and the global have to be held in a fine balance. The first large economic venture of the Sekem community initiative was production of a medicinal compound, ammoidin, an extract of *Ammi majus* (laceflower). The manufacture of herbal teas and a company to market fresh biodynamic produce in Europe followed. The needs of these companies led to many farms throughout Egypt switching to biodynamic methods; the SEKEM organization began an active advisory service to aid these farms in the transition to and the maintenance of biodynamic standards.

It was here that community projects also began: a medical clinic using anthroposophic medicine, and a Society for Cultural Development sponsoring lectures, concerts and other cultural activities, a center for adult education, a school educating children from kindergarten up to 18 years of age on the basis of Waldorf education. "The school serves Muslim and Christian children alike, encouraging them to live in harmony and have respect for the other's religious practices."

In response to the use of child labor in Egypt, SEKEM founded the project *Chamomile Children,* which offers children between ten and fourteen an education, vocational training, meals, and medical care in conjunction with their work. There is the Cooperative of SEKEM Employees, an independent organization with members from all the businesses and cultural institutions associated with SEKEM.

Faced with pesticide residues in their products that came from aerial spraying on nearby farms, SEKEM took up an initiative to eliminate such spraying in Egypt. As cotton production depended upon the sprays, SEKEM explored organic cotton production on initially small fields. The experiments were successful and yields actually were better than nonorganic production achieved. The Egyptian Ministry of Agriculture sponsored further and more extensive tests. Within three years, the ministry agreed that organic pest suppression was superior for cotton farming and began converting the entire area of Egyptian cotton, 4,000 square kilometers, to organic methods for controlling pests; the conversion took two years. The conversion resulted in a reduction in the use of synthetic pesticides in Egypt by over 90 percent and an increase in the average yield of raw cotton of almost 30 percent. SEKEM then created a company to process organic cotton using mechanical rather than chemical methods, Conytex.[14]

Local Food Systems

Imagine if women focused even a portion of their innate capacity to collaborate—and their natural systems-thinking intelligence—to restoring the abundance of local food systems. Vicki Robin and Thais Corral, the authors of *Women Strengthening Local Food Systems*, are remarkable pioneers of innovation in agriculture. They believe that local food systems are the way to catalyze a local community's creativity, collaboration, and connections for greater local food prosperity and abundance.[15]

Imagine the creativity, empowerment and satisfaction we would get from restoring community sovereignty by reclaiming, year by year, project by project, our right to produce and consume foods grown closer to home. . . .

Imagine the grassroots power from growing food in the soils of our regions and feeding our families without always feeding the corporate domination of our seeds and food supply. . . .

Pre-liberation, feeding the family was women's work. Post-liberation, in the twenty-first century, feeding our communities with fresh, whole, natural food can again be women's work—not just in kitchens or gardens, but in politics and social change.

In the developing world, according to the FAO, women comprise 43 percent of the agricultural labor force—possibly more, since horticulture isn't distinguished as work for many women in rural communities. When claiming economic independence, women often start food businesses.

We who have benefited from development are perfectly poised to be leaders in reclaiming sustainable food systems—as farmers, chefs, heads of NGOs, public officials, corporate CEOs, educators, researchers and innovators. As Vicki Robin, cofounder of the Local Food Labs, says: "The shift from anywhere-eating in an industrial system to relational-eating in a real living community not only gives us access to more wholesome food, it restores our sense of belonging and brings us a sense of security and sovereignty. Relational eating nourishes body and soul. The fact that most of our food now comes from unknown sources beyond our control means relational eating is also an exciting frontier of change."

The industrial food system arises from an industrial mindset: nature as feedstock for an ever-expanding economy. Agriculture, stripped of *culture,* becomes a matter of inputs and outputs; vertical integration and scale are the logical path to a profitable business.

Consumers are the end users—not participants in—the system. The challenges are all in the supply chain: getting product from farm or feedlot as efficiently as possible and at the lowest cost possible. Farmers are simply factors of production—as are the sun, soil, wind, rain, seeds, microorganisms, and pollinators. Nature is either useful (and thus harnessed) or useless (and thus ignored or eliminated).

Slowly we are emerging from this mindset. Nature is being granted rights. Species heading for extinction are being rescued. Now it's time to rescue our local, living food systems from the grip of the industrial mindset—to understand food production in a context of wholeness.

Life is a collaborative project, an ecological web of giving and receiving, of being born, living, and returning our borrowed bodies to the earth for recycling. Restoring our food systems comes from this understanding of wholeness and reciprocity, because a food system includes the free services of nature as well as all the "hands that feed us"—the farmers and all the workers at every step of the delivery process. The hands that feed us are also tilling other "fields"— those who tend to policy, research, education, governance, conflict resolution, design . . . well, we have to admit that food is woven into almost every aspect of our lives. Food is nature, nourishment, and culture.

Understanding a food system in this way, we will have to rethink our assumptions:

- We must understand ourselves as engaged producers, not just passive consumers.
- We must understand that we each have a role in inching our food systems away from corporate dependencies and toward local productivity.
- We must experience the profound value of food—all that brings it to our table—and shift away from overeating and waste, which are habits of excess and dishonoring.
- Currently we waste 40 percent of our food, most of which ends up in landfills; very little of it is composted. Food recovery is a growing movement.
- We must give up hopelessness, impotence, and unconsciousness about how industrial food is stripped of nature and spirit, and we must embrace the nourishment and power that growing our own food gives us.

Eastern and Western Medicine for Profound Good Health

Just imagine if we could have the benefit of the best of Western and Eastern systems of medicine. Western medicine has discovered drugs that have stopped epidemics and vaccines that have wiped out killer diseases, such as smallpox. It has developed brilliant surgical interventions—hip replacements that have prolonged the mobility of innumerable older people and major organ transplants that have saved people of all ages. There are many more examples of the achievements of allopathic medicine.

But as psychiatrist Andrew Powell says, Western culture "has pioneered life-saving prostheses like heart valves and yet at the same time makes and sells junk foods that clog the arterial tree. At best, it has saved countless lives with the help of antibiotics. Yet, due to their profligate misuse, we now have bacteria that are resistant to every known antibiotic."[16]

Since Western medicine is based in a mechanistic understanding of the human body, one that puts the part before the whole, it has trouble coping with systemic illnesses resulting from modern Western living, such as stress, anxiety, or addiction. Take, for example, the epidemic of human misery known as depression. The main treatment that doctors can offer for depression is based on drugs, which simply dull the symptoms and do not address the causes of the problem. Many observers believe that the drug "offers" communicated by the pharmaceutical industry to doctors actually pressurize them to over prescribe.

More Britons die each year from prescription drugs than from heroin and cocaine. In 2012, 807 people died as a result of taking tranquilizers and painkillers—16 percent more than five years previously. Critics say the high death toll is partly down to doctors overprescribing certain drugs. There has been a four-fold increase in the number of prescriptions for strong painkillers since 1991; it's estimated that 1.5 million people are addicted to prescription drugs such as Valium. [17]

Traditional Chinese medicine, on the other hand, after flourishing in ancient times and declining in modern times, is now on the path of resurgence. Instead of the approach of Western medicine, which splits the body into parts and looks for a single cause for a problem, Chinese medicine views the human body as an integrated system, using such traditional knowledge as the meridian system, the theory of *yin* and *yang*, and the Five Elements theory. Treatment includes acupuncture, herbal medicine, and medical *Chi Kung*. With a systemic and integral understanding of human health, doctors of Chinese medicine advocate living in harmony with the environment and teach patients the relationship between mind and body.

Each system offers a patient profound advantages; the difference in approach can be simply explained. So it makes sense, as has happened widely in China, for patients to be offered a choice of treatments—Eastern or Western, according to which is more appropriate for their case. A collapsing hip joint is better repaired with hip-replacement surgery than with acupuncture. A child with asthma may recover better with herbal medicine or acupuncture than with Western drugs that may produce unpleasant side effects.

Imagine if doctors could be paid according to how many of their patients are healthy. For hundreds of years, this was the practice in China. Suppose a substantial part of all national health budgets were invested in prevention—for example, encouraging all high school students—as part of their studies—to experiment with preventive practices, such as healthy eating to prevent or reverse obesity. Younger children could be taught the basics of nutrition in primary school to prepare them to live healthy lives, as well as to benefit the lives of their parents.

Imagine if parents and employees everywhere were offered courses in mindfulness-based stress reduction, which has been shown to reduce anxiety, improve the immune system, and reduce negative feelings like anger, tension, and depression. American businesses that have included mindfulness training within their organizations include Target, Google, General Mills, and many others. Not only are employees sharper, more professional, and responsive, but productivity has risen alongside the decrease in stress-related illness and absenteeism.[18]

The Healing Potential of Plants

Ayurvedic medicine is a system of traditional medicine native to the Indian subcontinent that uses plants to heal physical, emotional, and mental ailments. Because of its efficacy in healing complex health issues, its use is spreading worldwide. If that sounds ambitious, here's the experience of Annie MacIntyre, leading Ayurvedic practitioner in the United Kingdom:

> The natural world gives us herbs, incredible healing plants, which are manifestations of the conscious intelligence of the universe. . . . Each herb has its own unique blend of many different attributes. It has myriad chemical constituents and physiological actions . . . and with time and experience it is possible to become acquainted with each individual herb almost like a different personality. Plants have long been associated with healing, and not only for our physical ills but also in imbalances of the mind and the spirit that may give rise to our bodily symptoms.
>
> We have lived side by side with plants since the dawning of our existence, been fed and clothed by them, sheltered and housed by them, they provide the oxygen we breathe and for thousands of

years have given us medicines for almost every ill. By trapping the sun's energy through photosynthesis they enable solar energy or life energy on which all life depends, to be accessible to every inhabitant of the earth. By resonating with us at all speeds of vibration from the spiritual to the material, plants have the potential to heal us on all levels of our being.[19]

Conscious Death, or Dying with Dignity

The British National Health Service estimates that currently 50 percent of health-care costs are incurred in the last six months of life. Patients are often not sufficiently conscious to indicate whether or not they wish to be kept alive by artificial means, and the end of their lives is frequently troubling for themselves and their relatives.

Suppose, just as lawyers and families encourage older people to make a will, doctors and families encouraged older people to make a living will, also known as an advance health-care directive.[20] Such a document enables a person to make detailed decisions as to their care in later life. They may opt, for example to be resuscitated after a stroke (or not) or to be artificially fed (or not). The document is agreed with their general practitioner, with relatives, and if so desired, with a lawyer.

Such decisions normally relieve stress both for relatives and for patients at the close of life. The savings in costs could then be invested in preventive health education, to warn of the dangers of obesity leading to diabetes, cardiovascular disease resulting from a high-stress sedentary lifestyle, and the morbidity associated with alcohol, drugs, and tobacco consumption. Increased preventative health care would lead to people living longer, healthier lives, needing fewer drugs and less surgery, and dying more naturally.

When I heard about the advance health-care directive, I jumped at it. Having watched miserably as four members of my family died slowly from dementia, I wanted to take action to prevent my nearest and dearest from suffering as I did. I now know that certain key decisions have been made, so if I become senile, they will know what to do without having to agonize about what I want.

In the future, we shall also overcome our taboo against talking about death. It will normal for parents to discuss death with children and to tell stories about what may happen after death. Adults will make clear plans for how they would ideally like to die and prepare themselves consciously before the actual time comes, assuming death is not sudden. When a parent or grandparent dies, children will be actively included in several days of mourning, undertaking rituals that are uplifting rather than morbid.

Laurie Anderson described the death of her husband, the singer Lou Reed, who died as they meditated together. "As meditators we had prepared for this. . . . I have never seen an expression as full of wonder as Lou's as he died. His hands were doing the water flowing 21-form of tai chi. His eyes were wide open. I was holding in my arms the person I loved most in the world, and talking to him as he died. His heart stopped. He wasn't afraid. I had gotten to walk with him to the end of the world. And death? I believe that the purpose of death is the release of love."[21]

A World Where Conflict Is Transformed

The news flashes up on the screen of my phone with a photo of a man surrounded by heavily armed young fighters from DR Congo. The story reads:

A decade ago, tens of thousands of children were being kidnapped by armed fighters in the heart of Africa. These children were made into killing machines, and made to murder their own families, usually after being drugged.

Henri Bura Ladyi knew how the system worked and knew that the fighters were hungry. So he bought herds of goats and drove them to the militia encampment deep in the bush. He risked his life doing this but managed to strike a deal: he swopped one goat [price $5] for one child, and brought them back to their families. Then began the tireless work of rehabilitation to treat the trauma the children had experienced and to train them in a skill so they can survive.

Henri enabled over five thousand militia fighters to put down their weapons and leave the bush. But he has never been recognized for these years of exceptional courage and self-sacrifice. It is therefore our privilege to name him as "Unarmed Hero of the Year."

Photo: Fiona Lloyd-Davies

This is how I imagine the future could be, in a world in which we made heroes out of those who put their lives on the line so that others don't get killed. Every day—without us hearing about it—hundreds of ordinary citizen peace builders—as well as NGO personnel, envoys, and diplomats—are risking their lives to resolve violent conflicts. They intervene to stop killing, mediate between warlords, rescue child soldiers, persuade young people not to become suicide bombers, negotiate cease-fires, free hostages, and build bridges between people who hate each other. These are some of the most courageous and determined people on earth, yet the media doesn't feature them. Imagine if they became our heroes and heroines, their stories told on the front pages.

Imagine if every region of the world had its own Infrastructure for Peace—a network of skilled councils who would be immediately involved if a dispute arose, who would set in motion their culture's preferred methods of transforming that dispute.[22] This is already happening in countries that have established a Ministry of Peace—instead of a ministry of "defense." In March 2007, the government of Nepal decided to create a Ministry of Peace and Reconstruction, becoming the second nation in the world to have such a ministry, after the Solomon Islands; Costa Rica became the third in 2009. One of the first countries to start establishing an entire Infrastructure for Peace was South Africa: Local Peace Committees were set up as a result of the National Peace Accord, signed in 1991 between the main protagonists in South Africa's conflict. This helped to avoid a civil war after Mandela was released from jail. Two decades later, the governments of Ghana and Kenya are pioneering the implementation of their own Infrastructures for Peace.

Imagine if every town and village in the world could call on its own trusted "agents of transformation"[23]—respected people who had learned since childhood how to embrace the energy of conflict and provide a strong enough "container" for conflicted parties to listen to each other "for as long as it takes."[24]

Imagine a world in which we systematically trained peace builders in every part of the planet in the skills of Gandhi, Mandela, and Aung San Suu Kyi, developing the kind of courses that combine the practical skills of peace building with the development of inner intelligence or self-knowledge.[25] Imagine if graduating from such a course became a basic qualification for standing for election to any public office.

In areas and among populations who have suffered great trauma, systematic healing processes are required. The classic cycle of violence develops in the following way as depcited on the next page—and repeats itself if nothing is done

The cycle of violence can be turned around—before anger turns to hatred—on four different levels:

- By building physical security—through, for example, peacekeeping by the United Nations Peace Keeping Force, decommissioning weapons (as in Northern Ireland), or disbanding militias, as in Mozambique (where Albino Forquilha, having himself been a

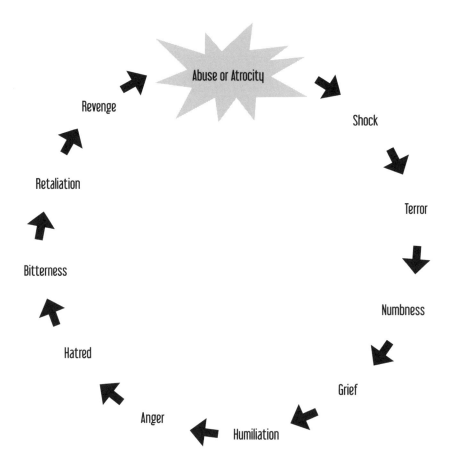

child soldier, is devoting the rest of his life to exchanging bicycles for caches of weapons and turning those weapons into sculptures, examples of which are now in the United Nations).

- By building political security—through mediated negotiations (as in Camp David), the introduction of free and fair elections (as enforced by the student movement OTPOR in Serbia), or supporting the right to demonstrate (as in Northern Ireland).
- By building psychological security—through, for example, cross-border humanitarian initiatives (such as Doctors without Borders), trauma counseling (for populations devastated by ethnic cleansing, as in Bosnia and Croatia), or deep listening processes (as in Rwanda).

- By working at a spiritually transformative level—for example, in Truth and Reconciliation processes (in South Africa and many countries in South America) or using the ancient Hawaiian process of Ho'opono pono or the practice of restorative justice (as in Brazil and countless inner cities in United Kingdom and elsewhere).

The last group listed—the spiritually based initiatives—are especially important, because they go to the root of the problem of violence, address the deepest pain, and light up the deepest longing in human beings: to know that we are all, ultimately, part of the same whole.

They are also the most sustained—and sustainable. They work at grassroots level, from the bottom up. They are perhaps impossible to measure, perhaps impossible to evaluate—yet they have access to unimaginable power.

These results underline what we have discovered at Peace Direct. In 1999, when we first researched the number of grassroots peace initiatives in the world—places where local people are risking their own lives to stop war—we were able to identify about 350 viable initiatives in hot conflict areas worldwide.

Now, that number is five times as many. This is because local people, who know best what needs to be done to prevent and resolve conflict in their own areas, are becoming empowered by better communications and some access to funding. This locally led peace building is one of the factors contributing to the decline of well over 50 percent in the number of major conflicts worldwide and in the number of people killed as a result of them, observed in chapter 4.

Awaken Your Own Visionary Power

The crises faced by humanity today are so vast and so far reaching that our creativity can freeze. Our capacity to imagine a positive future can simply wither. Instead, we look to others—politicians and movement leaders—and expect them to come up with answers. And, of course, they can't. This is the moment when grassroots, bottom-up creativity is most needed. So this section will offer a process whereby you can clear your mind of exhausted thought patterns and open up to the kind of playful energy that produces ingenuity, brilliant ideas—eureka moments.

Step 1. The first necessity is to allow your mind to become quiet and stop endlessly processing your to-do list and all your oughts and shoulds. Use whatever method works best for you: go for a long walk in nature and really see what's around you; listen to music that utterly absorbs you; meditate; contemplate a flower or the flame of a candle; sit quietly with an animal.

Step 2. Align yourself calmly with the two interlinked aspects of our crisis—the extremity of its destructiveness and the extraordinary opportunities that it offers to your creativity. Ask the divine—in whatever way you understand it—to be given the strength, wisdom, and energy to become one of the pioneers of the possible. There's a very simple practice that can help: imagine inhaling a brilliant golden light, which goes down to your toes and breaks out from the center of your head into a great golden ball that expands and encloses your whole being. In this golden light are all the qualities—power, clarity, fearlessness, energy—that you will need to be the visionary that you are. When you breathe out, consciously surrender all doubts and fears. Do this nine times, slowly and consciously, and you'll find that by the end you'll be in a state of radiant intelligent calm.

Step 3. Choose a field that interests you—the environment, for example, or education or health or money—some area that matters to you or affects your life. Then examine the assumptions you have about this subject. Be honest about the position you hold on it, delve into the shadowy reasons you have for thinking this way, the prejudices or foregone conclusions you may have adopted. For example:

- On the environment—do you feel deep down that it's too late to save the rainforests? Or do you think that a technical fix will be invented in time to reverse the effects of methane release?
- On education—are you putting up with teaching methods that

are training your children to simply pass exams, rather than think for themselves?

- On the economy—do you content yourself with complaining about greedy bankers, while worrying that your savings may be unsafe?
- On health—do you take medicine without fully understanding what it may do to your body? Have you resigned yourself to weighing more than is good for you?
- On peace—do you feel peace is desirable but, in reality, unattainable? Do you think that the world is becoming more violent and that nothing can be done?

Sit with these thoughts for a while. Are they troubling or uncomfortable? Do they feel like the real you? If not, release them. If they really feel like your truth, hold them more tightly, and see how this feels.

Step 4. Now, find a question for yourself, along the lines of the following:

- What *could* our environment be like?
- What is the most creative and freeing kind of education you can imagine?
- How could a lending structure be created, without banks?
- When did you feel really well, and what led to that feeling?
- What do you imagine as a peaceful world?

Be fully imaginative with your question, going far beyond these suggestions, if you can.

Sit with your question, with a notebook at hand, and simply wait for inspiration. It may arrive as a bolt from the blue, or it may be a little wisp of an idea that you catch just before it vanishes and gradually develop.

When ideas begin to form, share them with friends. If other people are interested, invite them to expand your idea. Go for as big a restructuring as you dare. Don't be daunted by things like government restrictions because—well, because you can be sure that someone, somewhere else will be having ideas about how to replace government regulations with something more human-friendly.

Step 5. When your vision has formed, dedicate the whole process to the inspiration of all human beings. Imagine the essence of your vision being communicated instantly through ripples emanating from your heart outward into the world.

Imagine that as you're doing this process, a light comes on a Google map of the world. Imagine that all over the world there are people like you pouring their creativity into a far better future. See the map of the world lighting up, so that your vision is linked with all the others now arising.

Step 6. Now make a plan to put your vision into action. Begin by developing ideas with friends around your kitchen table; all the best projects start around someone's kitchen table. As soon as you can, write a short paragraph about what it is you want to happen. This could start with a sentence of intention, then a sentence saying how it will work, then a sentence saying what you expect the outcome to be. The plan doesn't have to be perfect, as it will be amended many times. Make doable stages. Think about people you know who would be interested; form what Andrew Harvey calls a Network of Grace—a group of six to ten people who meet to dedicate themselves to making dreams come true in the real world.[26] Ponder how you could raise money to get traction for your ideas—or even better, design the ideas themselves to produce their own revenue. Write lists. Write letters. Don't give up. The leap from the mundane to the magnificent is worth anything it may cost. Doors open when you least expect them to.

> O Beloved,
> Do not let me pray for the poor
> Without working tirelessly
> To end the systems that thrive on poverty.
> Do not let me pray for the animals
> Without working to end
> The systems that are slaughtering them.
> Do not let me pray for justice and compassion

And the coming of your kingdom
Without being willing to give my life
To make them real.
Save me from the subtle and lethal hypocrisy
That would make me believe I love you
When I risk nothing
To make this love real in your world.

—Andrew Harvey[27]

CHAPTER 9

GREEN SHOOTS THROUGH CONCRETE

If you look at the science that describes what is happening on earth today and aren't pessimistic, you don't have the correct data. If you meet people in this un-named movement and aren't optimistic, you haven't got a heart. What I see are ordinary and some not-so-ordinary individuals willing to confront despair, power and incalculable odds in an attempt to restore some semblance of grace, justice and beauty to this world.

—Paul Hawken, *Blessed Unrest*

There appear to be two phenomena happening simultaneously in the twenty-first century.

The first is a disaster: humans are stripping the earth of its natural resources so fast that entire ecosystems are collapsing, technological breakdowns are releasing toxic materials that threaten all life, and the unimaginable beauty of the planet is being destroyed. Most human beings seem unaware of the tragedy happening around them.

The second is an awakening: a fast-growing number of highly energized humans waking up to an entirely new perception of the functioning of the universe and how, by working *with* its energy systems instead of against them, they can assist the regeneration of the planet.

In this final chapter, I want to try to assess how the second phenomenon affects the first, and what this means for you who are reading this.

When people realize the state of the planet, they seem to have one of two reactions. One is to simply shut down—"it's too big a problem," "governments should be dealing with it," and/or "simply surviving is challenge enough." The other is to be sufficiently shocked or personally affected that inaction is not an option. The result is campaigns and initiatives springing up all over the world—in the poorest places as in the richest.

The problem is that revolutionaries are often driven by fear and adrenaline, and they often are thrown into leadership roles before they have an opportunity to heal their fear. Their unconscious fear dictates their initiatives, and if the revolution is successful, they can become as oppressive as the regime they replaced. We tend to expect that "the new will be different," without recognizing the interconnection between the individual and the system.

It is therefore essential to take the extra steps to develop our own consciousness to a level able to transform the situation we are faced with and one aligned with the values we want to see implemented. That is what this book is about. This development of our consciousness is the current evolutionary process that most people can't see: *the desired outer change cannot come about without the inner change.* This is what Einstein meant when he said, "You cannot solve a problem from the consciousness that created it."

The gist of the now famous Theory U described by Otto Scharmer is equally plain: "The quality of results produced by any system depends on the quality of awareness from which people in the system operate." In a later book, Scharmer puts it thus: "The success of our actions as change-makers does not depend on what we do or how we do it, but on the inner place from which we operate."[1]

When the issue is profound social change, of the kind needed now, will it come about through bureaucracies? Or will it come about through the formidable power of individuals and groups who have realized their inner strength, and the authority this gives them? When Mandela and his colleagues were released from jail in 1990, the regime they opposed was armed to the teeth and profoundly violent, but they were made of sterner stuff. They were solid, honed, authentic, and determined, but there was something more—an inner resilience and courage that exuded extraordinary force. It was immediately apparent and unmistakable; if you look at film clips from that time, you will see it in Mandela's very bearing, his authority. And what made his authority so moving was that he remained humble and full of humor.

Inner change, and access to inner power, is happening globally now and examples spring to mind on every continent. Dr. Rama Mani is so brilliant and talented that she would, without a doubt, have become a top United Nations official had she not been woken up by Chögyam Trungpa's book *Shambhala: The Sacred Path of the Warrior*, which enabled her to see what constitutes real change. She is now the dynamic hub of a large social movement, and she has sparked at least three others.

At a personal level, it seems possible to maximize available energy to be able to work all the hours of the day on world issues *and* have a great time doing it. At a group level, an energy field can be built that affects the outcome of what that group does; it is tangibly felt, even at distance, as we saw in the example of Zimbabwe in chapter 2. At an organizational level—particularly with the turbocharge of social media—the energy that informs a global campaign can have tangible, measurable influence, of which there are now countless examples, not least that of the Avaaz campaigns described in chapter 6.

So what is this energy? Well, it's a bit different from the buzz that you get from those caffeinated energy drinks that may send your blood pressure sky-high. This energy makes your body feel whole (rather than "wired"), and your heart—instead of going into overdrive—is emanating ripples or waves that connect you to others. Mind, body, and spirit are aligned to produce a focus or intention that is charged with capability, a feeling that you can do whatever is necessary. It feels pliable and competent, and—needless to say—it feels good.

When people who have this energy gather in a group, it seems something special is beginning to happen. When like-minded, like-hearted, aware friends gather just because they love being together, they discover that there is something they want to do together. The quality of energy—and how it is to be used—seems to inform a particular quality of action. This is apparently the coming phenomenon of our age. I've noticed at least five such groups spring up in the past six months.

Let me offer an example. I'm a member of a group of midcareer professionals (who work in the media, consultancy, public service, business, education, and commerce) that meets in London one afternoon a month to share our ideas, training, and experiences. All are reasonably well informed about the state of the world, about half meditate regularly, and most are interested in some form of inner reflection.

In November 2013, after a check-in to find out how everyone was doing, we spent the afternoon investigating how pure presence can bring authenticity. We did a listening exercise (described in the appendix), and one of the results we noticed was exactly this—that telling our own deepest truths revealed to each of us a level of authenticity that was tangible, which every one of us became aware of.

We noticed that a "field" was developing during the afternoon—the sum of our energies was becoming more than the parts. How did we know this? There was synchronicity—two or more people thinking or saying the same thing at the same time—which made us laugh. There were bodily sensations of shivers, goose bumps, or frissons, experienced independently by various people. There were unusual bursts of imagination and creativity. Above all, people felt an extraordinary amount of love in the room and compassion for each other.

We started talking about how our authenticity is in direct relation to the influence (or personal power) that we have in the workplace and in the world. Many of us had experienced how the atmosphere in a room—during a speech or a training course—changes to pin-drop level when the speaker is fully authentic (open, connected, and loving). Perhaps it's because people in general are longing for honesty, for straight-forwardness, for transparency—for a bedrock they can trust.

Someone asked if we could put this field we seemed to have created to good use. Someone mentioned Fukushima and the fact that the Japanese Nuclear Agency had recently approved the removal of spent fuel rods from reactor 4, reporting what Yale University professor Charles Perrow had said about the dangers of those rods: that if they are not properly handled, they could trigger an uncontrollable nuclear reaction that could threaten the world.[2] We also talked about the threat of another earthquake bringing down reactor 4.

We agreed that there is no point is simply spreading fear when there is little or nothing that ordinary people can do. But after discussion, we discovered, by sending our loving care in our daily meditation, that we could extend the field of our attention and compassion to all those involved, focusing one at a time:

- One of the workers risking his or her life to remove the spent fuel rods
- One of the children in the area reported to have thyroid cancer
- One of the mammals or fish in the Pacific affected by radioactivity from the damaged plant
- One of the policy makers in the Japanese government responsible for making decisions

This exercise is not being undertaken to "prove" anything; it is simply to exercise the muscles of the power of love and care. In any case, it is virtually impossible to measure the results; if the fuel rods are safely removed and the four reactors safely decommissioned, there may be hundreds of contributing factors.

Until the fall of 2013, the general public was not necessarily in denial about the dangers still lurking in Fukushima, but simply not informed, largely on account of the lack of news in the global media. Slowly, toward the end of 2013, Fukushima began to play out on a bigger stage, thanks to the internet and social media waking people up to the problem. Information emerged steadily and on a global scale, amplified and sustained by individual contributions from many sources.

Electromagnetic Energy

What is fascinating, as the American expert on child development Joseph Chilton Pearce says, is that the heart produces two and a half watts of electrical energy at each pulsation, creating an electromagnetic field that is like a holograph of the electromagnetic field around the earth. "The electromagnetic field of the heart produces, holographically, the same field as the one produced by the earth and solar system. Now, physicists are beginning to look at the electro-magnetic auras as, simply, the organization of energy in the universe. All these are operating holographically—that is, at the smallest, unbelievably tiny level between the dendrites at the synapse [in the human brain], the body, the earth, and on outward."[3]

Could it then be said that humans are waking up to an entirely new perception of how the universe functions and how, by working with its energy systems instead of against them, we can assist the regeneration of the planet?

If this is the case, I'd like to describe what appear to me to be two of the most powerful forces in that direction: first, the energy, alertness, and skills of young social entrepreneurs the world over, and second, the empowerment of women to share with men the responsibilities of decision making.

The Energy of Young Social Entrepreneurs

During the summer of 2013 I helped train young social entrepreneurs from Colombia, Morocco, Egypt, Lebanon, Kenya, Mauritius, India, Pakistan, Azerbaijan, Bosnia, Germany, the Netherlands, Russia, Uganda, Ukraine, and United Kingdom to become builders of the kind of world they want.

Besides all the technical skills they needed—to do their research, build a website, raise start-up funds—they learned the inner skills that are vital in really transforming the world: skills to build trust in their teams, to resolve conflict quickly and effectively, to speak truth to power. Self-awareness at the individual level is what can enable each person to wake up and do what's needed to ensure a future for us on this planet—to change the world from the bottom up. And that's what they learned in this course.

There's a growing passion out there to do this work—there were two thousand applicants for this yearlong course at the Do School in Hamburg, Germany. The alumni of previous courses are back home, cascading the skills they learned. In 2013, over 5,200 young change makers applied for a Do School fellowship. Do School fellows worked on their start-ups in over fifty countries, spending a total of over thirty thousand hours working on innovative ventures to solve local problems in their communities, touching the lives of over one hundred thousand people. In response to demand, there are hundreds of such courses becoming available now around the world.

And it's not only the young. Remember Anupam Jalote in India, who produces renewable energy from organic and farming waste (profiled in chapter 3)? There are thousands and thousands of highly paid professionals in their forties and fifties hearing something similar to the interior message he heard—"Do not disappoint your soul"—and quitting well-paid jobs to devote their skills to the good of the planet. But work like theirs is below the radar—it doesn't make headlines. It's at street level—and you might well miss what Anupam is doing out there, and all the people like him. The media certainly have.

What's going on seems to me to be a movement without a name—*like green shoots coming up through concrete.* These are the people who are hunting truth, who are awake to the earth, who have woken up to what previous generations have done and refuse to resign themselves to simply wait out the crisis or relax into mindless consumption. They have the intelligence to see through the fog of spin, to piece together a global picture of trends, and to realize the extent of our present crisis.

They have courage enough

- to enter the darkness of what humans do to humans,
- to see the worst results of destruction,
- to stand up to put a stop to it,
- to create something alive and dynamic in its place.

This was foreseen by Martha Graham, considered one of the greatest artists of the twentieth century. "There is a vitality, a life force, an energy, a quickening that is translated through you into action. And because there is only one of you in all time, this expression is unique. . . . You have to keep open and aware directly to the urges that motivate you. Keep the channel open. . . . There is no satisfaction whatever at any time. There is only a queer divine dissatisfaction, a blessed unrest that keeps us marching, and makes us more alive than the other."[4]

The energy awakened in young social entrepreneurs is like a lightning flash—it jumps from one to another over considerable distances, *without a word said*.

> A secret smile of recognition,
> a frisson from this special frequency,
> a confidence in the skill of each other to find a way through.
> And do they come through!
> —They're cleaning up crime in Rio,
> —raising women's rights in Tahrir Square,
> —teaching computer skills to young men at risk of terrorism in Kenya,
> —setting up safe transport for girls in Islamabad,
> —enabling scavenger kids in the Philippines to go to school,
> —stopping knife fights in East London.

The connections are now happening quickly between those who have woken up and those waking—whether young social entrepreneurs, NGOs, or business people—because all have, to some extent, moved from "me" to "we." They care less about how much they have and more about how much they can offer. They want to improve things for others rather than impress.

Paul Hawken, one of the world's leading researchers, describes a worldwide movement largely unseen by politicians or the media. He spent a decade researching civil organizations dedicated to social justice. In *Blessed Unrest: How the Largest Movement in the World Came into Being and Why No One Saw It Coming,* he shows how "these organizations collectively comprise the largest movement on earth. It is organizing from the bottom up and is emerging as an extraordinary and creative expression of people's needs worldwide."[5]

Basically, there seem to be three responses of people to the current crises:

- They ignore the news; it's business as usual.
- They think we're all doomed, so do nothing.
- They think we're at a great turning point, that a shift in consciousness is taking place.

And these young social entrepreneurs know the secret. The mantra of last century was *What can I get?*—these young people know that the mantra of this century is *What can I give?* What they're willing to do is to risk all that others would guard so jealously—career, fame, wealth—to do what they can to make the world a better place. What's more, they love the adventure in this. As more citizens begin to wake up to what's possible, we seem to be realizing that the earth really is ours to protect and defend.

And I am by no means the only one who sees this happening. Monica Sharma, from her vantage point of years of experience at the United Nations, describes the new pathways being charted that are generating results—leaders reducing maternal mortality in parts of South Asia, transforming the lives of miners and neighboring communities in the world's second largest platinum-mining company in Africa, involving artists to share their wisdom and create new approaches to violence at home and in society. "These leaders are pattern-makers, not just problem-solvers. They deal with what is not working by creating alternatives. They are able to identify, distinguish, design and generate responses that integrate the different domains related to the entangled hierarchies of any given situation. They do not only solve complex societal problems at a surface level. They actively address the deeper dimensions."[6]

Remember how the "imaginal cells" started a major transformation in the caterpillar in chapter 2?

Here's the rest of the story:

The new imaginal cells continue to appear. More and more of them! Pretty soon, the caterpillar's immune system cannot destroy them fast enough. More and more of the imaginal cells survive. And then an amazing thing happens! The little tiny lonely imaginal cells start to clump together, into friendly little groups. They all resonate together at the same frequency, passing information from one to another. . . . A long string of clumping and clustering imaginal cells, all resonating at the same frequency, all passing information from one to another there inside the chrysalis. . . . A wave of good news travels throughout the system—it lurches and heaves . . . but is not yet a butterfly. . . . Then at some point, the entire long string of imaginal cells suddenly realizes all together that it is Something Different from the caterpillar. Something New! Something Wonderful!

... And in that realization is the shout of the birth of the butterfly! Happy Birthday Butterfly! . . . Since the butterfly now "knows" that it is a butterfly, the little tiny imaginal cells no longer have to do all those things individual cells must do. Now they are part of a multi-celled organism—A FAMILY who can share the work. . . . Each new butterfly cell can take on a different job. There is something for everyone to do. And everyone is important. And each cell begins to do just that very thing it is most drawn to do. And every other cell encourages it to do just that. A great way to organize a butterfly![7]

Humanity has reached the stage of knowledge and creativity when we must acquire a global and cosmic consciousness, and a long term consciousness into the future. An age of unprecedented, flourishing ideas has come which will make of humanity an entirely new species, a transcendent, elevated, cosmic species.

—Dr. Robert Muller, chancellor of the UN University for Peace, former assistant secretary-general of the United Nations

The Empowerment of Women to Share with Men the Responsibilities of Decision Making

On March 5, 2014, Desmond Tutu wrote:

We men have made a mess of things. I want a world run by women!

I think we are beginning to realize that we cannot have a fair world, a peaceful world, when we exclude half the population. It is not right that a child of God should be condemned to a life that is less than full, just because she is a girl. Give her the power to become all she can be and her world—which is ours, too—will be transformed.

Until I can have a world run by women, I want male leaders to do more for equality for girls and women. My fellow Elder Jimmy Carter calls women's inequality the most widespread human rights violation on earth, and sadly, I believe he is correct. [8]

Please observe how something strange has happened in the news: for centuries, the rape of women in India has been frequent, largely un-reported, and seldom punished. On December 16, 2012, in New Delhi, a twenty-three-year-old female physiotherapy intern was beaten and gang-raped by six men in a bus; she died from her injuries thirteen days later. Suddenly everything changed. The incident generated global coverage and was widely condemned, both in India and abroad. Thousands of protesters clashed with security forces in New Delhi and in major cities throughout India—furious with the government for not providing adequate security for women.

On February 14, 2013, a one-day event was held—One Billion Rising—a call for one billion women around the world to join together to dance in a show of collective strength.[9] The word *billion* refers the statistic that one in three women will be raped or beaten in her lifetime—about one billion worldwide. On February 14, 2014, the rally was held in more than 190 countries. Around five thousand organizations joined the campaign, which has also been aided or endorsed by religious ministers, movement builders, actors, and politicians.

Jean Houston writes:

> In this time of extraordinary transition, we can no longer afford to live as remedial members of the human race. A new set of values—holistic, syncretic, relationship and process-oriented, organic, spiritual—is rising within us and around us. . . . Many women are coming to see themselves as pilgrims and parents of this new emerging world and no old formulas and stop gap solutions will do. In the past, men in governments and the private sector have been partners in determining how the world works. It is time now to focus on the role that women, formerly largely excluded, should play in the development process. This is indispensable if we seek a future that is different from the past.[10]

Another example: even five years ago, a schoolgirl being shot by the Taliban would not have been a news item. Instead, via social media coverage in 2013, the shooting of Malala Yousafzai leapt into the headlines worldwide; the Pakistan government saluted her courage and bowed to popular opinion to nominate her for the Nobel Peace Prize. When she had recovered from the shooting, Malala made a speech to the General Assembly of the United Nations. It was broadcast live on television, and people around the world, along with the General Assembly, listened spellbound to the sixteen-year-old schoolgirl:

Dear brothers and sisters, do remember one thing. Malala Day is not my day. Today is the day of every woman, every boy and every girl who have raised their voice for their rights. There are hundreds of human rights activists and social workers who are not only speaking for human rights, but who are struggling to achieve their goals of education, peace and equality. Thousands of people have been killed by the terrorists and millions have been injured. I am just one of them.

The wise saying "The pen is mightier than sword" was true. The extremists are afraid of books and pens. The power of education frightens them. They are afraid of women. The power of the voice of women frightens them. And that is why they killed fourteen innocent medical students in the recent attack in Quetta. And that is why they killed many female teachers and polio workers in Khyber Pukhtoon Khwa and FATA. That is why they are blasting schools every day. Because they were and they are afraid of change, afraid of the equality that we will bring into our society.

Honorable Secretary-General, peace is necessary for education. In many parts of the world especially Pakistan and Afghanistan, terrorism, wars and conflicts stop children to go to their schools. We are really tired of these wars. Women and children are suffering in many parts of the world in many ways. In India, innocent and poor children are victims of child labour. Many schools have been destroyed in Nigeria. People in Afghanistan have been affected by the hurdles of extremism for decades. Young girls have to do domestic child labour and are forced to get married at early age. Poverty, ignorance, injustice, racism and the deprivation of basic rights are the main problems faced by both men and women.

Dear fellows, today I am focusing on women's rights and girls' education because they are suffering the most. There was a time when women social activists asked men to stand up for their rights. But, this time, we will do it by ourselves. I am not telling men to step away from speaking for women's rights, rather I am focusing on women to be independent to fight for themselves."

It is not only that women's organizations worldwide are multiplying exponentially and that women are becoming better educated worldwide and slowly taking up positions in parliaments and jobs in the media. There is another phenomenon that suggests something different. It suggests a fast-growing global sensitivity, accelerated by social media, to what is happening to the planet. People do mind that polar ice caps are melting, that toxic waste is polluting oceans, and that so many women are suffering violence—and they have found a way to show that they mind. Voters are beginning to wake up and act, to exert pressure on policy makers, to bring bottom-up forces to interact with top-down forces in ways not seen before.

This is symptomatic of the vast power unleashed by riding the dragon—it is the beginning of the rebalancing of masculine and feminine. I believe it is the key to building a future world that works for everyone. We may look back in a hundred years and realize that what we are witnessing now is a revolution more massive than the abolition of slavery.

This is how this awakening is taking place worldwide.

These are the new forces gathering speed.

This is the company you may be in, if you so choose.

The future hangs in the balance.

And what happens next depends on all of us.

AFTERWORD BY ANDREW HARVEY

My dear friends,

If you have read this book, you know by now that the crisis we are in is an extreme one and that the opportunity being offered to us all by this crisis is one that could radically change us and the world we live in. There is a great birth possible and a new world appearing out of the chaos of the old.

Everything depends now on us—you and I. And everything depends too on how deeply we go within to source, what it is we choose to do in response to what's happening. Action is urgently needed on every level, but the situation is far too serious for such action to be taken from fear or blame or rage or unhealed suffering. Only the action that arises from an increasingly healed inner being—and that is grounded in the deep feminine balanced with the deep masculine—can be of any real use now. I know that this is within your reach.

The good news is that there are hundreds of thousands of people waking up to this vision of sacred action and starting to embody it. My hope and prayer for you is that you become one of them and that you discover the joy and purpose that can only come from stepping up to the secret mission of your life and playing a part in the great evolutionary leap we are all summoned to.

In love and hope,
Andrew Harvey

APPENDIX

EXERCISES, TOOLS, AND RESOURCES

Strengthening the Immune System

(See chapter 6: last section.) This exercise is to address the inner, personal challenges of trying to change the world. It gives attention to the internal residues of emotion left by tackling some of the harshest realities of the planet. It takes about fifteen to twenty minutes.

Step 1: Find a quiet place where you are comfortable and not likely to be disturbed.

Step 2: Allow your intuition to trace some of the feelings you may have had recently, for example:

- When you see huge wealth being squandered, it can leave you with feelings of *outrage*.
- As we find out about the corruption and dishonesty of some political systems or the greed of some corporations, it can leave us feeling *furious but powerless*.
- The indifference of the media to issues we care passionately about can make us *cynical*.
- When we witness technology out of control, as, for example, in Fukushima, we are naturally filled with *fear*.

- Those who witness the brutal human casualties of war can be left with a residue of *suffering* that's almost unbearable.
- Those who are constantly seeing ecosystems being trashed can endure a sense of *acute loss or even heartbreak*.
- *Fury* can affect those who witness the results of financial decisions that rip off the poorest of the poor.

Step 3: Feel whatever feelings are there, as fully as you can. Take care of the feelings as if they were those of a child. Be as kind as you would be to a frightened, lost or heartbroken child.

Step 4: Don't offer solutions; just allow the feelings to simply be there, while you make space for them and listen to them, for about five minutes, breathing deeply.

Step 5: With your quiet, caring attention—that's all it takes—the feelings will transform. You will be left calmer and wiser.

Working on world issues can be compared to being a doctor going into an area where there is cholera or typhoid. That doctor will need a strong immune system. Taking care of emotions will strengthen your immune system and allow you to develop the self-awareness that is essential to doing effective work in the world.

The Listening Exercise

(See chapter 7, signpost 1.) The listening exercise has four benefits:

- It allows a profound deepening of your understanding of what's really going on inside you and another person.
- It helps you discover the authentic self from deep within—what you didn't know you knew.
- It allows you to check your ability to give another person your full attention without "helping."
- It reveals compassion and opens the heart.

I've done this exercise with corporate leaders, top executive teams, and young social entrepreneurs from all over the world. They all found it quite tough to do at first but came out of it astonished at what they found—their own truths as well as others. You can also do it with your lover or partner; if you've hit a sticky patch in your relationship, it's an incredible way of getting past the blame game and learning what's happening inside yourself and inside your partner.

It's important to agree to absolute confidentiality, because you may be saying or hearing things that are extremely private, tender, and vulnerable—things that may never have been said before.

Sit down opposite each other in a comfortable place where you won't be disturbed for twenty minutes. Have a timer there to ensure each person listens for the same amount of time. One partner is A and one is B. Agree on a nontrivial question, for example, "tell me who you really are?" or "tell me what you long for most in your life?" Set the timer for five minutes.

Partner A asks the question: "Tell me, [name of partner], who you really are?" then he or she does nothing else except to give *full listening attention*. That means keeping eye contact but not reacting—not nodding, smiling, laughing, or grimacing. This isn't easy, but it is essential, because when we encourage another person with a nod—or react in any way—we subtly affect what they decide to say.

Partner B undertakes the following sequence:

1. Gives his or her full attention to the question,
2. Puts his or her full intention on finding out the truth of the answer,
3. Takes the question down from the brain into the belly (the *hara*, the center of gravity of the body)
4. Reports whatever answer is there.

It's important for Partner B to report *only* what is there—not give all the back story—and then continue to do the technique again. The more honestly you can report what is there, be it embarrassing, shameful, astonishing or funny, the more you will discover. Partner B may not say a great deal before going silent again while repeating the four-part sequence over a period of five minutes. Meanwhile Partner A simply continues to give full attention and does not repeat the question.

When the timer indicates five minutes have elapsed, you change roles. Partner B asks partner A the same question and then follows the same instructions, simply giving full attention and eye contact. Partner A undertakes the sequence above.

You can use this method with just one question, which will take about ten minutes, or you can go on and do four questions of your choice, which will take about forty minutes. Other questions people sometimes use are:

- Tell me what's disturbing you in your life?
- Tell me what are you yearning for?
- Tell me what unlocks your heart?
- Tell me what gives you energy?

When you finish, you can decide if you want to simply write in your journal or share feedback. You'll be amazed what you find out about yourself, your listening skills, and about what really matters to your friend.

Some Choices for Starting a Meditative Practice

(See chapter 7: signpost 2.) There are so many choices available, to suit all tastes:

- Vipassana
- Zen
- Buddhism
- Christian meditation
- Sufism
- Transcendental meditation
- Yoga
- T'ai chi
- Chi gong
- And many, many more.

See which one attracts you and try it out. Within a short time, settle on one practice that you like and keep doing it regularly (at the same time of day, if possible) for six months. Then evaluate. Below, in more detail, are two that work for me: mindfulness and Heartmath.

Mindfulness

This simple exercise, mentioned in chapter 7, has been shown to reduce stress, improve concentration, and relieve pain.[12] It can take as little as five minutes, though it can be extended. Half an hour is recommended, and daily practice is highly effective.

You need to be sitting in a place where you will not be disturbed. Sit with a straight back and your legs and arms uncrossed. Close your eyes.

- Give full attention to relaxing the body, starting with the toes, then the ankles, calves, knees, thighs, hips, abdomen, and the vital organs of the body, including the liver, stomach, kidneys, lungs, and the heart. Go to the base of the spine, called the sacrum, and relax the spine—vertebra by vertebra—up to the shoulder blades. Take the attention down the arms to the elbows and the hands and fingers. Then finally take the attention to the top of the spinal column up into the bones of the skull and the brain, relaxing the forehead, eyes, ears, nose, mouth, and finally the jaw.
- Breathe in slowly and mindfully, noticing the air gradually swelling the lungs and the torso. Breathe in for a count of four and breathe out for a count of four, noticing how the air is cooler as it enters the nostrils and warmer as it leaves through the mouth.
- Continue to breathe like this deeply for twenty times.
- Now allow yourself to watch the screen of your mind as if it were a blue sky.
- Watch as your thoughts pass across the blue sky, like white clouds, observing your thoughts in a passive and relaxed way, as you continue to breathe.
- When you feel this is enough, gently allow yourself to come back into the room. You can continue for as long as you wish. Half an hour is considered very beneficial.

You may notice after doing this for half an hour that you feel a feeling of emptiness and calmness and joy. The secret is that you distance yourself from the repetitive thoughts in your mind and that you become the "watcher." This space that you create gives you freedom.

Institute of HeartMath:
A Change of Heart Changes Everything

(See chapter 8.) The heart needs to be the new focus of consciousness, rather than the mind, because it is the first and most important organ in the body.[13]

- The electrical field of the heart is about sixty times greater in amplitude than the electrical activity generated by the brain. The magnetic field produced by the heart is more than five thousand times greater in strength than the field generated by the brain and can be detected twelve to twenty-five feet away from the body in all directions.
- 60 to 65 percent of all the cells in the heart are neural cells, which are precisely the same as brain cells and function in the same way, but they monitor and maintain control of the entire mind, brain, body, and organism.
- The heart is the coordinating center of the major endocrine glandular structure of the body, which produces the hormones that profoundly affect the operations of body, brain, and mind and coordinate the functioning of the other systems in the body, including the immune system.

To open the heart, do the first exercise below as many times during the day as you can, as that reinforces the habit of always returning to the heart center. Ultimately, this sets a calm, regular heart rhythm rather than a jagged, chaotic one. It sets up a cascade of calm neurological responses in the brain and throughout the different systems in the body.

Exercise 1

1. Focus on the center of your chest, in the heart area.
2. Breathe deeply in and out through the heart.
3. Activate a positive feeling of some kind: gratitude for what you have, love for people you hold close to you, compassion, peace.
4. Radiate that feeling—first throughout your own body field and then out into the wider field of the world.

Exercise 2

1. If you are feeling stressed, anxious, angry, frustrated, depressed, or something similar, acknowledge this state before you activate the positive feeling in step 3 of exercise 1 above.
2. Do the heart-focused breathing, slowly.
3. Activate the positive feeling—whatever it is. As you breathe in, imagine that you are drawing in a feeling of inner ease from your heart.
4. When the stressful feelings have diminished, affirm that you want to maintain and anchor this state of ease for yourself rather than sending it out to others or the world. This will establish a specific heartbeat frequency that will strengthen in regularity as you do this exercise.
5. Revisit steps 1–4 during the day to reset the system so that you feel relaxed, present, energized, and in the flow of life.

These two exercises align heart and mind so that each works with rather than against the other. When you have practiced this for several days, several times a day, or whenever you feel fraught, upset, or anxious, you will get the feeling that things are just right.

Cocounseling Is Reciprocal Peer Counseling:

(See chapter 7: signpost 3.) *Reciprocal:* cocounselors take it in equal turns to be client and counselor.

Peer: everyone is equal, there are no experts trying to sort out other people.

Counseling: it is a bit like other forms of counseling, in that one person listens while the other talks, but there the similarity ends. It is the person in the role of the client who is in charge of the session, and the person in the role of the counselor mainly just gives very good attention.

Cocounselors make their own arrangements to meet, usually in pairs, for cocounseling sessions. Cocounseling sessions are free.[14] Cocounseling can be used to help us get better at most things and in most ways. It can be used to deal with day-to-day life problems or it can be used to deal with deep personal distress. It is for anyone, not just for people with serious problems—we do not have to be ill to get better. The basic idea (shared by many humanistic approaches) is that if we are given time and compassionate attention (rather than questions and advice), we will be able to explore whatever is blocking us or hurts us or prevents us realizing our potential. Cocounseling trains us to give that sort of attention to others and to use it to work on ourselves, so we spend equal time in each role.

Conflict Transformation Technique

(See chapter 7: signpost 5.) Conflict is not good or bad; it's simply energy. As such, it does not have to be prevented or resolved, but transformed.[15] This exercise enables us to move

- from the head (being "right" and having a "position")
- to the heart (being connected, with the possibility to discover a common interest).

Ask the person with whom you have a conflict if he or she would be willing to sit with you for half an hour and talk in a structured way. Explain that this will give both parties an opportunity to express feelings safely, without going into the rights and wrongs of the situation.

Two people involved [A and B] sit opposite each other, preferably with a neutral facilitator, and preferably with some flowers nearby. During this process the facilitator can coach the participants to be more specific and remind them stick to the first person, to express feelings clearly, and to be more authentic.

1. A starts to describe his or her feelings in the conflict, speaking in the first person and not accusing B. For example, saying, "When this happens, I feel—sad, angry, frustrated, miserable, fearful."
2. A continues until has said enough. B simply gives full attention and listens, without interrupting.
3. B is asked to repeat to A what B has heard, as accurately as possible, and to include what he or she has observed of the feelings behind the words.
4. A is asked, "Was that correct? Was anything omitted?" A can then add anything that was left out.
5. Change roles and do the same with B speaking and A listening, following steps 1–4.
6. Then facilitator can ask A to express his or her needs: "What do you need?" while B listens to the answer.
7. Then the same question to B, while A listens.
8. Then move to requests. The facilitator asks A, "What do you request B to do or not do?" B can agree or not, and they can set a time frame, if necessary, by which time B will do what A requests.
9. The same is asked of B—to make a request of A. A agrees or not, and they set a time frame, if necessary, by which time A will do this.

To repeat, what this process does is to shift the issue from the head (where the focus is on the thought "I'm right and you're wrong") to the heart, which allows you to understand what it is like to be the other person. This means you can move from your opposing positions to a place where you can both look at the problem from a perspective of your mutual interests—what you both need. If all goes reasonably well, you're moving toward a place of communication, a softening of what was previously hard and harsh.

The Practical Bit:
How to Hold Meetings That Energize

Ask employees of any large company or organization, and they will complain that they spend too much time in meetings. This frustrates and drains people of energy; they feel they are wasting time and are bored and impatient. The art of holding meetings that energize people is well worth learning. Here are some ground rules that produce more fruitful meetings and help to build trust in the team.

- Start meetings with a few moments of silence to allow everyone to "arrive"—not just physically but for the heart and mind to be present, leaving distractions behind.
- Hold a check-in—set aside a moment for each person to say briefly how he or she is in that moment or express any concerns or expectations about the meeting.
- Agree total confidentiality, if appropriate.
- Agree when the meeting will end, and stick to this.
- Listen while another is talking and not interrupt (a talking stick is useful).
- Talk without raising the voice or using accusing language.
- Appoint two facilitators, one responsible for process and one for content.

The *process facilitator* monitors the quality and focus of the meeting by periodically taking the temperature of the meeting, pointing out if there appears to be anger in the air, for example, or sadness. The facilitator sometimes asks people to share briefly how they are feeling at that moment. If necessary, the facilitator calls for a brief pause—an agreed silence—to allow the participants to collect themselves and digest what has been said. It's good to start and end the meeting with a check-in and check-out, times when each person can say a sentence or two about how he or she doing. This builds trust and enables participants to become aware of the emotional state of their fellow stakeholders.

The *content facilitator* keeps the conversation on topic. He or she points out when the conversation is going off topic; periodically sums up the meeting (saying something like "this is where we've gotten to so far"); ensures the agenda items are covered in the time available; and makes sure that at the end of meeting, everyone is clear about next steps.

It's essential to practice these skills, because establishing trust between mutually suspicious parties—who may have caused each other harm—is not easy. That's why we say we are *holding* a meeting: the facilitators are literally *holding the space* in which transformative results can be developed. To build resilient trust between stakeholders, one has to go beyond concerns of physical or psychological security. Very often, exposing vulnerability or a trace of humanity can be the doorway to building deeper trust. An example, one of the key inspirational moments of reconciliation in South Africa was when Nelson Mandela had tea with Bessie Verwoerd, the widow of former president Henrik Verwoerd—the grand architect of apartheid. For many, this encounter was unthinkable. It had an incredible impact on Afrikaner extremists—the man they were trying to portray as a dangerous criminal had the trust and integrity to pay a civilized visit and have a cup of tea with someone who could have been his sworn enemy.

NOTES

Chapter 1: Riding the Dragon

1. The Oxford Research Group, www.oxfordresearchgroup.org.uk/about.
2. Scilla McLean, ed., *How Nuclear Weapons Decisions are Made* (London: MacMillan, 1986).
3. "Our Approach" on Peace Direct's webpage, www.peacedirect.org/about /our-approach.
4. Scilla Elworthy, "Waiting for the Dawn: A Baghdad Diary," *Open Democracy,* January 14, 2003, www.opendemocracy.net/conflict-iraqwarquestions/article _885.jsp.

Chapter 2: The Leap in Consciousness

1. Edgar Mitchell, quoted on the webpage of the Institute of Noetic Sciences, www.noetic.org/about/history.
2. Yann Arthus-Bertrand and Luc Besson, *Home,* 2009, https://archive.org /details/HOME_English. *Home* is an exceptional movie. The producer says, "We are living in exceptional times. Scientists tell us that we have 10 years to change the way we live, avert the depletion of natural resources and the catastrophic evolution of the Earth's climate. The stakes are high for us and our children. Everyone should take part in the effort, and *Home* has been conceived to take a message of mobilization out to every human being. For this purpose, *Home* needs to be free. A patron, the PPR Group, made this possible. EuropaCorp, the distributor, also pledged not to make any profit because

Home is a non-profit film. *Home* has been made for you: share it! And act for the planet."

3. I've since read about this sensation in a book by Douglas Harding, entitled *On Having No Head: Zen and the Rediscovery of the Obvious* (Carlsbad, CA: InnerDirections, 2002).

4. Eknath Easwaran, trans., *The Upanishads* (Petaluma, CA: Nilgiri Press, 1987).

5. "Episode Five: A Deeper Look at Love and Intimacy," narrated by Gangaji, *A Conversation with Gangaji*, February 20, 2012.

6. Fritjof Capra, *The Tao of Physics: An Exploration of the Parallels Between Modern Physics and Eastern Mysticism* (New York: Bantam Books, 1975).

7. Robert Muller, *The Third Five Hundred Ideas of Two Thousand Ideas for a Better World: A Countup to the Year 2000*, vol. 3 (Santa Barbara, CA: Media 21 Global Public Relations, 1998), http://robertmuller.org/voladnl/v3adnl.htm.

8. Anne Baring, *The Dream of the Cosmos: A Quest for the Soul* (Dorset, England: Archive Publishing, 2013), 332.

9. Institute of HeartMath, "Global Coherence Initiative," www.glcoherence.org.

10. "Can Group Meditation Bring World Peace? Quantum Physicist, John Hagelin explains," YouTube video 4:05 posted by "Transcendental Meditation," October 6, 2009, www.youtube.com/watch?v=yVFa6Wtuxu8.

11. Elisabet Sahtouris, "Ecosophy—Nature's Guide to a Better World," Paper presented at the the conference The Emerging Future, Oxford, England, October 2013.

12. The Tree of Life is a healing and empowerment process of storytelling and time in nature with circles of around eight participants and two facilitators using the tree as a metaphor for life (roots, trunk, branches, wounding, fruit), which takes place over three days.

13. Bev Reeler, Tarisiro, email to author, August 2013.

14. Poetry by Bev Reeler, Tarisiro, September 2013.

15. Sally Dearman Cummings, email to author, January 5, 2014.

16. Lynne McTaggart, *The Field* (Shaftesbury, England: Element 2001), 125.

17. McTaggart, *The Field*, 277.

18. Daniel J Siegel, Mindsight: The New Science of Personal Transformation (New York: Bantam, 2010).

19. Christopher Bache, in *Mind Before Matter*, edited by Paul Devereux (Alresford, England: Iff Books, 2012), 274.

20. Scilla Elworthy, *Power and Sex: A Book About Women* (Shaftesbury, England: Element, 1996), 5.

21. Lynn Margulis and Dorion Sagan, *Acquiring Genomes: A Theory of the Origins of Species,* 1st ed. (New York: Basic Books, 2002).

22. Greg Ray, "The Ocean Is Broken," *Newcastle Herald* (Australia), October 18, 2013, www.theherald.com.au/story/1848433/the-ocean-is-broken.

23. IUCN, "Changes in Numbers of Species in the Threatened Categories (CR, EN, VU) from 1996 to 2013 (IUCN Red List version 2013.1) for the major taxonomic groups on the Red List," table 2, *The IUCN Red List of Threatened Species,* last modified June 8, 2013, www.iucnredlist.org/documents/summary statistics/2013_1_RL_Stats_Table_2.pdf.
24. National Snow and Ice Data Center (NSIDC), http://nsidc.org.
25. E. Rignot, I. Velicogna, M. R. Broeke, A. Monaghan, and J. T. Lenaerts, "Acceleration of the Contribution of the Greenland and Antarctic Ice Sheets to Sea Level Rise." *Geophysical Research Letters* 38, no. 5 (2011): doi:10.1029/2011GL046583.
26. Arthus-Bertrand and Besson, *Home.* If you do nothing else, watch the movie *Home.* It shows the diversity of life on earth and how humanity is threatening the ecological balance of the planet. It received over four hundred thousand combined views within the first twenty-four hours on YouTube.
27. Andrew Harvey, "The Gospel of Thomas: A Road Map to Transfiguration," *Patheos,* August 12, 2013, www.patheos.com/blogs/christpathseminar/2013/08/the-gospel-of-thomas-a-road-map-to-transfiguration, quote altered with permission.
28. Karen Armstrong, *The Great Transformation: The World in the Time of Buddha, Socrates, Confucius and Jeremiah* (London: Atlantic, 2006).
29. Cultural historian and theologian Thomas Berry, in *The Great Work* and *The Dream of the Earth,* biologist and business consultant Dr. Elisabet Sahtouris in *Biology Revisioned,* physicist Fritjof Capra in *The Web of Life,* biology professor Christopher Uhl in *Developing Ecological Consciousness: Path to a Sustainable World,* and many others—all give the same urgent message.
30. Andrew Harvey, *Radical Passion* (Berkeley, CA: North Atlantic Books, 2012), 3.
31. Eckhart Tolle, *A New Earth: Awakening to Your Life's Purpose* (New York: Penguin, 2005).

Chapter 3: Learning How World Changers Use Inner Power

1. Thich Nhat Hanh, *Being Peace* (Berkeley, CA: Parallax Press, 1987).
2. Scilla Elworthy, "Dekha Ibrahim Abdi Obituary: Schoolteacher in Rural Kenya Who Became a Global Peacemaker," Guardian, August 9, 2011, www.theguardian.com/global-development/2011/aug/09/dekha-ibrahim-abdi-obituary.
3. Elizabeth Grice, "Ellen MacArthur: 'I can't live with the sea any more,'" *Telegraph,* August 31, 2010, www.telegraph.co.uk/sport/othersports

/sailing/7966301/Ellen-MacArthur-I-cant-live-with-the-sea-any
-more.html.

4. Ellen MacArthur, *Full Circle: My Life and Journey* (London: Michael Joseph, 2010), 361.

5. Grice, "Ellen MacArthur: 'I can't live with the sea any more.'"

6. Ellen MacArthur Foundation, "The Circular Model—An Overview," www.ellenmacarthurfoundation.org/circular-economy/circular-economy /the-circular-model-an-overview.

7. Grice, "Ellen MacArthur: 'I can't live with the sea any more.'"

8. "Mark Rylance Performs 'The Peacebuilder,'" YouTube video, 34:23, posted by "Peace Direct" on June 13, 2011, www.youtube.com/watch?v=xcE_eLR 1JKc.

9. "Congo: 4,532 Militia Fighters Lay Down Their Guns," Peace Direct, www.peacedirect.org/dr-congo-4532-fighters-demobilise.

10. From a speech read on video on August 31, 1995, before the NGO Forum on Women, Beijing, China.

11. "Celebrate Life 2011," YouTube video, 3:05, posted by "Celebratelife2011," February 22, 2011, www.youtube.com/watch?v=wofSzf-xVGM.

12. "Thomas Hübl," Thomas Hübl, www.thomashuebl.com/en/thomas-huebl .html.

13. "News," Thomas Hübl, www.thomashuebl.com/en/news.html#shift.

14. Personal account of teleconference with Thomas Hübl, February 2013.

15. Pema Chödrön, *When Things Fall Apart: Heart Advice for Difficult Times* (Boston: Shambhala, 1997), 10.

16. "Pema Chödrön," Shambhala International, www.shambhala.org/teachers /pema/shenpa3a.php.

17. Evite se Perron, www.evita.co.za/inthenews.html.

18. *The Star* (Johannesburg, August 12, 1981), quoted in Allen John, *Rabble-Rouser for Peace: The Authorized Biography of Desmond Tutu* (Johannesburg: Random House, 2006), 347.

19. Desmond Tutu, *No Future Without Forgiveness* (London: Rider, 1999), 51–52.

20. This may not be his exact words, but my impression of what he said—I was present in the room.

21. "The 'Democratization of Power': An Interview with Anupam Jalote, CEO of GreenOil," *Beyond Profit*, http://beyondprofit.com/?p=1513wableenergye ntrepreneur.

22. Of course, extremely destructive people can also have presence, such as Hitler and Saddam Hussein.

23. Quoted anonymously in Joe Simpson, *The Beckoning Silence* (Seattle, WA: Mountaineers Books, 2003).

Chapter 4: Changing the Values That Underlie Our Decisions

1. "Measuring the Daily Destruction of the World's Rainforests," *Earth Talk* (blog), *Scientific American*, November 19, 2009, http://www.scientific american.com/article/earth-talks-daily-destruction.

2. Adapted from Dr. Vandana Shiva, "The Uttarakhand Disaster: A Wake Call to Stop the Rape of Our Fragile Himalaya," June 24, 2013.

3. Vandana Shiva, "From Seeds of Suicide to Seeds of Hope: Why Are Indian Farmers Committing Suicide and How Can we Stop This Tragedy?" *Huffington Post*, April 28, 2009, www.huffingtonpost.com/vandana-shiva/from-seeds -of-suicide-to_b_192419.html.

4. David Attenborough, "State of the Planet," BBC 2, 2000.

5. Reported in "Are We in the Middle of a Sixth Mass Extinction?" *Science*, March 2, 2011.

6. UN Food and Agriculture Organisation expert prediction.

7. Worldwide Institute: *Vision for a Sustainable World*.

8. Anne Baring, *The Dream of the Cosmos*, 334.

9. Milne says this in *Metaphysics and the Cosmic Order*, quoted in Baring, *The Dream of the Cosmos*, 334.

10. Baring, *The Dream of the Cosmos*, 335.

11. Richard Dawkins, *The Selfish Gene*, 2nd revised edition (Oxford, Oxford Paperbacks, 1989), 3.

12. Sally Dearman Cummings, email communication with author, January 5, 2014. The TED talk presented by neuro-anatomist Jill Bolte-Taylor illustrates this quite well: "Jill Bolte-Taylor: My Stroke of Insight," filmed February 2008, TED video, 18:19, www.ted.com/talks/jill_bolte_taylor_s_powerful _stroke_of_insight.html.

13. United Nations: International Investment Disputes on the Rise, SUNS News, April 18, 2013.

14. Dr. Maude Barlow, *Blue Future: Protecting Water for People and the Planet Forever*, forthcoming.

15. Hazel Henderson, "Looking Back from 2030: Humanity's Transition to the Ethical Green Global Economy." Manuscript sent to the author, November 2013.

16. "The World's Billionaires," Forbes, www.forbes.com/billionaires/list.

17. Jason Hickel, "The Truth about Extreme Global Inequality," Al Jazeera, April 14, 2013, www.aljazeera.com/indepth/opinion/2013/04/2013 49124135226392.html. Hickel is a lecturer at the London School of Economics.

18. "Into the Shadows," directed by Andrew Scarano (2009), www.intothe shadows.org.

19. John Thomas Didymus, "Oxfam: World's 100 Richest Individuals Earn

Enough to End Poverty," Digital Journal, January 20, 2013, http://digital
journal.com/article/341755#ixzz2bqdeWCHb.

20. "Global Wealth Inequality—What You Never Knew You Never Knew,"
YouTube video, 3:50, posted by "TheRulesOrg," April 3, 2013, www.youtube
.com/watch?v=uWSxzjyMNpU.

21. The next seven paragraphs were contributed by John Bunzl, author of *Global
Domestic Politics, Global Briefing Series* (London: ISPO, 2013), www.simpol
.org.

22. See John Bunzl's talk for TEDxBerlin: John Bunzl, "The Political
Prisoner's Dilemma," TED video, 16:24, 2012, www.tedxberlin.de/
tedxberlin-2012-crossing-borders-john-bunzl-the-political-prisoners-dilemma.

23. "Global Competitiveness," World Economic Forum, www.weforum.org
/issues/global-competitiveness.

24. John Bunzl, *Global Domestic Politics: A Citizen's Guide to Running a Diverse
Planet, Global Briefing Series* (London: ISPO, 2013).

25. Bunzl, *Global Domestic Politics*, 45.

26. Stockholm International Peace Research Institute figures.

27. Gareth Evans, "The Global March toward Peace," *Project Syndicate*, December 27, 2012, www.project-syndicate.org/commentary/the-decline-of
-violent-conflict-by-gareth-evans This "New Peace" phenomenon was first
publicized by Andrew Mack's Human Security Report Project, supported by
the superb database of the Uppsala Conflict Data Program. For statistics on
the number of people killed, Evans cites The Human Security Report 2012,
http://hsrgroup.org/docs/Publications/HSR2012/Figures/2012Report
_Fig_5_2_GlobalSBBDs46–08.pdf.

28. *International Control of the Arms Trade* (Oxford: Oxford Research Group,
1992).

29. "Prince Andrew: "Cheerleader in Chief for the Arms Industry,'" *Channel 4
News*, March 10, 2011.

30. Suhbet Karbuz, "US Military Oil Pains," *Energy Bulletin*, February 17, 2007,
detailed the oil consumption just for the Pentagon's aircraft, ships, ground vehicles, and facilities that made it the single largest oil consumer in the world.

31. "Scientists Gain New Insight into Climate Change, and What to Do about
It," *Washington's Blog*, August 14, 2013, www.washingtonsblog.com
/2013/08/scientists-gain-new-insight-into-.

32. Barry Sanders, *The Green Zone The Environmental Costs of Militarism* (Oakland, CA: AK Press, 2009).

33. See information at Peace Direct, www.peacedirect.org.

34. Michael Gross, "Silent War," *Vanity Fair*, July 2013, www.vanityfair.com
/culture/2013/07/new-cyberwar-victims.

35. Gross, "Silent War."

36. Hermann Goering, Hitler's Reich-Marshall speaking at the Nuremberg Trials after WWII.

37. Gabrielle Rifkind and Giandomenico Picco, *The Fog of Peace* (London: I.B. Tauris, 2014), 167.

38. Rifkind and Picco, *The Fog of Peace*, 167.

39. Diana Francis, "Making Peace Global," *Peace Review: A Journal of Social Justice*, 25, no. 1 (2013), 42–50.

40. Jakob von Uexkull, MA Oxon. Founder, The World Future, Council Keynote Speech, World Judiciary Summit, CMS Lucknow, India, December 14, 2013.

41. Javier Gimeno, "The Perils of Short-Term Thinking," *INSEAD*, July 17, 2013, http://knowledge.insead.edu/leadership-management/the-perils-of-short-term-thinking-2544.

42. Victor Anderson, "Addressing Short-Termism in Government and Politics," *Guardian Sustainable Business* (blog) *Guardian*, March 2, 2011, www.theguardian.com/sustainable-business/government-politics-short-termism-unsustainability.

43. Oxford Martin Commission for Future Generations, Oxford Martin School, University of Oxford, www.oxfordmartin.ox.ac.uk/commission.

44. Kehkashan Basu, World Future Council, www.worldfuturecouncil.org/kehkashan_basu.html.

45. I am indebted to Dr. Andrew Powell for his summary of the effects of these two events in "Technology and Soul in the 21st Century," a paper based on talks given at the 2013 "Interfaces" series, Edinburgh International Festival and "Beyond the Brain X. Shifting Consciousness: Mind, Self and Brain in the 21st Century," Scientific and Medical Network, 2013, drawing on A. Yablokov, "Chernobyl: Consequences of the Catastrophe for People and the Environment," *Annals of the New York Academy of Sciences*, 1181 (2010). Even more serious figures on thyroid abnormalities have emerged: "Report: Now over 44% of Fukushima Children Have Thyroid Abnormalities in Latest Tests," Energy News, February 14, 2013, http://enenews.com/report-now-over-44-of-fukushima-children-tested-have-thyroid-abnormalities. The official report now says, "The results compiled up to January 21, 2013 revealed that 41,947 (44.2%) of 94,975 children had thyroid ultrasound abnormalities. Together with 38,114 children (13,645 or 35.8% had thyroid ultrasound abnormalities) tested in the last half of Fiscal Year Heisei 23 (FYH23) from October 2011 through March 2012, a total of 55,592 (41.8%) of 133,089 Fukushima children have been found to have ultrasound abnormalities."

46. Rupert Wingfield-Hayes, "What Have We Learned from Fukushima?" *BBC*, September 20, 2013, www.bbc.co.uk/news/science-environment-24332346.

47. Harvey Wasserman, "More than 80,000 Demand a Global Takeover at

Fukushima," *Huffington Post*, October 1, 2013, www.huffingtonpost.com /harvey-wasserman/more-than-80000-demand-a-_b_4020673.html.

48. Indigenous Council Statement, October 2013, www.indigenousaction.org.

49. For details, see GeoEngineering Watch, www.geoengineeringwatch.org.

50. For details, see "Solar Radiation Management," International Risk Governance Council, www.irgc.org/issues/climate-engineering.

51. David Krieger, "Hubris vs. Wisdom," *The Sunflower* 197 (December 2013) (newsletter of the Nuclear Age Peace Foundation).

52. "The Battle for the Coasts," World Ocean Review, http://worldoceanreview .com/en/wor-1/coasts/living-in-coastal-areas.

53. John O'Donohue, *Divine Beauty: The Invisible Embrace* (London: Bantam Books, 2003), 15.

54. Martha Chen, Joann Vanek, Francie Lund, and James Heintz, "Women Work and Poverty," UNIFEM, 2005, www.un-ngls.org/orf/women-2005.pdf.

55. Data compiled by the Inter-Parliamentary Union on the basis of information provided by National Parliaments by July 1, 2013, www.ipu.org/wmn-e /classif.htm.

56. See Nicholas Kristof and Sheryl Wudunn, *Half the Sky* (Virago, 2010), 94.

57. For more information, see "Violence Against Women," WHO, factsheet 239, updated October 2013, www.who.int/mediacentre/factsheets/fs239/en.

58. Nicholas Kristof, "Raped, Kidnapped, and Silenced," *New York Times*, June 14, 2005, www.nytimes.com/2005/06/14/opinion/14kristof.html.

59. Pam Grout, *E2* (Carlsbad, CA: Hay House, 2013), 77.

60. The Club of Rome has a tradition of addressing the root causes of the challenges facing humankind and has initiated a program called ValuesQuest to explore these issues and to map out a path forward. This paragraph is related to an article by Martin Palmer and Karl Wagner, "ValuesQuest," *Eruditio* 2 (March 13, 2013), http://eruditio.worldacademy.org/issue-2.

61. Dr. Andrew Powell, "Technology and Soul in the 21st Century."

62. Video available at: Annie Leonard, "From the Story of Stuff to the Story of Solutions," Daily Good, November 21, 2013, www.dailygood.org/story/598 /from-the-story-of-stuff-to-the-story-of-solutions-annie-leonard.

63. Television statistics available at www.statisticbrain.com/television-watching -statistics and www.csun.edu/science/health/docs/tv&health.html.

Chapter 5: The Shift to Different Norms

1. UN Secretary-General Ban Ki-moon lecture, "The UN in a World in Transition," delivered at Stanford University in Palo Alto, California, January 17, 2013.

2. "The Next Scientific (R)evolution," a course at the Shift Network, http://nextscientificrevolution.com/course/NextScientificRevolution.

3. The Gaia Foundation has made a five-minute animation about our throw-away culture. It's the best I've seen and brilliant for kids as well as adults: "Wake Up Call," www.gaiafoundation.org/wakeupcall.

4. For more on Steiner-Waldorf schools, see www.goodschoolsguide.co.uk /help-and-advice/school-types/alternative-schooling/316/alternative -education-steiner-waldorf-philosophy.

5. Baring, *The Dream of the Cosmos*, 195.

6. Dr. Andrew Powell, "Technology and Soul in the 21st Century."

7. "Naomi Klein: 'Big Green Groups Are More Damaging than Climate De-niers,'" *Guardian Environment Network, Guardian*, September 10, 2013, www.theguardian.com/environment/2013/sep/10/naomi-klein-green -groups-climate-deniers.

8. Dustin R. Rubenstein and James Kealey, "Cooperation, Conflict, and the Evolution of Complex Animal Societies," *Nature Education Knowledge* 3, no. 10 (2010), available at http://www.nature.com/scitable/knowledge/library /cooperation-conflict-and-the-evolution-of-complex-13236526.

9. "The Next Scientific (R)evolution," a course at the Shift Network, http://nextscientificrevolution.com/course/NextScientificRevolution?inf _contact_key.

10. Ibid.

11. Donella Meadows, Jorgen Randers, and Dennis Meadows, *Limits to Growth: The 30-Year Update* (White River Junction, VT: Chelsea Green; Earthscan, 2004), 57.

12. Meadows, Randers, and Meadows, *Limits to Growth*, 52.

13. CORO's website is at www.coroindia.org. Kamble and Lavhande are also fel-lows of Leaders' Quest in Mumbai.

14. For more on Leaders' Quest fellowships, see www.leadersquest.org/quest -fellowships.

15. Human Security Centre, University of British Columbia, Canada, *Human Security Brief 2006*, see chapter 3, "How Wars End," available at www.hsrgroup.org/human-security-reports/2006/text.aspx.

16. Maria J. Stephan and Erica Chenoweth, "Why Civil Resistance Works: The Strategic Logic of Nonviolent Conflict," *International Security* 33, no 1 (Sum-mer 2008), 7–44.

17. This and the previous examples are case studies in Dylan Mathews, *War Prevention Works* (Oxford: Oxford Research Group, 2000).

18. Kofi Annan, "Progress Report on the Prevention of Armed Conflict: Report of the Secretary-General" United Nations General Assembly, July 18, 2006, available at http://daccess-dds-ny.un.org/doc/UNDOC/GEN/N06/393 /22/PDF/N0639322.pdf.

19. Rifkind and Picco, *The Fog of Peace*, 176

20. American Friends Service Committee, "Shared Security: Re-Imagining US Foreign Policy," April 2013, http://sharedsecurity.files.wordpress.com/2013/05/shared-security-discussion-guide_v6.pdf.

21. The full story is told by Dan Baum, "Battle Lessons: What the Generals Don't Know," *New Yorker*, January 17, 2005 www.newyorker.com/archive/2005/01/17/050117fa_fact.

22. Quoted in Rifkind and Picco, *The Fog of Peace*, 164.

23. "Defence Secretary Publishes Update on Progress with Trident Replacement," Nuclear Information Service, December 18, 2013, http://nuclearinfo.org/article/future-submarines/defence-secretary-publishes-update-progress-trident-replacement.

24. Peter Burt, "News Analysis Reveals Full Impact of Trident Replacement on Defence Budgets" Nuclear Information Service, December 18, 2013, http://nuclearinfo.org/article/government-uk-trident-future-submarines/new-analysis-reveals-full-impact-trident-replacement.

25. In 2012, the most recent year for which complete data is available, the United States approved $645.7 billion in defense budget authority (fiscal year 2013 dollars). This figure includes funding for the Pentagon base budget, Department of Energy-administered nuclear weapons activities, and the war in Afghanistan. This number is six times more than China, eleven times more than Russia, twenty-seven times more than Iran and thirty-three times more than Israel. In 2012, the United States consumed 41 percent of total global military spending: http://armscontrolcenter.org/issues/securityspending/articles/2012_topline_global_defense_spending.

26. *Global Policy Action Plan*, The World Future Council, June 2013.

27. Bunzl, *Global Domestic Politics*, 86, quoting Sahtouris, Koestler, and Vermeij.

28. Laicie Heeley, "U.S. Defense Spending vs. Global Defense Spending," The Center for Arms Control and Non-Proliferation, April 24, 2013, http://armscontrolcenter.org/issues/securityspendingarticles/2012_topline_global_defense_spending.

29. Diana Francis, "Making Peace Global," *Peace Review: A Journal of Social Justice* 25, no. 1 (2013), 42–50.

30. C. G. Weeramantry, Ashok Khosla, and Scilla Elworthy, "Guardians for the Future: Safeguarding the World from Environmental Crisis," *Environmental Blog, Guardian*, April 20, 2012, www.theguardian.com/environment/blog/2012/apr/20/guardians-for-the-future-environment.

31. "A Dedicated Representative of Future Generations—Judge C. G. Weeramantry Calls for the UN to Provide Leadership," Future Justice, October 9, 2013, www.futurejustice.org/blog/news/judge-c-g-weeramantry-calls-for-the-un-to-appoint-a-dedicated-representative-of-future-generations.

32. An email from The Elders August 2, 2013.

33. Lindsay Levin, *Invisible Giants: Changing the World One Step at a Time* (New Delhi, Rupa, 2013), 116–22.
34. Shelley Reciniello, "Is Woman the Future of Man? An Exploration of the Potential of Women in the Knowledge Economy and of the Problem of Gender Inequality in the Workplace," *Organisational and Social Dynamics* 11, no. 2 (2011): 151–74.
35. Peter Senge, American scientist and director of the Center for Organizational Learning at the MIT Sloan School of Management, interviewed by Prasad Kaipa, "Exerpt from an Interview with Peter Senge," *Collective Wisdom Initiative*, www.collectivewisdominitiative.org/papers/senge_interv.htm.
36. After the Vietnam War, Buddhist monks and nuns regularly guided people across minefields.
37. Steinmetz questioned by Roger Babson, "The Study of God," *Next Future*, September 28, 2013, http://nextfuture.aurosociety.org/the-study-of-god-2.
38. *UN Economic and Social Council's Commission on the Status of Women*, after the Fourth World Conference on Women, 1995, http://www.un.org/documents/ecosoc/docs/1995/e1995-26.htm.
39. Liz Rivers, "Women's Hormones: The Key to World Peace" *Liz Rivers*, November 4, 2013, www.lizrivers.com/2013/11/womens-hormones-the-key-to-world-peace.
40. Azra and Seren Bertrand, "The Essence of the True Masculine," *Fountain of Life*, 2012, www.thefountainoflife.org/true-masculine-essence. I'm indebted to Guy Marson for guiding me to this.
41. Rose von Thater-Braan, in *Mind Before Matter*, edited by Paul Devereux (Alresford, England: Iff Books, 2012)
42. Richard Barrett, *Building a Values-Driven Organization: A Whole System Approach to Cultural Transformation* (Boston: Butterworth-Heinemann, 2006) 159–67.
43. "The Next Scientific (R)evolution," a course at the Shift Network, http://nextscientificrevolution.com/course/NextScientificRevolution/homepage.

Chapter 6: Strategies to Get from Here to There

1. John Bunzl, *Global Domestic Politics: A Citizen's Guide to Running a Diverse Planet* Global Briefing Series (London: ISPO, 2013).
2. George Papandreou, "George Papandreou: Imagine a European Democracy without Borders" TEDGlobal talk, YouTube video, 20:06, posted by "TED," June 12, 2013, www.youtube.com/watch?v=y9ALB39wRKo.
3. For details, "What People Are Saying about Simpol," Simpol website, www.simpol.org/index.php?id=11.
4. Their video is quite remarkable: "The Climate Parliament and UNDP:

Introduction" YouTube video, 3:16, posted by "Ben Martin," March 21, 2013, www.youtube.com/watch?v=230H25ZB1ls.

5. These paragraphs draw on M. H. Jeucken and J. J. Bouma. "The Changing Environment of Banks." *Greener Management International* (1999): 21–35.

6. The Global Alliance for Banking on Values, www.gabv.org.

7. Abridged (with the permission of the author) from Pua Hershlag, "Navigating a Big Bank towards a New Era," *SKGR* 1 (January 2011) www.selfknowledgeglobalresponsibility.org/wp-content/uploads/2011/09 /SKGRissue1.pdf

8. Otto Scharmer, *Theory U: Leading from the Future as It Emerges* (San Francisco: Berrett Koehler, 2009).

9. Felia Salim, email to author, July 13, 2013.

10. "What Is Timebanking?" Timebanking UK, www.timebanking.org/about /what-is-a-timebank/#sthash.qZPMxWqG.dpuf.

11. For more on Margrit Kennedy, see her website: www.margritkennedy.de.

12. Jo Confino, "Richard Branson and Jochen Zeitz Launch the B Team Challenge," *Guardian Sustainable Business* (blog), *Guardian*, June 13, 2013, www.theguardian.com/sustainable-business/blog/richard-branson -jochen-zeitz-b-team.

13. Ian Christie, Research Fellow, Centre for Environmental Strategy, University of Surrey, Guildford, UK. Email to author.

14. Patagonia is a California-based clothing company that makes primarily high-end outdoor clothing. Rohan Narse, meetrohan.com/thoughts/26/2013–12 /what-would-love-doa-real-story.

15. For more on Leaders' Quest, see www.leadersquest.org/who-we-are.

16. Levin, *Invisible Giants*, 53.

17. Anonymous participant on Leaders' Quest, email to author, September 13, 2013.

18. Andrew Winston, "The Most Powerful Green NGO You've Never Heard Of," *HBR Blog Network, Harvard Business Review*, October 5, 2010, http://blogs.hbr.org/winston/2010/10/the-most-powerful-green-ngo.html.

19. "UK Universities Urged to Pull Cash from Fossil Fuel Giants," Positive TV, n.d., http://positivetv/news/ uk-universities-urged-to-pull-cash-from-fossil-fuel-giants.

20. For more on People and Planet's Fossil Free Campaign, see http://people andplanet.org/fossil-free.

21. For more on feed-in tariffs, see http://www.worldfuturecouncil.org/5762.html.

22. For more on the World Future Council's Global Policy Action Plan, see http://www.worldfuturecouncil.org/gpact.html.

23. World Future Council founder Jakob von Uexkull delivered a keynote address at the 14th International Conference of Chief Justices of the World (The

World Judiciary Summit 2013), http://www.worldfuturecouncil.org /recent_events.html.

24. SolarAid can be found at www.solar-aid.org; SunnyMoney at www.sunny money.org.

25. Maria Alexopoulou, "Solar Lanterns on the Verge of Mainstream Acceptance in Africa," *Solar Power Portal*, February 28, 2013 www.solarpowerportal. co.uk/news/solar_lanterns_on_the_verge_of_mainstream_acceptance_in _africa_2356.

26. Lester Brown, "Wind Surpasses Nuclear in China," *Tree Hugger*, www.treehugger.com/renewable-energy/wind-surpasses-nuclear-china. html. Also see the REN21 Renewable Energy Global Status Report + the nuclear/renewable surpass comparison of the Earth Policy Institute.

27. International Energy Agency, "Redrawing the Energy-Climate Map," June 10, 2013, www.worldenergyoutlook.org/media/weowebsite/2013 /energyclimatemap/RedrawingEnergyClimateMap.pdf.

28. See TED presentation by Capt. Charles Moore of the Algalita Marine Research Foundation: Charles Moore, "Charles Moore: Seas of Plastic," Filmed February 2009, TED video, 7:20, www.ted.com/talks/capt_charles_moore _on_the_seas_of_plastic.

29. The United Nations University, in its *Our World 2.0 series*, published an article in April 2009 about the invention of this plastic-to-oil converting machine, republished here: Carol Smith, "Plastic to Oil Fantastic," United Nations University, October 27, 2010, http://ourworld.unu.edu/en/plastic-to-oil-fantastic. The accompanying video instantly exceeded 115,000 views on YouTube and has been seen many more times since: "Plastic to Oil Fantastic," YouTube video, 5:08, posted by "UNUChannel," April 13, 2009, www.you tube.com/watch?v=R-Lg_kvLaAM.

30. Though the company still mainly produces larger, industrial-use machines, Blest Co. will be more than happy to hear from you. Please contact them directly at info@blest.co.jp.

31. Gene Sharp, *From Dictatorship to Democracy* (London: Serpent's Tail, 2011), first published in Bangkok in 1993.

32. See case study in Dylan Mathews, *War Prevention Works* (Oxford: Oxford Research Group, 2000).

33. Michael Caster, "A Sea of Dissent: Nonviolent Waves in China," *Open Democracy*, September 24, 2013, www.opendemocracy.net/civilresistance /michael-caster/sea-of-dissent-nonviolent-waves-in-china.

34. See Kristof and Wudunn, *Half the Sky*.

35. Avaaz, email to author, July 17, 2013.

36. "Occupy Yourself," on Richard Branson's blog, www.virgin.com/richard -branson/occupy-yourself.

37. Greg Ray, "The Ocean Is Broken," *Newcastle Herald* (Australia), October 18, 2013, www.theherald.com.au/story/1848433/the-ocean-is-broken /?cs=2452.

38. Michael Houseman, "Make Love Not War: Sex and Peacebuilding in Mindanao," *Insight on Conflict*, March 22, 2013, www.insightonconflict.org /2013/03/sex-peacebuilding-mindanao.

39. Adapted from Joanna Macy, *World as Lover, World as Self* (Berkeley, CA: Parallax Press, 1991) and Joanna's memoir, *Widening Circles* (Gabriola Island, British Columbia: New Society Publishers, 2001).

40. John-Paul Flintoff, "Local, Self-Sufficient, Optimistic: Are Transition Towns the Way Forward?" Guardian, June 14, 2013, www.theguardian.com /environment/2013/jun/15/transition-towns-way-forward.

41. Embercombe has a website, www.embercombe.co.uk.

42. Harry de Quetteville, "The 13-Year-Old Who Has the World Planting Trees," Telegraph, April 29, 2011, www.telegraph.co.uk/earth/8476747 /The-13-year-old-who-has-the-world-ting-trees.html.

43. Plant for the Planet: www.plant-for-the-planet.org/en.

44. The United Kingdom's National Endowment for Science, Technology and the Arts (NESTA) recently published a research paper, "Radical Efficiency: Different, Better, Lower Cost Public Services," which describes an approach for rethinking social services based on a set of core principles. The restorative circles model pioneered by Dominic Barter in Brazil is one of the case studies used to illustrate how these principles look in action, and this account is adapted from the NESTA report.

45. "TEDxBerkeley—Nipun Mehta—Designing For Generosity," YouTube video, 18:09, posted by "TEDx Talks," February 26, 2012, www.youtube .com/watch?v=kpyc84kamhw.

46. Gareth Evans, "The Global March toward Peace," *Project Syndicate*, December 27, 2012, www.project-syndicate.org/commentary/the-decline-of -violent-conflict-by-gareth-evans This "New Peace" phenomenon was first publicized by Andrew Mack's Human Security Report Project, supported by the superb database of the Uppsala Conflict Data Program. For statistics on the number of people killed, Evans cites The Human Security Report 2012, http://hsrgroup.org/docs/Publications/HSR2012/Figures/2012Report _Fig_5_2_GlobalSBBDs46–08.pdf.

47. See Insight on Conflict's page "Gender and Women's Rights: Peacebuilding Organisations": www.insightonconflict.org/themes/gender-womens /peacebuilding-organisations.

48. Aware Girls: www.awaregirls.org.

49. Madeleine Bunting, "Young Women Fight the 'Talibanisation' of Rural Pakistan," *Guardian*, May 16, 2011, www.guardian.co.uk/global-development/

poverty-matters/2011/may/16/pakistan-young-women-fight-prejudice.

50. Jonathan Granoff, "It's Time to Make the Middle East WMD-Free," World Policy Institute (blog), September 12, 2013, www.worldpolicy.org /blog/2013/09/12/its-time-make-middle-east-wmd-free.

51. Extract from Baring, *The Dream of the Cosmos*, 238.

52. Save Somali Women and Children (SSWC), Arab.org, http://arab.org /index.php/index.html?sobi2Task=sobi2Details&sobi2Id=50,

53. "Eradication of Female Genital Mutilation in Somalia," Unicef, www.unicef .org/somalia/SOM_FGM_Advocacy_Paper.pdf.

54. See Insight on Conflict's page "Gender and Women's Rights: Peacebuilding Organisations": www.insightonconflict.org/themes/gender-womens /peacebuilding-organisations.

55. "Women's Participation in Peace Negotiations: Connections between Presence and Influence," United Nations Entity for Gender Equality and the Empowerment of Women, available at http://reliefweb.int/sites/reliefweb .int/files/resources/03AWomenPeaceNeg.pdf.

56. Ibid.

57. Kristin Williams, "Survey Report: Syria Peace Talks Fail to Engage Women," *The Institute for Inclusive Security*, January 22, 2014, www.inclusivesecurity .org/survey-report-syria-peace-talks-fail-to-engage-women.

58. International Crisis Group, "Beyond Victimhood: Women's Peacebuilding in Sudan, Congo, and Uganda," June 28, 2006, www.crisisgroup.org/en /regions/africa/horn-of-africa/112-beyond-victimhood-womens-peace building-in-sudan-congo-and-uganda.aspx.

59. "Meet the Peacebuilders of the Women Waging Peace Network," *Institute for Inclusive Security*, www.inclusivesecurity.org/women-waging-peace -network.

60. Levin, *Invisible Giants*, 122.

61. Tatyana P. Soubbotina, *Beyond Economic Growth: An Introduction to Sustainable Development*, 2nd ed., chap. 3, (Washington, DC: The World Bank, 2004), www.worldbank.org/depweb/english/beyond/global/chapter3.html.

62. Unicef, "The State of the World's Children 2007," Unicef, New York, 2007, 4–6.

63. United Nations Population Fund, "Empowering Women through Education," www.unfpa.org/gender/empowerment2.htm.

64. Kristof and Wudunn, *Half the Sky*, 187.

65. Kristof and Wudunn, *Half the Sky*, 189.

66. Kristof and Wudunn, *Half the Sky*, 190.

67. Barbara Herz and Gene B. Sperling, *What Works in Girls' Education: Evidence and Policies from the Developing World* (New York: Council on Foreign Relations, 2004), 2–3.

68. Andrew Harvey, *The Hope: A Guide to Sacred Activism* (London: Hay House, 2009), 185.
69. Harvey, *The Hope*, 92–100.
70. Harvey, *The Hope*, 92–100.
71. Quoted by the students of Lalaji Memorial Omega International School, Chennai, India in their Opening Statement at the United Nations Student Leadership Conference on Development, March 3, 2014.
72. Bronnie Ware, *The Top Five Regrets of the Dying: A Life Transformed by the Dearly Departing* (London, Hay House, 2011).

Chapter 7: Waking up to Who We Really Are

1. Such ideas are described by C. G. Jung in the book he contributed to in his eighties, *Memories, Dreams, Reflections*, reissue edition (New York: Vintage, 1989).
2. Pam Grout, *E2* (Carlsbad, CA: Hay House, 2013), 12.
3. Lao Tzu, *Tao Te Ching*, translated by Stephen Mitchell (New York: Harper and Row, 1988). Lao Tzu lived in the sixth century BCE.
4. Elders update: Myanmar visit, October 4, 2013.
5. Bill George, Peter Sims, Andrew N. McLean, and Diana Mayer, "Discovering Your Authentic Leadership," *Harvard Business Review* 85, no. 2 (February 2007), 133.
6. Cathy Lynn Grossman, "'Life's Purpose' Author Eckhart Tolle Is Serene, Critics Less So," *USA Today,* April 15, 2010, http://usatoday30.usatoday.com/news/religion/2010–04–15-tolle15_CV_N.htm.
7. Eckhart Tolle, *Practising the Power of Now* (London: Hodder and Stoughton, 2001).
8. Susan David and Christina Congleton, "Emotional Agility: How Effective Leaders Manage Negative Thoughts and Emotions," *Harvard Business Review* (November 2013), http://hbr.org/2013/11/emotional-agility/ar/1.
9. Dan Hurley, "Breathing In vs. Spacing Out," *New York Times,* January 19, 2014, www.nytimes.com/2014/01/19/magazine/breathing-in-vs-spacing-out.html.
10. All these from Pema Chödrön, *When Things Fall Apart: Heart Advice For Difficult Times* (Boston: Shambhala, 1997).
11. "What Is NVC?" *Center for Nonviolent Communication*, www.cnvc.org/about/what-is-nvc.html.
12. For more on Marshall Rosenberg, see www.cnvc.org/about/marshall-rosenberg.html.
13. For more about restorative justice, see www.cnvc.org/about-us/projects/-restorative-justice-project/cnvc-restorative-justice-project.

14. Joshua Wachtel, "Toward Peace and Justice in Brazil: Dominic Barter and Restorative Circles," *International Institute for Restorative Practices*, March 20, 2009, www.iirp.edu/pdf/brazil.pdf.

15. Jeremy Rifkin, "The Empathic Civilisation," lecture at the Royal Society of Arts www.thersa.org/__data/assets/pdf_file/0011/558938/RSA-Lecture -Jeremy-Rifkin-transcript.pdf.

16. For more on Transparent Communication, see www.thomashuebl.com/en /approach-methods.html.

17. "Thomas Hübl—Working Method," *Academy of Inner Science*, www.innerscience.info/en/thomas-huebl/approach-and-methods.html.

18. For more on Ushahidi, see www.ushahidi.com.

19. Lao Tzu, *Tao Te Ching*, translated by Stephen Mitchell (New York: Harper Perennial, 1992), verse 43.

20. John O'Donohue, *Divine Beauty: The Invisible Embrace* (London: Bantam Books, 2003), 27.

21. Larry Page's University of Michigan Commencement Address, May 2, 2009, can be found at http://googlepress.blogspot.co.uk/2009/05/larry-pages -university-of-michigan.html.

22. Jonathan Sacks, "Five Rules for Life," *The Times*, January 5, 2013, www.thetimes.co.uk/tto/faith/article3648354.ece.

23. Joseph Campbell, in one of his lectures.

24. Harvey, *The Hope*, 18.

25. O. Scharmer and K. Kaufer, *Leading from the Emerging Future* (San Francisco: Berrett Koehler, 2013).

26. Saki Santorelli, *Heal Thy Self* (New York: Three Rivers Press, 2000).

27. Joseph Campbell, *The Hero with a Thousand Faces* (Novato, CA: New World Library, 2008).

28. Nelson Mandela, *Long Walk to Freedom* (Boston: Abacus, 1994); Anthony Sampson, *Mandela: The Authorized Biography* (New York: Harper Collins, 1999); Ed Kader Asmal, *Nelson Mandela in His Own Words* (Boston: Abacus, 2003).

29. See the Lao Tzu quote in chapter 7.

30. Tolle, *A New Earth*, 48.

31. Robert Rabbin, *Invisible Leadership* (Lakewood, CO: Acropolis Books, 1998).

32. Caroline Myss, interview with Andrew Harvey in his *Radical Passion—Sacred Love and Wisdom in Action* (Berkeley, CA: North Atlantic Books, 2012), 328.

33. Ibid., 327.

34. Robert Greenleaf, "The Servant as Leader," an essay that he first published in 1970.

35. Lao Tzu, *Tao Te Ching*, translated by Stephen Mitchell (New York: Harper Perennial, 1992).

36. Barbara Marx Hubbard, *Emergence: The Shift from Ego to Essence* (Charlottes-ville, VA: Hampton Roads, 2001).

37. Barbara Marx Hubbard, *Agents of Conscious Evolution Training*, Emergence Process Session One, Step 1: creating an inner sanctuary, http://theace training.com/ACE.

38. Ibid.

39. Ibid.

40. Rumi, *The Essential Rumi*, translated by Coleman Barks (New York: Harper Collins, 1995).

41. For details of how to set up a dialogue, see Janet Bloomfield, Rosie Hould-sworth, and Charlotte Smith, eds. *Everyone's Guide to Achieving Change: A Step-By-Step Approach to Dialogue with Decision-Makers* (Oxford: Oxford Research Group, 2007).

42. "Do Not Lose Heart—We Were Made for These Times," by Clarissa Pinkola Estés, author of *Women Who Run With the Wolves: Myths and Stories of the Wild Woman Archetype* (New York: Ballantine, 1992).

43. An excerpt from "Turn on Your Light," by Ben Okri.

Chapter 8: Recipe for Imagining a World That Works for You

1. Lawrence Bloom, email to author, November 7, 2013.

2. Prof. Jean Houston, personal communication, March 2013.

3. For more on Transparent Communication, see www.thomashuebl.com/en /approach-methods.html.

4. For more on the Bee School and the Do School, see http://scillaelworthy.com and http://thedoschool.org.

5. Such as those from the Open University and the Khan Academy (www.khan academy.org).

6. Dr. Monica Sharma, "Future Systemic Transformation: Leadership for Paradigm Shifts in an Interdependent World," paper presented at The Emerg-ing Future: Women Co-creating a World that Works, Oxford, UK, October 28–November 1, 2013.

7. *Home* is on YouTube: "Home," YouTube video, 1:33:17, posted by "homepro-ject," May 12, 2009, www.youtube.com/watch?v=jqxENMKaeCU. "Life on Earth," David Attenborough's groundbreaking study of the evolution of life on our planet, www.bbc.co.uk/programmes/b01qjcmb.

8. The National Trust: www.nationaltrust.org.uk.

9. "Best Oceans Policies Awarded at UN Biodiversity Summit," *World Future Council*, Octover 17, 2012, www.worldfuturecouncil.org/fpa-ceremony.html.

10. Janne Rohe and Anisha Grover, *Oceans Survey*, World Future Council,

www.worldfuturecouncil.org/fileadmin/user_upload/Future_Policy
_Award/FPA_2012/oceans_survey.pdf.

11. Visit, for example, the West Kennet Long Barrow in Wiltshire, near the Avebury stone circle in Wiltshire, UK.

12. This poem, written by Bev Reeler, comes from the *Tree of Life* people in Zimbabwe, who are discussed in chapter 2.

13. I. Abouleish, in *Sekem—An Image Brochure*, 2010. Internal Document. Sekem's website is www.sekem.com.

14. Alexander Schieffer and Ronnie Lessem, *Uni-versity = Unity in Diversity, Actualizing Integral Development via the Integral University*, chap. 24, "Integral University Pioneer: Sekem and Heliopolis University for Sustainable Development."

15. The following passage is from Vicki Robin and Thais Corral's *Women Strengthening Local Food Systems*, an unpublished paper submitted to the *Rising Women Rising World* initiative in October 2013. Corral is the founder of Network for Human Development in Brazil and the cofounder of Women's Environment and Development Organization. Robin (http://vickirobin.com/about) is also the author of *Blessing the Hands that Feed Us; What Eating Closer to Home Can Teach Us about Food, Community and Our Place on Earth* (New York: Penguin, 2014) and coauthor (with Joe Dominguez) of the international bestseller, *Your Money or Your Life: Transforming Your Relationship With Money and Achieving Financial Independence* (New York: Viking Penguin, 1992).

16. Dr. Andrew Powell, "Medicine and Its Role in Today's World," paper prepared for the Scientific and Medical Network Round Tables Conference "Transforming World-Views in Science, Medicine and Psychology" 5–7 July 5–7, 2013.

17. Jon Ungoed-Thomas, "Deaths Soar as Britain Turns into Nation of Prescription Drug Users," *Sunday Times*, September 8, 2013, www.thesundaytimes.co.uk/sto/news/uk_news/Health/article1311141.ece; also see *The Week*, September 12, 2013.

18. Mindfulness-Based Stress Reduction for Business: www.mindfulofjoy.com/mindfulness/mbsr-for-business.

19. Anne McIntyre and Michelle Boudin, *Dispensing with Tradition—A Practitioner's Guide to using Indian and Western Herbs the Ayurvedic Way*, (n.p.: Anne McIntyre and Michelle Boudin, 2012) http://annemcintyre.com.

20. For more on advanced health-care directives and living wills, see www.mayoclinic.org/healthy-living/consumer-health/in-depth/living-wills/art-20046303.

21. Kyle Anderson, "Laurie Anderson on Lou Reed's Last Hours: 'I Have Never

Seen an Expression as Full of Wonder,'" *Entertainment Weekly*, November 6, 2013, http://music-mix.ew.com/2013/11/06/laurie-anderson-lou-reed-tribute.

22. "Issue Brief: Infrastructure for Peace," United Nations Development Programme, March 7, 2013, www.undp.org/content/undp/en/home/librarypage/crisis-prevention-and-recovery/issue-brief—infrastructure-for-peace; the Global Alliance for Ministries and Infrastructures for Peace, www.gamip.org.

23. For more on agents of transformation, see www.Trans4mationAgents.org.

24. The words of Senator George Mitchell, negotiating the Good Friday Agreement in Northern Ireland.

25. Building on courses already available in universities such as Bradford, Strathclyde, Essex, York, Lancaster and Woodbrooke College in the United Kingdom; Oberlin, Georgetown, Texas, Columbia, American, Brandeis and Utah in USA; in Lady Sri Ram College in Delhi; in CapeTown University and others across the globe.

26. For more on Networks of Grace, see www.andrewharvey.net/networks-of-grace.

27. Andrew Harvey, *Light the Flame: 365 Days of Prayer* (Carlsbad, CA: Hay House, 2013), 181.

Chapter 9: Green Shoots through Concrete

1. O. Scharmer and K. Kaufer, *Leading from the Emerging Future* (San Francisco, CA: Berrett Koehler, 2013), 18.

2. Charles Perrow, "Fukushima Forever," The Huffington Post, September 20, 2013, www.huffingtonpost.com/charles-perrow/fukushima-forever_b_3941589.html.

3. *The Importance of the Heart* by Joseph Chilton Pearce, quoted in Baring, *The Dream of the Cosmos*, 403.

4. Martha Graham to Agnes de Mille, quoted in *Dance to the Piper and Promenade Home* by Agnes de Mille (Da Capo, 1982).

5. Paul Hawken, *Blessed Unrest: How the Largest Movement in the World Came into Being and Why No One Saw It Coming* (New York, Viking Press, 2007) a *New York Times* bestseller.

6. Monica Sharma, "Future Systemic Transformation: Leadership for Paradigm Shifts in an Interdependent World," paper for The Emerging Future: Women Co-creating a World that Works, Oxford, UK, October 28—November 1, 2013.

7. Norie Huddle, *Butterfly*, published on Earth Day, 1990, can be found at http://blogofcollectiveintelligence.com/2004/05/27/the_collective_intelligence_of.

8. Desmond Tutu, email to author March 5, 2014

9. One Billion Rising, www.onebillionrising.org.

10. Jean Houston, email to author, March 9, 2014.

11. The full text: "Malala Yousafzai Delivers Defiant Riposte to Taliban Militants with Speech to the UN General Assembly," *The Independent*, July 12, 2013, www.independent.co.uk/news/world/asia/the-full-text-malala -yousafzai-delivers-defiant-riposte-to-taliban-militants-with-speech-to-the -un-general-assembly-8706606.html; it's also at http://pdc-afpak.blogspot. co.uk/2013/07/the-full-text-malala-yousafzai-delivers.html.

12. Dan Hurley, "Breathing In Vs. Spacing Out" *New York Times*, January 19, 2014, www.nytimes.com/2014/01/19/magazine/breathing-in-vs-spacing -out.html.

13. The Institute of HeartMath: www.heartmath.org.

14. Cocounseling can be found at Co-Counseling International: www.co-counselling.org.uk.

15. This exercise is based on the concepts of Nonviolent Communication, developed by Marshall Rosenberg: www.nonviolentcommunication.com /aboutnvc/4partprocess.htm.

SUGGESTED READING

Baring, Anne. *The Dream of the Cosmos: A Quest for the Soul*. Dorset, England: Archive, 2013.

Barrett, Richard. *Building a Values-Driven Organization: A Whole System Approach to Cultural Transformation*. Oxford: Butterworth-Heinemann, 2006.

Bloomfield, Janet, Rosie Houldsworth, and Charlotte Smith, eds. *Everyone's Guide to Achieving Change: A Step-By-Step Approach to Dialogue with Decision-Makers*. Oxford: Oxford Research Group, 2007.

Bucko, Adam, and Matthew Fox. *Occupy Spirituality*. Berkeley, CA: North Atlantic Books, 2013.

Bunzl, John. *Global Domestic Politics*. London: ISPO, 2013.

Chödrön, Pema. *When Things Fall Apart: Heart Advice for Difficult Times*. London: Element, 2005.

Elworthy, Scilla. *Power and Sex: A Book about Women*. London: Element Books, 1996.

Goleman, Daniel. *Emotional Intelligence*. New York: Bantam Books, 1996.

Houston, Jean. *The Wizard of Us*, New York: Atria Books; Hillsboro, OR: Beyond Words, 2013.

Harvey, Andrew. *The Hope: A Guide to Sacred Activism*. London: Hay House, 2009.

Harvey, Andrew. *Radical Passion: Sacred Love and Wisdom in Action*. Berkeley, CA: North Atlantic Books, 2012.

Kabat-Zinn, Jon. *Wherever You Go, There You Are: Mindfulness Meditation for Everyday Life*. New York: Hyperion, 1994.

Kristof, Nicholas, and Sheryl Wudunn. *Half the Sky: How to Change the World*. London: Virago, 2010.

Lao Tzu. *Tao Te Ching*. Translated by Stephen Mitchell. New York: Harper Perennial, 1992.

Macy, Joanna. *World as Lover, World as Self*. London: Random House, 1993.

Moore Lappé, Frances. *Liberation Ecology*. Cambridge, MA: Small Planet Media, 2009.

Moore, Thomas. *Care of the Soul*. London: Piatkus Books, 2012.

Porritt, Jonathan. *The World We Made*. London: Phaidon, 2013.

Rabbin, Robert. *Invisible Leadership*. Lakewood, CO: Acropolis Books, 1998.

Rosenberg, Marshall. *Nonviolent Communication: A Language of Life*. Encinitas, CA: PuddleDancer Press, 2003.

Senge, P. M., C. O. Scharmer, J. Jaworski, and B. S. Flowers. *Presence: An Exploration of Profound Change in People, Organizations, and Society*. New York: Crown Business, 2005.

Scharmer, O., and K. Kaufer. *Leading From the Emerging Future*. San Francisco, CA: Berrett Koehler, 2013.

Tan, Chade-Meng. *Search Inside Yourself*. London: Harper Collins, 2012.

Thich Nhat Hanh. *Being Peace*. Berkeley, CA: Parallax Press, 1987.

Tolle, Eckhart. *The Power of Now: A Guide to Spiritual Enlightenment*. London: Hodder and Stoughton, 2001.

———. *Stillness Speaks*. Novato, CA: New World Library, 2003.

———. *A New Earth: Awakening to Your Life's Purpose*. New York: Penguin, 2008.

Tutu, Desmond. *No Future Without Forgiveness*. London: Random House, 1999.

INDEX

ABOUT THE AUTHOR

Photo by Joanna Vestey

Scilla Elworthy PhD founded the Oxford Research Group in 1982 to develop effective dialogue between nuclear weapons policy makers worldwide and their critics, work that included a series of dialogues between Chinese, Russian, and Western nuclear scientists and military, and for which she has been three times nominated for the Nobel Peace Prize. She founded Peace Direct in 2002 to fund, promote, and learn from local peace-builders in conflict areas, leading to the acceptance by the United Nations of the value and cost-effectiveness of locally led initiatives. Peace Direct was voted "Best New Charity" in 2005. Scilla was awarded the Niwano Peace Prize in 2003 and was adviser to Peter Gabriel, Archbishop Desmond Tutu, and Sir Richard Branson in setting up The Elders. She is chair of the Civil Society sector of the Hanwang Forum in China, a councillor of the World Future Council, author of numerous books, and patron of *Gender Rights and Equality Action Trust*, *Voice of a Woman, Oxford Research Group*. She also advises the executive leadership teams of selected international corporations. Scilla has one daughter and two grandchildren and lives in the heart of England.

SACRED ACTIVISM SERIES

SACRED
ACTIVISM SERIES

Heart in Action

When the joy of compassionate service is combined with the pragmatic drive to transform all existing economic, social, and political institutions, a radical divine force is born: Sacred Activism. The Sacred Activism Series, published by North Atlantic Books, presents leading voices that embody the tenets of Sacred Activism—compassion, service, and sacred consciousness—while addressing the crucial issues of our time and inspiring radical action.

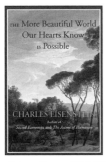

*The More Beautiful World
Our Hearts Know Is Possible*

Charles Eisenstein

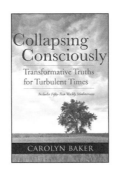

Collapsing Consciously

Carolyn Baker

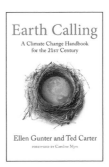

Earth Calling

Ellen Gunter
and Ted Carter

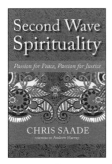

*Second Wave
Spirituality*

Chris Saade

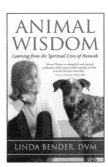

Animal Wisdom

Linda Bender

Spiritual Democracy

Steven Herrmann
OCTOBER, 2014

The Sacred Activism Series was cocreated by Andrew Harvey, visionary, spiritual teacher, and founder of the Institute for Sacred Activism, and Douglas Reil, associate publisher and managing director of North Atlantic Books. Harvey serves as the series editor and drives outreach efforts worldwide.